Digital literacies
for learning

Digital literacies for learning

Edited by

Allan Martin and Dan Madigan

facet publishing

© This compilation: Allan Martin and Dan Madigan 2006
The chapters: the contributors 2006

Published by Facet Publishing
7 Ridgmount Street, London WC1E 7AE
www.facetpublishing.co.uk

Facet Publishing is wholly owned by CILIP: the Chartered Institute of
Library and Information Professionals.

First published 2006

British Library Cataloguing in Publication Data
A catalogue record for this book is available from the British Library.

ISBN-13: 978-1-85604-563-6
ISBN-10: 1-85604-563-3

Typeset from editors' disks by Facet Publishing Production in
11/13 Elegant Garamond and Humanist.
Printed and made in Great Britain by MPG Books Ltd, Bodmin, Cornwall.

Contents

For Vivien, Alison and Calum

The contributors

Neil Anderson
Associate Professor and Deputy Head of Education
James Cook University, Queensland, Australia
Neil Anderson's main area of research has concerned equity and learning technologies with an emphasis on the intersection of socio-economic disadvantage and the implementation of computers and associated peripherals in classrooms. Current research interests include leading an Australian Research Council funded collaborative study to address low rates of female participation in IT professional occupations and education pathways. This study involves academic researchers (Professor Colin Lankshear and Associate Professor Mary Klein) and personnel from Education Queensland and Queensland-based ICT companies such as Technology One. He wrote the training and research plan for the Island Watch Digital Network, a $5.5 million Networking the Nation programme to enhance the provision and use of communication networks and ICT in the Torres Strait region. He is a chief investigator in Phase 1 of Success for Boys – a DEST-funded $19 million national research and professional development project. He is the co-ordinator of SiMERR QLD – the state hub of the National Centre for Maths, Science and ICT research for regional and rural Australia – and leader of the ICT stream of the EIDOS research community partnership (www.eidos.org.au).

www.faess.jcu.edu.au/soe/staff/neil.anderson.html
neil.anderson@jcu.edu.au

Claire Bélisle
Research Engineer
Institut des Sciences de l'Homme, Lyon, France
Claire Bélisle is a socio-psychologist, with a doctorate in cognitive psychology, presently working as a human and social sciences research engineer for the National Scientific Research Centre. She is based in Lyon, in the research unit LIRE (University Lumière Lyon 2 – CNRS). Her main interests focus on the integration of information and communication technology in education and research. She has conducted several international research projects (for example, on telepresence, the digital campus), managed research teams, given presentations and conferences, published articles and edited books, such as *Pratiques Médiatiques* (Editions du CNRS, 1999) and *Lecture Numérique, Réalités, Perspectives et Enjeux* (Presses de l'ENSSIB, 2004). She is now conducting user studies on reading and digital corpuses, focusing on digital reading and cognitive navigation in hypermedia contents, such as online encyclopedias. She also does consulting work for educational organizations and the European Commission.

www.ish-lyon.cnrs.fr/labo/LIRE/Belisle_page.htm
claire.belisle@ish-lyon.cnrs.fr

Catherine Cardwell
Associate Professor
Chair, Department of Library Teaching and Learning, and Instruction Coordinator, University Libraries
Bowling Green State University, USA
Catherine Cardwell has been a member of the library faculty at Bowling Green State University since 1998. Collaboration, student learning and information literacy in the disciplines are frequently the topics of her publications and professional activities. As Chair of University Libraries' Department of Library Teaching and Learning, she is leading her department's effort to integrate information literacy into the undergraduate and graduate curriculum. Catherine was the principal investigator of a major Ohio Board of Regents Technology Initiatives grant, the aims of which were to promote collaboration among librarians, faculty development centre directors and faculty members; and to promote the development of discipline-specific information literacy content.

cardcat@bgnet.bgsu.edu

Johannes Cronjé
Professor of Computers in Education and Training
University of Pretoria, South Africa
Johannes Cronjé has been involved in the development and facilitation of Masters and Doctoral studies in the field of ICT in education and training since 1994. His

main field of interest lies in the functioning of virtual learning communities and the development of a digital culture. He has been a visiting professor or visiting scholar at the Universities of Bergen (Norway), Khartoum (Sudan), Addis-Ababa (Ethiopia) and Joensuu (Finland). His current research focus is on the dynamics of blended learning support across cultural and linguistic divides in Africa.

http://hagar.up.ac.za/catts/abchome.html

jcronje@up.ac.za

Chris Fowler
Director, Chimera
University of Essex, UK

Chris has a BSocSc in psychology and sociology and a PhD in cognitive psychology. Until 1990 he taught in higher education institutions both in the UK and abroad, until joining the Human Factors Division at BT Labs in Martlesham Heath, Suffolk. While there, he worked on projects in the area of usability engineering. In the mid-1990s he established and ran BT's Education and Training Research Group within HF Research. The work looked at developing constructive models and frameworks for innovative learning systems across all the main education sectors (from schools to universities) as well as learning in the workplace. In 1998 he became the part-time Director of the Institute of Education's new Centre for Future Learning. In 2000 he took up the new job of establishing BT's Asian Research Centre in Malaysia, returning in 2001 to run the newly established Customer Behaviour Laboratory (CBL) in BT's Research Department at Adastral Park (formerly BT Labs). His current areas of interest are: cross-cultural psychology (cognitive styles, memory and attention; methodological issues), HCI (user-centred design methodologies, particularly user needs and requirements capture), education (conceptual frameworks that bridge theories and design; learning communities; learning relationships and the importance of dialogue in learning; managing change and organizational learning) and methodologies (scenario-based user needs analysis; market proposition validation from user needs; discounted techniques).

www.essex.ac.uk/chimera/team/chrisf.html

cfowler@essex.ac.uk

Paul Gilster
Freelance writer/columnist

Paul Gilster is a writer who focuses on technology and its implications. He is the author of seven books including *Digital Literacy* (John Wiley & Sons, 1997) and *Centauri Dreams: imagining and planning for interstellar flight* (Copernicus, 2005); the latter is a study of the technologies that may one day make it possible to send a probe to the nearest star. He tracks ongoing developments in areas of interstellar research from propulsion to robotics on the *Centauri Dreams* website (www.centauri-dreams.org). He has contributed to numerous technology and business magazines, and has published essays, feature stories, reviews and fiction in a wide range of publications both in and out of the technology arena. In addition, he has for the last 17 years written the weekly 'Computer Focus' column, which now appears in *The News & Observer* (Raleigh NC). He is a graduate of Grinnell College (IA); he did six years of graduate work at UNC-Chapel Hill, specializing in medieval English literature.

gilster@mindspring.com

Stephen Griffiths
Assistant Registrar (Learning and Teaching)
Cardiff University, Wales
Stephen Griffiths has responsibility for overseeing Cardiff University's Learning Environment Strategy, and has led and participated in many projects on information literacy, the accessible curriculum, learning and teaching space, and the development of programmes to support academic staff development. He was formerly a lecturer in international politics at Leeds University and a research fellow at the Stockholm International Peace Research Institute (SIPRI), and holds degrees from the University of Wales, Aberdeen University and Sheffield University. He is the author of *Nationalism and Ethnic Conflict: threats to European security* (Oxford University Press, 1993) and other articles on political and social issues.

griffithss4@cardiff.ac.uk

Denise Haywood
European Projects Co-ordinator, School of Education
University of Edinburgh, Scotland
Denise Haywood is the European Projects Co-ordinator in Higher and Community Education, School of Education at the University of Edinburgh. She has a background in social work and administration. Her work on evaluating the effectiveness of ICT in learning and in surveying university student and staff skills and attitudes across Europe has led to her interest in the effects that e-learning has on individuals, and in particular on the nature of informal support. She has been involved in many European e-learning projects including SEUSISS, SPOT+, UNIGAME, SIG-GLUE, SEEQUEL and EUCEBS, and most recently VICTORIOUS (www.victorious-project.org) and MASSIVE (www.massive-project.org). Recent research includes Haywood, J., Haywood, D., Macleod, H., Mogey, N. and Alexander, W. (2004) The Student View of ICT in Education at the University of Edinburgh: skills, attitudes and expectations, in J. Cook, (ed.), *Blue Skies and Pragmatism: learning technologies for the next decade*, Proceedings of the 11th Association for Learning Technology Conference.

denise.haywood@ed.ac.uk

Jeff Haywood

Professor of Education and Technology, School of Education
University of Edinburgh, Scotland

Jeff Haywood is Professor of Education and Technology, School of Education, and Deputy Director of Information Services at the University of Edinburgh. His research interests are in the development of strategies for effective use of e-learning at institutional, national and international levels, and in the attitudes of adult learners towards ICT in education, particularly in universities. Within the University of Edinburgh, he is responsible for the e-learning strategy and its implementation. He is particularly interested in measures of the effectiveness of the strategy, and how well it enhances the student experience. He is Chair of the Coimbra Group Taskforce on E-learning (www.coimbra-group.be), and international member of the board of the Open Source Portfolio Initiative (www.osportfolio.org) in the USA. Recent works are Tosh, D., Light, T. P. , Fleming, K. and Haywood, J. (2005) Engagement with Electronic Portfolios: challenges from the student perspective, *Canadian Journal of Learning Technology*, **31** (www.cjlt.ca/index.html); and Haywood, J. et al. (2004) A Comparison of ICT Skills of Students Across Europe, *Journal of e-Literacy*, **1** (www.jelit.org/33/).

http://homepages.ed.ac.uk/jhaywood
jeff.haywood@ed.ac.uk

Renee Hobbs

Associate Professor, Temple University, USA
Department of Broadcasting, Telecommunications and Mass Media
Director, Media Education Lab

Renee Hobbs is one of the leading authorities on media literacy education in the USA. She is an Associate Professor of Communication at Temple University's School of Communications and Theater, where she directs the Media Education Lab. Her research examines media literacy education in the context of English-language arts, health education and social studies in K-12 and after-school environments, and the development of students' literacy and critical-thinking skills in relation to multimedia and popular culture. She co-authored the best-selling secondary language arts textbook *Elements of Language* (Holt, Rinehart, Winston, 2000), and her new book, *Teaching the Media in High School*, is published by Teachers College Press in 2006. She holds a BA in English Literature and Film/Video Studies from the University of Michigan, MA in Communication from the University of Michigan, and EdD in Human Development from Harvard University Graduate School of Education.

www.reneehobbs.org/
renee.hobbs@temple.edu

Martin Jenkins

Academic Manager, Centre for Active Learning
University of Gloucestershire, UK

Martin Jenkins is Academic Manager of the Centre for Active Learning (CeAL) (a national Centre for Excellence in Teaching and Learning) at the University of Gloucestershire (www.glos.ac.uk/ceal). CeAL will be conducting pedagogic research into active learning and Martin has a particular interest in the use of learning technology. Prior to this he was Head of Learning Technology Support at the University, responsible for centrally supported e-learning developments. He has been actively involved in staff development and student skills support since the late 1980s, initially as a chartered librarian and latterly as a learning technologist. In 2004 he was awarded a National Teaching Fellowship.

www.glos.ac.uk/ceal/contacts/martinjenkins.cfm
mjenkins@glos.ac.uk

Maryann Kope

Co-ordinator, Learning Services
University of Guelph, Canada

Maryann has an MEd from the University of Toronto and degrees from Wilfrid Laurier University and Queen's University. She has worked in student learning support at the university level since 1986. Within the unique collaborative environment of Guelph's Learning Commons, she manages a range of services to support and enhance student learning, including programmes and resources for undergraduate and graduate students, and specialized services for faculty and teaching assistants. She is also responsible for the Learning Commons' award-winning website and time-management webshop. Her research interests include e-literacy and the impact of computer technologies on student learning strategies. Recent projects include an investigation into the use of PDAs as an academic tool. She invites comments on her chapter and can be reached by e-mail.

mkope@uoguelph.ca

Jesús Lau

Director, USBI VER Library
Universidad Veracruzana, Boca del Río, Veracruz, Mexico

Jesús Lau holds a PhD in Information Studies from Sheffield University, and a Masters degree in Library Science from Denver University. He has received the National Researcher Award in Mexico four times. He is Chair of the Information Literacy Section, IFLA, where he co-ordinates the UNESCO-funded International Information Literacy Resources Directory. He is founder and organizer of the biannual Mexican Information Literacy Conference that began in 1998. He has published more than 120 articles, papers and books in Mexico and abroad.

jlau@uv.mx

Hamish Macleod
Senior Lecturer, School of Education
University of Edinburgh, Scotland

Hamish Macleod is Senior Lecturer within the Centre for Teaching, Learning and Assessment (CTLA), School of Education, University of Edinburgh. His research and teaching interests are in the psychology of computer use, particularly the applications of information technology in teaching and learning. Part of his activities within the CTLA over recent years has been to support the University's IT Literacy Programme. He taught for many years in the University's Department of Psychology and still retains close links with colleagues there. Recent publications include: Koubek, A. and Macleod, H. (2004) Game Based Learning, in Pivec, M., Koubek, A. and Dondi, C. (eds) *Guidelines for Game-Based Learning* PABST Science Publishing; and Ellaway, R., Dewhurst, D. and Macleod, H. (2004) Evaluating a Virtual Learning Environment in the Context of its Community of Practice, *ALT-J*, **12**, 125–46.

http://homepages.ed.ac.uk/ejua41/
h.a.macleod@ed.ac.uk

Dan Madigan
Director, Scholarship of Engagement
Bowling Green State University, USA

Dan Madigan was the Founding Director of the Center for Teaching, Learning and Technology (CTLT) at Bowling Green State University, and he served in that capacity until recently. He is currently the Interim Director of the Scholarship of Engagement, a campus-wide initiative to strengthen outreach within the external community. As the director of CTLT for the past ten years Dan was instrumental in establishing faculty learning communities that provided faculty with an opportunity to participate in an interdisciplinary forum that focused on sharing ideas and information about topics that promote professional growth in the areas of learning, teaching and research. He also developed a staff that supports a variety of faculty development initiatives on topics such as assessment of student learning, tenure and promotion portfolios, active learning strategies and the integration of technology into the classroom. Dan's research interests are in the area of literacy and he has published a book, numerous articles and chapters in this area. His most recent literacy interests have expanded into the area of digital literacy – specifically, how the digital world is helping to shape a new kind of literacy that is necessary for the intellectual and social growth of the world's populations.

dmadiga@bgnet.bgsu.edu

Allan Martin
Director, IT Education Unit
University of Glasgow, Scotland
Allan Martin was born in Glasgow, and has degrees in sociology, folklore and education and a diploma in computer education. He taught in secondary schools for ten years (sociology, history, English, French, geography), ending as Head of Faculty and Head of Sixth Form. Then he moved to teacher education, lecturing in sociology and IT at St Andrews College, Glasgow, and then training computing/IT teachers at the University of Leeds. He went to Glasgow University in 1995 to develop the University's IT Literacy Programme (now evolving towards a broader Digital Literacy Programme). His research interests focus on the digital society, digital literacy and education. He has been involved in a number of funded projects in these areas, and currently leads the DigEuLit project, funded from the EC's e-Learning initiative, focused on developing a European digital literacy framework (www.digeulit.ec). He is founder and editor of the open-access peer-reviewed online *Journal of eLiteracy* (JeLit) (www.jelit.org) and convener of the Foundation Committee for the eLit conference series (www.elit-conf.org). He edited, with Hannelore Rader, *Information and IT Literacy: enabling learning in the the 21st century* (Facet Publishing, 2003).

www.iteu.gla.ac.uk/staff/amartin.html
a.martin@educ.gla.ac.uk

Terry Mayes
Centre for Research in Lifelong Learning
Glasgow Caledonian University, Scotland
Terry Mayes is currently a research professor at Glasgow Caledonian University. He has long experience as both researcher and practitioner in learning technology. He was Director of Research at the Institute for Computer-based Learning at Heriot-Watt University, Edinburgh, from its formation in 1990. His early work with teaching machines was followed by 14 years as a lecturer in psychology at the University of Strathclyde, during which period he researched cognitive aspects of learning. Since the mid-1980s he has worked extensively on the development of interactive learning through technology. During the late 1990s he led collaborative projects funded through the UK Research Councils involving research on the educational potential of vicarious learning. Recently he has acted in a variety of advisory roles for the Scottish higher education sector. He has published widely on human aspects of learning technology.

http://apu.gcal.ac.uk/pages/staff/TMhome.htm
j.t.mayes@gcal.ac.uk

Hester Mountifield

Assistant University Librarian, Information Commons and Learning Services
University of Auckland, New Zealand

Hester Mountifield has been with the University of Auckland Library in various roles since 1996, and prior to that worked in the university and secondary school sector in South Africa. Her current role includes the management of the University Library's Information Commons services and the development and co-ordination of information literacy and integrated learning support initiatives in collaboration with institutional partners. She is interested in the pedagogical and learning support issues raised by the blending of e-learning technologies with digital libraries, resources and services, the educational design role of librarians and the learning support and e-literacy needs of the Net Generation. She holds a Masters degree in library and information science and a postgraduate diploma in higher education. Her publications include conference papers and articles on the information commons and e-literacy. She has also contributed chapters to books on these topics.

h.mountifield@auckland.ac.nz

David Murphy

Director, Centre for the Advancement of Learning and Teaching
Monash University, Australia

Professor David Murphy is Director of the Centre for the Advancement of Learning and Teaching (CALT). He returned to Monash University in 2005 after four years at the Open University of Hong Kong (OUHK), where he was most recently professor and head of the Centre for Research in Distance and Adult Learning. He was also senior course designer at the OUHK, a position he held during previous tenure there from 1994 to 1998. He spent three years at Monash (1998–2001) as Associate Professor in Flexible Learning in the Centre for Higher Education Development, and has also worked at Deakin University and the Hong Kong Polytechnic University. He has a long association with distance and open education, along with staff development in higher education, and he is on the editorial boards of a number of journals. His consultancies include work with the Commonwealth of Learning, Austrade, the United Nations High Commissioner for Refugees and the World Health Organization. Specific projects have included development and evaluation work in India, Seychelles, Malaysia, Taiwan and Thailand. His research has most recently focused on information and communication technologies in higher education. His latest publications include three edited books, titled *Online Learning and Teaching With Technology: case studies, experience and practice*, *Advancing Online Learning in Asia* and *Distance Education and Technology: issues and practice*.

David.Murphy@calt.monash.edu.au

Gill Needham

Head of Strategic and Service Development,
Open University Library and Learning Resources Centre
The Open University, UK

Gill Needham's current post is Head of Strategic and Service Development in the Open University Library. Since joining the Open University in 1998 she has taken a leading role in developing the Library's electronic services to its 200,000 students, has launched and developed an information literacy strategy for the University and has been a major author on three Open University courses. Previously she worked for 15 years in the National Health Service, initially as a librarian and subsequently as an R&D Specialist in Public Health, responsible for promoting evidence-based practice and public involvement in healthcare decision-making. During her career she has managed a wide variety of projects at local, regional and national levels, published a range of articles and project reports and presented papers at various national and international conferences. Current interests include e-learning, use of new technologies in learning and teaching, information literacy, evidence-based practice and digital libraries.

g.needham@open.ac.uk

Ola Pilerot

Deputy Head Librarian
University of Skövde, Sweden

Ola Pilerot is Deputy Head Librarian at Skövde University Library, Sweden. His main area of interest is information literacy in theory and practice. He is a member of the Swedish Library Association's Steering Group for Library Pedagogy and of the Swedish Association for Information Specialists' Committee for Information, Conference and Training.

www.his.se/bib/ola
ola.pilerot@his.se

Alex Reid

Professorial Fellow
University of Western Australia

Alex Reid, now an honorary professorial fellow at the University of Western Australia (UWA), has been in the IT industry for over 44 years, most of that in universities. He directed the computing centre at UWA from about 1976 until 1993, and then at Oxford University until 2000; he was then involved in setting IT policy at UWA until 2005. He has always been interested in helping people develop and improve their IT skills, teaching Fortran to beginners from 1969, and writing an introductory Fortran compiler and reference book in 1971: Reid, T. A. *A Guide to Fortran Programming and Uniwaft* (UWA). He developed discussion papers and policies relating to IT literacy at both these universities (the first being in October 1992), and in 2003 convened a joint study of IT literacy by Australian Directors of IT, Library and Learning. He oversaw the introduction of the ECDL at Oxford University, and a doubling in student hours of IT training during his time there. He continues to teach professional ethics to computer science undergraduates.

http://people.csse.uwa.edu.au/info.php?name=alex
alex.reid@uwa.edu.au

Cornel J. Reinhart
International Consultant, Centre for e-Learning and Literacy
Bloemfontein, South Africa
Cornel 'Corky' Reinhart is an international consultant assisting faculty and institutions with the architecture and pedagogy of online learning. The former Director of the University Without Walls programme at Skidmore College (Saratoga Springs, USA), he is an historian with a background in African–American and American social history. He earned his PhD from the University of Oklahoma in 1972. He taught in upstate New York for some years at the State University of New York, Plattsburgh, and St Lawrence University, Canton NY. Among other publications, he has written an introduction to a recent edition of *The Life and Times of Frederick Douglass* (Wordsworth Editions Limited, 1996) and assisted in the republication, with new introduction, of Isaac Johnson's autobiography, the story of a black Civil War veteran born a slave (*Slavery Days in Old Kentucky*, Syracuse University Press, 1994). He maintains a long-standing interest in local history projects. He founded Skidmore College's University Without Walls web-based distance education programme for non-residential adult students. He offered UWW's first online course, *America in the Sixties*, and co-facilitated Skidmore College's faculty workshop devoted to online pedagogy, *Putting Your Course On-Line*. He has shared his work at numerous conferences, often published.

www.cornelreinhart.com
creinhar@skidmore.edu

Chris Sutton
Director, eLearning Australia
Chris Sutton holds degree and postgraduate qualifications in education. For many years she has provided support and leadership for teachers within all education sectors in Australia. She has been a primary/secondary school teacher and principal, a computer education adviser, the education manager in corporations, an instructional designer and internet training consultant for TAFE Queensland Online. In 2003, Chris was recognized as an Australian Flexible Learning Leader (FLL) by the Australian Flexible Learning Framework. The research grant made

it possible for her to investigate strategies for teacher professional development (PD) across Australia, New Zealand and the UK. She visited numerous universities, institutes and organizations to identify common issues and effective PD strategies, finding digital competence and multiliteracies significant factors in teachers' ability to teach effectively online. As a result, she has continued researching and publishing on multiliteracies and has developed a framework of instructional design, based on current pedagogy, for teachers new to e-learning. She delivers support services for e-learning and courses in e-learning facilitation and instructional design through eLearn Australia.

www.elearnaustralia.com.au
chris.sutton@elearnaustralia.com.au

David F. Warlick
Consultant and author
The Landmark Project, USA

David Warlick has 30 years of experience in the field of education. He has been a classroom teacher, district administrator and staff consultant with the North Carolina State Department of Public Instruction. For the past ten years, he has been the Director and Principle Consultant for the Landmark Project, a web development, consulting and innovations firm in Raleigh, North Carolina. His website, *Landmarks for Schools*, serves more than 6 million visits a month and hosts a variety of popular web tools for teachers and students. He is also the author of three books on instructional technology and 21st century literacy, and has spoken to audiences throughout the USA, Europe, Asia and South America.

www.landmark-project.com
david@landmark-project.com

Foreword

Digital Literacies for Learning is written for a diverse community of educators, librarians, information technologists and researchers to help them enable students to successfully learn in the technological and digital global environment. This is most important in the 21st century since information is generated more quickly than ever before and is becoming the foundation for economic development throughout the world. Information-seeking behaviour is changing at a faster pace than ever before owing to the internet and the emergence of powerful search engines. Academic institutions in the electronic age have been undergoing a variety of changes to deal with new ways of teaching to prepare students for productive futures in an electronic information environment featuring increasing online access to digital and electronic information.

Twenty-five authors from nine countries and four continents address new literacies such as information literacy, technological literacy, media literacy and digital literacy in the teaching and learning environment of higher education. The first part of this volume explores the landscape of digital literacy, learning and teaching environments and e-learning. Virtual learning environments are described and the change from traditional educational environments to the e-learning environment is explained. Online teaching and learning have been revolutionizing the entire academic environment and online scholarly communication is quickly emerging as a major academic enterprise and requires many changes in the publishing and research environments.

The second part of this volume addresses the enabling of digital literacies and the teaching of information competencies, and outlines the information commons as a student-centred environment. Learning management systems are becoming more important on campuses and are described in terms of social elements, student feedback and equity. Achieving information and computer technology (ICT) literacy is also becoming a major goal on many university campuses, and successes and failures regarding these efforts are documented. A number of universities are beginning to instruct graduate students in information and computer skills to prepare them for the future technological information environment.

It is important to note that not only do universities have to cope with major changes to be successful in the digital environment but academic libraries likewise are undergoing major changes at an increasingly fast pace to remain not only viable in the electronic information age but to evolve into major centres for learning, teaching and socializing. They are dealing with new ways to handle collection development for both print and electronic information. They are increasing the digitizing of print materials and they are struggling with the complexities and financial responsibilities to provide more complete online information access in all subject areas. Major changes are also occurring in the physical environments of libraries since library users are demanding more user-friendly spaces, wireless computer access and diverse information provisions. Users also need friendly, competent and expert advice and services in the digital information environment making it necessary to provide highly trained professionals who will receive continual staff development. The academic library challenges like the university challenges in the digital age are indeed enormous and very exciting.

This volume will be a most useful addition to the higher education literature related to the teaching of information skills and to the acquisition of ICT competencies for undergraduate and graduate students. Faculty and librarians in all parts of the world should find this publication useful in their endeavour to instruct students in all disciplines to ensure they acquire subject expertise and important information skills.

Hannelore Rader
Librarian and Dean of the University Libraries
University of Louisville, Kentucky

Preface

It is now nearly a decade since Paul Gilster published *Digital Literacy*. Gilster's book was stimulated by the emergence of the internet, which had 'grown from a scientist's tool to a worldwide publishing and research medium open to anyone with a computer and a modem'. (Gilster, 1997, 1). Since that point, the world of the digital has changed still further (not that we should be surprised about that, as change is endemic to human society and to the human condition). Eliana Rosado and Claire Bélisle summarize the way in which our relationship to knowledge has evolved:

> The use of technological tools to access information (such as databases, digital libraries, or simply the Web) has resulted in the need to cope with information of immeasurable quantities, with great levels of complexity, accessible at inconceivable speeds. Knowledge skills needed include knowing how to be able to gather vast amounts of information from varied sources, knowing how to select and synthesize it, how to interpret it and evaluate it taking into account diverse cultural contexts and formatting. Because the human mind cannot deal with great quantities of symbols simultaneously, technological tools become absolutely necessary to organise such complex information in readable patterns.
>
> (Rosado and Bélisle, 2006, 4)

The internet is still with us, as a means of communication – e-mail, instant messaging, chatrooms, discussion forums, blogs, virtual communities – as a publishing outlet and literally limitless source of 'information' – good or bad, true or false, beneficent or malicious, well crafted or careless, meaningful or incoherent, organized or random – and as a gigantic marketplace – for groceries, books (yes, they're still in demand!), holidays, houses, ideas and anything that can be bought and sold, auctioned, swapped or simply given away (although there's usually a catch). Cyberspace represents and purveys everything that exists in human society – it has become *coterminous* with it ('of equal extent or scope or duration' – http://word-net.princeton.edu/perl/webwn). But there's more. As Rosado and Bélisle point out, the amount of information out there is too great for us to handle – it is simply beyond imagining. In many ways, the only way to deal with it is by employing more digital tools. And deal with the digital world we must.

The virtual world does not sit 'out there' like a parallel universe – disturbing, creepy, but at least it is on the other side of the screen. Rather, it invades and conditions the 'real' world, the physical world. Information derived from the reality of our lived world is churned, processed, sieved, squeezed and ground for meaning by silent digital engines of great speed and even greater patience, so that in the cyberworld we become known better than we know ourselves. If I go to a well known online bookseller to look for a book, even before I have a chance to express an opinion, the system will tell me what it thinks I should buy, based on my entire previous buying history. I can't remember all the books I bought, so it knows better than I do. And it's not just books – almost everything I buy is recorded digitally. If all this data is collated with other data about me – date of birth, driver's licence, passport details, educational history, employment history, criminal record, secret service data and so on – there is clearly out there in the cyberworld an image of my identity that is very dense, very detailed, flawless, better informed than I am myself about myself. Confronted with the 'full picture', how can I disagree with what I am told of who I am?

And if it is not some database feeding information to the world about who I purport to be, it is myself. Through digital forums like MySpace.com and personal blogs, we share ourselves with the world. Who we are. Who we want to be. Who we might become. We are complicit in perpetuating a cyberworld that is redefining our cultural worlds as we once knew them, sometimes in isolation of other cultures.

In fact, the cyberworld is not 'out there' at all – it is part of the real world, the world we all inhabit and help shape. All the information in it is put there by people for a purpose – to inform, to publicize, to sell, to mislead, to denounce, to control, to resist – and all the data-mining engines and the giant databases have been made by men (and women) for the same purposes, to liberate, to enslave and to do everything in between. The digital environments in which we live are products of, and are embedded within, our social order (or disorder). They are made for purposes legitimated within our society, although many of those purposes may be contested by sections or by members of our society. The extent to which such goals can be legitimated and have resources allocated to them are social issues, not technological ones. Whether to provide, for instance, a digitally supported education which is liberating and empowering of the individual, or one which, on the other hand, is stultifying and controlling, is a decision made by people. Whether the decision is made fairly or justly or in the interests of the individual or of 'the group' or 'the market', or of some religious or political concept, is a product of the workings of the social, economic and political structure. As individuals, by our actions, we contribute daily to the re-making and re-shaping of the social order. And the more we are aware, the more we can make a difference, maybe only in small ways, to our own situation and to that of our society.

This is where we have to recognize that the digital is subject to human agency and to human understanding. It is not a technology which determines how we must act and how, for instance, we must be educated. It is a tool for the realization of human goals. And the things which it can do can be recognized, and described, in terms which humans can understand – the engines may be powerful and hideously complex, but the jobs they do are set by people who can talk in words we understand of profit or security, happiness, enlightenment.

This book is one bite at the apple of making the digital amenable to understanding and thereby to responsible control and empowering usage. Gilster (1997, 1) pointed out that 'digital literacy is about mastering ideas, not keystrokes'. Just as literacy theorists have come to recognize that developing literacy is about engaging with culture, and that the mastery of the mechanics of reading and writing is a key enabling skill, but no more than that, the thrust of this book is that the literacies of the digital are about engagement with the embeddedness of the digital in the culture and practices of society and, in particular, in educational actions. Giles and Middleton (1999, 24) define culture as 'the production and circulation of meaning'; culture is thus essentially dynamic – meanings are instantiated in actions that can in turn affect the meanings. Engagement with culture is therefore engagement with meaning and with change.

Technology as a cultural element is embedded within the mainstream of social action and meaning, for tools, as the defining characteristic of technology, are only meaningful in terms of tool-using situations. Thus, the significance of texting with mobile phones is related to the situations and patterns of social interaction and communication (which may or may not have changed due to the availability of texting). The situations and understandings of usage are more important than the techniques; and to gain a mastery of technique – the processes required to operate a tool – does not necessarily imply a mastery of usage. The meaning of the action is inherent in the situation, and not simply in the tool or the technique, although both of these are attributed meaning. The individual person is at the centre of the situation, for it is his or her interpretation that leads to action and hence change.

We can therefore understand the value of gaining understanding and adopting meaningful courses of action in respect of digital technology. In gaining digital literacies, digitally involved situations are rendered understandable and, hence, more controllable than they might otherwise be. The need for frameworks of understanding and of action will be the greater in those areas of social life where change is more rapid, and meaning is therefore less certain; changes in social life involving digital technologies are just such an area of uncertainty, where meanings, because they are being made new, are ambiguous, fluid and even contested. There is enormous benefit in regularizing an area of potential chaos, and the development of understanding of digital technology and its meaningful deployment, enabling individuals to map their own relationship to the digital, can be an important vehicle for empowerment, for both individuals and whole societies.

The intention behind this book is to explore some of those 'literacies' through which individuals can understand and develop their engagement with the digital, particularly (but not exclusively) in educational settings. However, this book will be of interest not just to librarians and educators, but to all those who are concerned with the participation of individuals as literate citizens and engaged learners in the 'information society', or whatever we call a culture that is infused with the digital.

The book is divided into two parts. In the first we address more general issues concerning the nature of the 'digital age' and the various literacies that enable individuals to survive in such a cultural milieu; in the second we present some examples of the development of 'digital literacies' in practice, and discuss some of the issues that arise as a result of such practices. Each chapter is written by different authors, from different backgrounds, countries and continents. Consequently, readers will enjoy a variety of writing styles, including the narrative and unique perspectives commonly found among those of similar yet sometimes distinct cultures. In this respect the book is more like a colloquium than a lecture. Voices from afar and near. Our task as editors was to identify notable contributors who have something to say in this area that is relevant and coherent, and which will both enlighten the reader and stimulate her (or him) to further thought – and perhaps an important transformational change.

Allan Martin
Dan Madigan

References

Giles, J. and Middleton, T. (1999) *Studying Culture*, Oxford, Blackwell.

Gilster, P. (1997) *Digital Literacy*, New York, John Wiley.

Rosado, E. and Bélisle, C. (2006) *Analysing Digital Literacy Frameworks*, DigEuLit project paper, Lyon, CNRS-LIRE, www.digeulit.ec/docs/public.asp.

Part 1
Literacies in the digital age

1

Literacies for the digital age: preview of Part 1

Allan Martin

Abstract

Our society is characterized by the use of numerous terms emphasizing the primacy of information technology. Although the pervasion of the digital is only a symptom of a listless and uncertain society, ability to cope with it is important to social survival. The idea of literacy is taken as a focus for coping with the digital: the notion of literacy itself has changed in response to the digital, and new literacies have been proposed, addressing elements of it. Some of these, and their possible convergence, are considered, and the notion of 'digital literacy' is suggested as a useful general concept. An overview is also given of the first part of the book.

Introduction: the 'digital society'

The world of the 21st century is digitally infused: an *e*-world, a world permeated by the effects and products of electronic technology. *E*-business, *e*-commerce, *e*-villages, *e*-health, *e*-government, *e*-learning: *e* is pervasive, although some parts of the world are more affected than others. In this e-world, *e*-encounters, that is, situations involving contact with electronic tools and facilities, are commonplace. E-encounters might encompass a washing machine or microwave oven, a camera, a telephone, a computer, or many other everyday items. E-encounters have become both ubiquitous and global: there are now few places in the world where electronic tools and facilities are not to be found, and, thanks to communications advances, e-encounters can themselves involve participants worldwide. Social activity can be enabled by and mediated through digital facilities. Electronic mail, discussion fora, mobile telephone texting, digital video conferencing and so on offer the enablement of social interaction at distances vastly greater than previous communication technologies, even those such as the telegraph and telephone, which offered immediate or almost immediate communication. Digitally enabled 'communities' have become a normal part of life. In addition to instantaneous communication, the internet also offers limitless information, extending beyond the scope of anything that might be considered for publication in a book, ranging from the products of governments, international agencies and multinational companies to the personal musings of bloggers or the whimsical websites of anyone who cares to invent one.

It is tempting to think that our society has been created by digital technologies, and the temptation is encouraged by the many technologically inspired names given, over the last 40 years, to the age in which we live. In 1967 Samuel Handel could write of *The Electronic Revolution* (Handel, 1967), while Peter Large in 1980 was referring to *The Micro Revolution* (Large, 1980). US National Security Adviser Zbigniew Brzezinski (1970) announced the 'technetronic age'. Dertouzos and Moses (1979) referred to *The Computer Age*, while for Forrester (1980) it was *The Microelectronics Revolution*. Nora and Minc refer to *L'Informatisation de la Société*, translated as *The Computerization of Society* (Nora and Minc, 1981). And the claims have continued up to the present, each successively trying to capture the ultimate superlative. Alvin Toffler warned in 1980 that: 'A new civilization is emerging in our lives, and blind men everywhere are trying to suppress it' (Toffler, 1980, 23). More recently, Bill Gates proclaimed that 'The information highway will transform our culture as dramatically as Gutenberg's press did the Middle Ages' (Gates, 1995).

Earlier terms have now largely been superseded by the 'information society', a term used routinely by both governments and international agencies as if it is self-evident. A European Commission report, *Europe and the Global Information Society*, stated that, 'throughout the world, information and communications technologies are bringing about a new industrial revolution which already looks to be as important and radical as those which preceded it' (European Commission, 1994, 4). 'The world is undergoing a technological revolution and entering the age of the Information Society' according to a House of Lords Select Committee report (House of Lords, 1996, §1.6). The UK government's 1998 Green Paper *The Learning Age: a renaissance for a new Britain* announced in its very first sentence: 'We are in a new age – the age of information and of global competition' (DfEE, 1998, 9). The term 'information society' is not new, being coined first in the 1960s (see Mattelart, 2003, for an 'archaeology of the information age'), but has found its time since the explosive spread of the internet in the 1990s , and the communication and information-accession possibilities it offers.

The main thesis underlying this notion is that information, or knowledge – the words are often used interchangeably – has become the key commodity in

the present age, that knowledge industries are the most central to global economic wellbeing, and knowledge workers the most essential to the maintenance
of progress. The 'knowledge revolution' has been enabled by developments in
information technology and communications, and has led to a 'knowledge
society' or 'information society'. However, while the term may be a useful way
of characterizing an IT-rich economic and social environment, some critics (e.g.
Lyon, 1988; Webster, 1995; May, 2002) argue that it fails as socio-economic analysis, since there is no convincing evidence that social and economic structures are
fundamentally changing. Relations between employers and employed, rich and
poor, powerful and powerless are unchanged; indeed, it has been argued that
owing to globalization they are getting worse. Even the argument that the
'information revolution' has had a significant social impact can be challenged:
Samuelson (2000) compares the social effects of the internet unfavourably with
those of the printing press or the railway.

The problem with notions such as the 'technological revolution' and the
'information society' is that they are powerful metaphors without clear content.
They create the impression that social change is determined by technology,
obscuring the fact that change, and indeed technology, are both products of
human action and interaction. And they suggest that social change is characterized by revolutions, i.e., sudden and simple shifts from one mode of activity to
another; whereas in reality social change is gradual and complex – even notable
'revolutionary' events are surrounded by other events that are all part of the
change process. However, while analytical notions of the information society
represent a perspective on social and economic development – and its relationship to technology – that may be strongly contested, as descriptive statements they
embody powerful symbols. Symbolic terms draw power from their assumed
grounding in reality, and their acceptance as real may give credence to particular
theoretical frameworks. Even as an avowedly superficial descriptor, the notion of
'information society' has power to change perceptions of the world, and to determine actions within it. Such symbols are knowingly used as agents of policy by
companies, governments and international bodies.

In fact the rise of the 'information society' and of the 'digital age' is bound
up with deeper social changes, which have been most elegantly characterized
by the Polish sociologist Zygmunt Bauman as the 'liquefaction' of social order
(Bauman, 2000):

> Society is being transformed by the passage from the 'solid' to the 'liquid' phases of
> modernity, in which all social forms melt faster than new ones can be cast. They are
> not given enough time to solidify, and cannot serve as the frame of reference for human
> actions and long-term life-strategies because their allegedly short life-expectation

undermines efforts to develop a strategy that would require the consistent fulfilment of a 'life-project.'

(Bauman, 2005, 303)

In this world uncertainty and unpredictability are normal. For those who do not belong to the global elite, life has become an individual struggle for meaning and livelihood in a world which has been termed 'the risk society' (Beck, 1992). Previous providers of long-term meaning, such as the state, institutional religion and local heavy industries, play a fast-diminishing role in giving life shape. Consumption has become the only reality, the main topic of TV and of conversation, and the focus of leisure activity. Lives are lived as short-term projects and past experience is of little or no value in a world where change is endemic.

The digital has a major part to play in the emergence and sustenance of this listless society. Instantaneous collection and analysis of data enables rapid and pinpoint responses to changes in worldwide patterns of consumption. And reliance on light and digitally driven equipment rather than immobile heavy plant enables global production relocation in months rather than years, leaving behind only deserted workshops and unemployed workers. Movement of capital often happens automatically, driven by software responding to the tiniest of changes in commodity or share prices by selling or buying raw materials, stocks, shares, bonds, rights, advances and anything considered a purchasable (and saleable) temporary asset. Commodities no longer need to move in the physical world for their digital shadows to travel thousands of miles. Information has become the bloodstream of the global capitalist elite. And a crucial effect is what Bauman calls the 'devaluation of place': 'The physical, non-cyber space where non-virtual communication takes place is but a site for the delivery, absorption and recycling of the essentially exterritorial, cyberspace information' (Bauman, 2001, 38). With digital games, mobile phones and iPods, a growing generation of 'digital natives' do not use digital technology to engage with reality, but to insulate themselves from it. Digital reality comes to seem more significant than actual. The technology also facilitates the coming together of 'communities' drawn through e-mail, chat rooms or mailing lists; such interest-based groupings are temporary and voluntary, requiring no commitment and no minimum level of participation.

The digital also plays a part in the increasing uncertainty of knowledge. First, the infinitude of information now accessible through the internet dwarfs any attempt to master a subject – it is simply no longer possible to know what is to be known in any area. The response is to focus on ever narrower or more esoteric disciplines or interests, or to admit that all that can be done is to sample the field. Second, the stature of knowledge is challenged, because the quality of what can be accessed is often unknown. In the printed book, the signs of quality – publisher, author affiliation, and so on – are usually clearly marked. But the quality of information on the internet is not always so obvious, sometimes deliberately veiled, sometimes simplistic but loud. Even the encyclopedic is not guaranteed: *Wikipedia* bills itself as 'the free encyclopedia that anyone can edit' (http://en.wikipedia.org/wiki/Main_Page). Despite the theory that correct material will usually overcome incorrect, there is nevertheless a caveat that knowledge is always relative.

In this context, out of all the challenges offered by a digitally infused society, the question of how individuals can understand, and cope with, the digital world becomes a significant one.

Literacy and literacies

The possession of multiple tools enabling the individual to cope in society is captured by the term 'literacy'. However, notions of literacy have changed substantially over time. Literacy in the Middle Ages had a twofold meaning: first, the ability to read and write – not necessarily simple abilities, for in many civilizations reading and writing were complicated and demanding activities to perform; and second, the idea of the learned person, participating in the activities of the community of the literate, the *literati*. This model persisted until the end of the Middle Ages. The rise of industrial society saw a change in the perception of literacy. It remained a mark of elite status, but for the middle classes literacy was also a functionality linked to their management roles of industrial society. There was also awareness that the ability to read and write was a benefit to the worker, justified by functionality (making them better workers) or social control (making them more obedient citizens). By the latter half of the twentieth century, the notion of literacy was based on psychological notions of competence in reading and writing, sustaining a deficit model of 'illiteracy', which encouraged focus on 'remediating' the problems of 'deprived' groups or individuals.

The limited skills approach to literacy has, however, over the past four decades, been joined by new approaches which question the exclusive focus on acquisition of the cognitive and manual mechanics of reading and writing. Thus, the concept of literacy is generalized, so that it consists of generic functionalities rather than the specific mechanics of reading and writing, and is set within a generic situation of usage. The UNESCO programme LAMP (Literacy Assessment and Monitoring Programme) defines literacy as

> the ability to identify, understand, interpret, create, communicate and compute, using printed and written materials associated with varying contexts. Literacy involves a continuum of learning enabling an individual to achieve his or her goals, develop his or her knowledge and potentials, and to participate fully in the community and wider society.
> (LAMP, 2004, 2)

For UNESCO, literacy development is linked to economic growth and the growth of civic consciousness and political maturity. The literate person lives within the literate society:

> Literacy is no longer exclusively understood as an individual transformation, but as a contextual and societal one. Increasingly, reference is made to the importance of rich literate environments – public or private milieux with abundant written documents (e.g. books, magazines and newspapers), visual materials (e.g. signs, posters and handbills), or communication and electronic media.
>
> (UNESCO, 2005, 159)

A more radical application of the general functionality approach was that of Paulo Freire, who saw literacy as an approach to learning and not as a specific, 'objective', intervention. Literacy becomes part of learning as a communal and critical activity, with the subject matter as important as the practice of reading or writing it. Literacy in this view becomes an instrument that can, indeed must, question and challenge power structures and legitimations of the social and cultural order. For Freire, literacy is a weapon against exploitation, and a vehicle for emancipation and democracy (Freire and Macedo, 1987).

The 'New Literacy Studies' approach focuses on the way in which literacy activities happen in a social and cultural context. Street (2001) identifies two key tenets, that literacy is a social product, and that language itself is interactive and dynamic. The implication of this view is that ideas of literacy, and actions taken in the pursuit of those ideas, are fully understandable only in terms of the contexts within which they occur; this echoes our earlier observations about the cultural embedding of technology.

Alongside these developments we should also note the appropriation of the term 'literacy' into English usage as a term denoting the set of abilities required to do something or associated with a particular sphere of activity. As mentioned below, 'visual literacy' dates from 1969, and 'computer literacy' from 1976, but the adoption of 'literacy' in this sense seems to have accelerated during the 1980s, and can now be applied willy-nilly to any set of abilities. Thus 'physical literacy' involves basic physical activities such as running, skipping, jumping and hopping, and needs to be developed because of a growing 'physical illiteracy', where children have never developed these abilities owing to an increasingly sedentary and indoor lifestyle (Denholm, 2005).

Digitally related literacies

We can identify a number of 'literacies' that have gained new or increased relevance with the emergence of digital environments, and which we can see converging with

the digital as suitable for special focus. Apart from ICT literacy, they have origi-
nated in the pre-digital world, but have successfully been able to draw digital activities within their ambits, and have recognized that the digital has had a transforming
impact upon their area of focus.

ICT literacy

The need for education systems to deliver ICT skills at all levels has been perceived
almost since the 1960s. We can see concepts of computer literacy as passing
through three phases: the *mastery* phase (up to the mid-1980s), the *application* phase
(mid-1980s to late-1990s) and the *reflective* phase (late-1990s onwards) (Martin,
2001, 2003). In the *mastery* phase the computer is perceived as arcane and powerful, and emphasis is placed on gaining knowledge and skill to master it.
'Computer basics', or whatever they were called, consisted of how the computer
works (simple computer science) and how to program it (using whatever languages
were current at the time), often with additional input on the social and economic effects of computers. This approach is exemplified in reports such as that of the
UK University Grants Committee on computing for university students
(UGC/CBURC, 1970), the Scottish Education Department reports on computers and schools (SED, 1969, 1972), and the US government's report *A Nation at
Risk* (NCEE, 1983). The term 'computer literacy' was proposed during this
phase, and reflects its concerns:

> Because of the widespread use of elementary computing skill, there should be an
> appropriate term for this skill. It should suggest an acquaintance with the rudiments
> of computer programming, much as the term literacy connotes a familiarity with the
> fundamentals of reading and writing, and it should have a precise definition that all
> can agree on. It is reasonable to suggest that a person who has written a computer pro-
> gram should be called *literate in computing*.
>
> (Nevison, 1976, 401, italics original)

Towards the end of the 1980s the demands of the market led to the development
of simple user interfaces and easy-to-use mass market applications, which opened
up computers to mass usage and stimulated a change in notions of computer literacy. In the *application* phase an intuitive graphical user interface was taken for
granted, and the computer was perceived as an everyday tool that can be applied
to a wide range of activities in education, work, leisure and the home. Windows
and similar interfaces are the norm, and applications software became more
powerful and simpler to use. IT (information technology) and ICT (information
and communications technology) become the normal terms of reference for computing activities. The focus of literacy activity was on how to use computer appli-

cations , and definitions of computer or IT literacy focused on lists of practical competences rather than specialist knowledge. This was accompanied by the production of training materials and the appearance of mass certification schemes focusing on basic levels of ICT competence.

Movement to the *reflective* phase was stimulated by recognition that ICT could be a vehicle through which student-centred pedagogies, championed by innovators in schools and higher education since the 1960s, could at last be realized. There was now an awareness of the need for more critical, evaluative and reflective approaches to using IT. The term 'fluency' was proposed by a US National Research Council report (NRC, 1999) to suggest the greater intellectual challenge proposed. The US Educational Testing Service report takes a clear position on the reflective nature of ICT literacy:

> ICT literacy cannot be defined primarily as the mastery of technical skills. The ... concept of ICT literacy should be broadened to include both critical cognitive skills as well as the application of technical skills and knowledge. These cognitive skills include general literacy, such as reading and numeracy, as well as critical thinking and problem solving. Without such skills . . . true ICT literacy cannot be attained.
>
> (ETS, 2002, 1)

The report defines ICT literacy as follows:

> ICT literacy is using digital technology, communications tools, and/or networks to access, manage, integrate, and create information in order to function in a knowledge society. (ibid., 2) . . .
>
> The five components represent a continuum of skills and knowledge and are presented in a sequence suggesting increasing cognitive complexity. ...

Access – knowing about and knowing how to collect and/or retrieve information.
Manage – applying an existing organizational or classification scheme.
Integrate – interpreting and representing information. It involves summarizing, comparing and contrasting.
Evaluate – making judgements about the quality, relevance, usefulness, or efficiency of information.
Create – generating information by adapting, applying, designing, inventing, or authoring information.

(ibid., 17)

At the reflective level, where specific skills are superseded by generic skills or meta-skills, there is also more overlap, or convergence, with the approach of other literacies. This is also evident in the definition formulated by the OECD-ILO PISA project:

> ICT literacy is the interest, attitude and ability of individuals to appropriately use digital technology and communication tools to access, manage, integrate and evaluate information, construct new knowledge, and communicate with others in order to participate effectively in society.
>
> (van Joolingen, 2004)

It is possible that this three-phase development of ICT literacy, from skills through usage to reflection, is paralleled in the evolution of the other literacies considered here. We should note that the earlier phases remain as subordinate layers, so that the literacy concepts become more complex and multi-layered as they develop.

Technological literacy

'Technological literacy' emerged in the 1970s as a response to two very different concerns: the growing awareness of the enormous potential danger of technological developments for the environment and for humanity; and the growing fear that ignorance of developing technologies would render the workforce, in countries such as the USA and Britain, vulnerable to competition from countries with more technological awareness (Waks, 2006). The result was an uneasy marriage of the two concerns, since one favoured a skills-based vocational approach (with a preference for a behaviourist pedagogy) and the other a critical, action-oriented 'academic' approach (with a liking for a more constructivist pedagogy) (Dakers, 2006). This compromise is reflected in the *Technology for All Americans* materials, funded by the US government:

> Technological literacy is the ability to use, manage, and understand technology:
> – The ability to use technology involves the successful operation of the key systems of the time. This includes knowing the components of existing macro-systems, or human adaptive systems, and how the systems behave.
> – The ability to manage technology involves insuring that all technological activities are efficient and appropriate.
> – Understanding technology involves more than facts and information, but also the ability to synthesize the information into new insights.
>
> (ITEA, 1996, 5)

Technological literacy was enthusiastically adopted by President Bill Clinton, although his agenda focused on computers, the four key points of his agenda being:

1.   Connect every school and classroom in America to the information superhighway;
2.   Provide access to modern computers for all teachers and students;
3.   Develop effective and engaging software and on-line learning resources as an integral part of the school curriculum; and
4.   Provide all teachers the training and support they need to help students learn through computers and the information superhighway.

(ed.gov, 1997)

A major criticism of these developments is that, despite the rhetoric, the critical element of technological literacy is insufficiently developed or implemented; it is necessary to engage the industrial application of technology with deeper understanding of the social and political involvement of technology (Michael, 2006). This will involve adopting a more critical philosophy of technology education:

> Technology education ... should have a 'relationship' with industry, but not a subservient one, not one that is simply in the service of industry. Critical debate about technology and the role that industry has in its development must be encouraged.
>
> (Dakers, 2006, 156)

Information literacy

The notion of 'information literacy' developed in the USA from the late 1980s as a re-focusing of 'bibliographic instruction' (the equivalent UK term is 'user education') in academic libraries, in the light of the trend towards student-centred learning, and thus arose in a largely pre-digital context. The report of an influential 1987 symposium noted that

> Reports on undergraduate education identify the need for more active learning whereby students become self-directed independent learners who are prepared for lifelong learning. To accomplish this, students need to become information literate.
>
> (Breivik and Wedgeworth, 1988, 187–8)

The 1989 report of an American Library Association committee (reprinted in Breivik, 1998, 121–37), defined the information literate person as one who 'must be able to recognize when information is needed and have the ability to locate, evaluate, and use effectively the needed information' (ibid., 121–2).

With the increasing perception of the worldwide web as a seemingly infinite source of information, the movement for information literacy gained more urgency. The US Association of College and Research Libraries, focusing on higher education, presented a set of performance indicators based on five 'standards':

The information literate student:

i.   determines the nature and extent of the information needed;
ii. accesses needed information effectively and efficiently;
iii. evaluates information and its sources critically and incorporates selected information into his or her knowledge base and value system;
iv. uses information effectively to accomplish a specific purpose;
v.   understands many of the economic, legal, and social issues surrounding the use of information and accesses and uses information ethically and legally.

(ACRL, 2000, 8–13, passim)

In the UK, SCONUL's 'Seven Pillars' model, intended for students in higher education, identifies seven 'headline skills' forming information literacy, each of which can be developed from a level of 'novice' to that of 'expert':

* recognizing an information need
* identifying what information will fulfil the need
* constructing strategies for locating information
* locating and accessing the information sought
* comparing and evaluating information obtained from different sources
* organizing, applying and communicating information
* synthesizing and building upon information.

(Adapted from Town, 2000, 17–18.)

In the Seven Pillars model, IT skills (along with basic library skills) are seen as a key element underpinning information skills.

Information literacy has influenced librarians worldwide (see Rader, 2003), and is seen as important by national and international bodies. In September 2003 an 'Information Literacy Meeting of Experts', organized by the US National Commission on Library and Information Science and the National Forum on Information Literacy, with the support of UNESCO, was held in Prague. The meeting resulted in the so-called 'Prague Declaration' (UNESCO, 2003) stressing the global importance of information literacy in the context of the 'Information Society'. It includes the statement that:

Information Literacy encompasses knowledge of one's information concerns and needs, and the ability to identify, locate, evaluate, organize and effectively create, use and communicate information to address issues or problems at hand; it is a prerequisite for participating effectively in the Information Society, and is part of the basic human right of life long learning.

(ibid., 1)

The meeting report emphasizes that information literacy is not only about digital information, but that there is a wider challenge of which digital environments form only one part. Research by Johnston and Webber suggests that digital factors have less impact on academics' perceptions of information literacy than do their pedagogical approaches. Johnston and Webber (2003) underline the media-independent nature of information literacy with their own definition:

> the adoption of appropriate information behaviour to obtain, through whatever channel or medium, information well fitted to information needs, together with critical awareness of the importance of wise and ethical use of information in society (http://dis.shef.ac.uk/literacy/project/about.html).

Media literacy

Media literacy has developed from the critical evaluation of mass media, and is a major educational and research activity in both the USA and Europe. The Alliance for a Media Literate America offers the following definition on its website:

> Within North America, media literacy is seen to consist of a series of communication competencies, including the ability to ACCESS, ANALYZE, EVALUATE and COMMUNICATE information in a variety of forms including print and non-print messages. Interdisciplinary by nature, media literacy represents a necessary, inevitable and realistic response to the complex, ever-changing electronic environment and communication cornucopia that surrounds us.
>
> (AMLA, 2005)

Media literacy is a major goal, along with digital literacy, of the EU eLearning Initiative:

> Media literacy helps citizens, particularly youth, develop the critical thinking and production skills they need to live in the 21st century media culture. It is the ability to communicate fluently in all old and new media, as well as to access, analyse and evaluate the powerful images, words and sounds that confront us in our daily lives.
>
> (European Commission, 2003, 15)

There is much similarity between definitions of media literacy and information literacy, suggesting that the generic competences are very similar. The difference seems to be one of approach, arising out of the separate histories of each movement. Media literacy is focused more on the nature of various genres of medium and the way in which messages are constructed and interpreted – in this perspective the characteristics of the author/sender and the receiver are crucial in understanding the meaning of the message and its content. Information literacy has tended to focus on the ways in which information is accessed – genre? – and the evaluation of the content. Both also include the creation of new messages or information.

Visual literacy

Visual literacy has developed out of art criticism and art education, and was initially concerned with both the physiology and psychology of perception, and the way in which artists and designers have used perspective, ratio, light, colour and other techniques of visual communication. The term was first coined in 1969 by John Debes:

> Visual Literacy refers to a group of vision-competencies a human being can develop by seeing and at the same time having and integrating other sensory experiences. The development of these competencies is fundamental to normal human learning. When developed, they enable a visually literate person to discriminate and interpret the visible actions, objects, symbols, natural or man-made, that he encounters in his environment. Through the creative use of these competencies, he is able to communicate with others. Through the appreciative use of these competencies, he is able to comprehend and enjoy the masterworks of visual communication.
>
> (IVLA, 2006)

Visual literacy is thus a key element of art and design education: Wilde and Wilde (1991, 12) link visual problem solving to 'the quest for visual literacy' and offer this as 'the best hope for creating future generations of visually literate designers'. Dondis however emphasizes that this approach can enable everybody (not merely the artistic elite) to engage with the visual aspects of culture, and thus sees visual literacy as very much parallelling classical literacy:

> Literacy means that a group shares the assigned meaning of a common body of information. Visual literacy must operate somewhat within the same boundaries. . . . Its purposes are the same as those that motivated the development of written language: to construct a basic system for learning, recognizing, making, and understanding visual messages that are negotiable by all people, not just those specially trained, like the designer, the artist, the craftsman, and the aesthetician.
>
> (Dondis, 1973, x)

Visual images have of course always been a powerful medium for the interpretation of information and the communication of meaning, in science as well as art, and in dealing with the exigencies of everyday life. Yet the wealth and complexity of visual imagery which is possible using digital tools emphasizes the power of the visual. For instance, the website www.visualcomplexity.com offers many examples of how visual structures are used in the processes of interpreting data and creating new knowledge. Kress argues that in the 'post-text' world, language is itself being affected by visual forms:

> The screen more than the page is now the dominant site of representation and com-
> munication in general, so that even in writing, things cannot be left there. ... The screen
> is the site of the image, and the logic of the image dominates the semiotic organiza-
> tion of the screen.

(Kress, 2003, 65)

New literacies and multiple literacies

Literacy theorists have also recognized the significance of the digital in shaping the contexts within which literacy is to be understood. Lankshear and Knobel (2003) talk about 'new literacies' although they also refer to 'new literacy practices' (Knobel and Lankshear, 2002). They describe 'new literacies' as follows:

> The category of 'new literacies' largely covers what are often referred to as 'post-typo-
> graphic' forms of textual practice. These include using and constructing hyperlinks
> between documents and/or images, sounds, movies, semiotic languages (such as ...
> emoticons ('smileys') used in email, online chat space or in instant messaging), manip-
> ulating a mouse to move around within a text, reading file extension and identifying
> what software will 'read' each file, producing 'non-linear' texts, navigating three-
> dimensional worlds online and so on.

(Lankshear and Knobel, 2003, 16–17)

To these new literacies, which do not all necessarily involve ICT, they add further literacies which are new in a chronological sense, or new to being considered as literacies. They offer an interesting range of examples: scenario planning, zines, multimediating, e-zining, meme-ing, blogging, map rapping, culture jamming and communication guerrilla actions (ibid., 23–49).

To underline the existence of a range of distinct but interrelated literacies, some commentators use the plural terms 'literacies', 'multiple literacies' or 'multiliteracies'. Kellner (2002, 163) prefers the term 'multiple literacies' which, 'points to the many different kinds of literacies needed to access, interpret, criticize, and participate in the emergent new forms of culture and society', but also refers to 'techno-literacies' (Kahn and Kellner, 2006). Snyder (2002) titles her book *Silicon Literacies* but tends in the text itself to refer to 'literacy practices' rather than 'literacies'. Kress (2003), however, argues against the multiplicity of literacies, suggesting that it leads to serious conceptual confusion, and believes that instead of taking this path, it is necessary to develop a new theoretical framework for literacy which can use a single set of concepts to address its various aspects. Tyner (1998, 63–8) recognizes the need to refer to multiliteracies, but prefers to identify groups of linked literacies while retaining 'literacy' as an overarching concept.

Convergence or overlap

It is clear that there is considerable overlap between the literacies outlined above. In some cases, the definitions of the different literacies are almost identical, and only nuanced in different directions. Tyner (1998, 104) points out that:

> The similarities between the stated competences of information literacy, visual literacy, and media literacy are so close that separating them seems unnecessarily artificial. … The need to set one literacy apart from another can only be explained by a need to use the concepts for other reasons, that is, to strengthen the professional status of its constituencies, or to take issue with the approaches used by its proponents

although she does admit that, 'there are some subtle differences in emphasis' between these three literacies.

What do we learn from the proliferation of literacies, and from their overlap, or convergence? The proliferation is not surprising, since each has come from a different route, each at the service of its own interest group and operating in a context important to, and perhaps even controlled by, the interest group. And, even if there is much overlap at the most generic level of definition, the nuances reflecting the perspective of the interest group will become more apparent as we approach the detailed description of competences, abilities, understandings and activities. We should also note that, apart from ICT literacy, they have all developed in pre-digital contexts, and digital applications only form part (albeit maybe a large and growing part) of their field. From the pre-digital time, the culture of the interest group has developed, so that it has a distinctive identity and sense of purpose. It may also have an institutional infrastructure which offers members of the interest group roles in which they can feel secure. As well as functional justifications for its distinctiveness, there are thus also powerful social reasons why an interest group should want to maintain the distinctiveness and independence of 'their' literacy. Assimilating a 'threatening' literacy may be an effective defensive response to maintain the culture and identity of the group.

The apparent (or real) convergence may be due to several reasons. The emergence of digital tools and environments may well have created a heightened awareness of the similarities or overlaps between various literacies, as literacy promoters from different areas home in on the same generic digital tools. The convergence of ICT and information literacies has been encouraged also by organizational changes in educational institutions, where IT support services and libraries have been brought together into a single organizational unit, often dubbed an 'information service'. Part of the convergence also involves the evolution of literacies from a skills focus through an applications focus towards a concern with critique, reflection and judgement, and the identification of generic cognitive abilities or processes. Thus there is a move to conceptualize literacies away from the specification of content – in the form of lists of skills or competences – towards identification of generic processes of problem-solution or task-achievement. This results in literacies re-defining themselves as being concerned with the application of similar critical/reflective abilities in slightly different fields of activity. Those who champion the idea of enabling students or citizens through literacy activities may also tend to favour the adoption of student-centred pedagogies, and will therefore tend to identify similar sets of learning abilities, addressed by similar generic literacy activities.

To seek in these circumstances 'one literacy to rule them all' may be a fruitless venture. It may seem attractive to bring an end to definitional confusion and regularize overlapping – and no doubt sometimes duplicating – activities, and to speak with one voice for the 'literacy of the information society', but the likely result will be that the voice will be that of the powerful, the institutional and the wealthy. A multitude of literacies may be confusing and inconvenient, but it represents the reality of social life, where perspectives and situations vary immensely and are constantly changing. Literacies point to perceptions of need and empowerment in society, and a changing society will inevitably continue to create new ones, since the perception of modes of empowerment is a corollary of the perception of what it is, or what it should be, to be a functioning member of society. Concepts of literacy are pieces of the visions of the social order.

Digital literacy

'Digital literacy' may have some merit as an integrating (but not overarching) concept that focuses upon the digital without limiting itself to computer skills, and which comes with little historical baggage. The term was popularized by Paul Gilster, who defined it as 'the ability to understand and use information in multiple formats from a wide range of sources when it is presented via computers' (Gilster, 1997, 1). Gilster identifies critical thinking rather than technical competence as the core skill of digital literacy, and emphasizes the critical evaluation of what is found on the web, rather than the technical skills required to access it. He also emphasizes the relevant usage of skills in real life, that digital literacy is more than skills or competences. These sentiments are echoed in *Digital Horizons*, a report of the New Zealand Ministry of Education:

Digital literacy is the ability to appreciate the potential of ICT to support innovation in industrial, business and creative processes. Learners need to gain the confidence, skills, and discrimination to adopt ICT in appropriate ways. Digital literacy is seen as a 'life skill' in the same way as literacy and numeracy.

(Ministry of Education, 2003, 5)

The EC-funded DigEuLit project (www.digeulit.ec), defines 'digital literacy' as:

the awareness, attitude and ability of individuals to appropriately use digital tools and facilities to identify, access, manage, integrate, evaluate, analyse and synthesize digital resources, construct new knowledge, create media expressions, and communicate with others, in the context of specific life situations, in order to enable constructive social action; and to reflect upon this process.

(Martin, 2006: 15)

In this view, digital literacy is only achieved when digital competences are thoughtfully deployed in authentic life situations, in solving a problem or completing a task. Digital literacy is thus much more than the mastery of skills. The reflective element also enables digital literacy to become a transformative activity, since reflection on one's digital usage can enable changes in one's own practice and that of others. It is therefore important for individuals to be aware of their own development as digitally literate people, in the context of the life, work and study trajectories they see ahead of them.

The reflective and lifelong aspects of digital literacy is emphasized by Søby, who, in a report for the Norwegian Ministry of Research and Education, draws attention to the concept of 'Digital Bildung':

Digital *Bildung* expresses a more holistic understanding of how children and youths learn and develop their identity. In addition, the concept encompasses and combines the way in which skills, qualifications, and knowledge are used. As such, digital *Bildung* suggests an integrated, holistic approach that enables reflection on the effects that ICT has on different aspects of human development: communicative competence, critical thinking skills, and enculturation processes, among others.

(Søby, 2003, 8)

Søby uses the german term *Bildung* to suggest the integrated development of the individual as a whole person. The process of *Bildung* goes on throughout life, affects all aspects of the individual's thought and activity, and affects understandings, interpretations, beliefs, attitudes and emotions as well as actions. It represents the making of the individual both as a unique individual and as a member of a culture. We can therefore see the digitally literate person being aware, throughout their life, and across all its aspects, of their development as an empowered member of a digitally infused society.

The assertion of digital literacy for any person or group is always provisional. Digital literacy is an ongoing and dynamic process – it is not a threshold that, once achieved, guarantees familiarity with the digital for ever after. It cannot therefore be certificated with a one-off certification like a driver's licence, since digital literacy needs are a characteristic of the individual. It is dependent on the needs of the situation; when those needs change, what constitutes digital literacy for that situation may well change. To remain digitally literate, it may be necessary to return again and again to the well of digital competence – which is itself changing in content as technology evolves – to acquire the competence elements that are now required to succeed in the life-situation, whether it be learning, work or leisure. Digital literacy is a condition, not a threshold.

Literacies for the digital age

The developments described above raise many issues, some of which are only touched upon, that one volume cannot resolve. Contributors to this book engage with them in a range of different ways and in a range of contexts. The more general issues are addressed in the first half of the book.

Chapters 2 and 3 focus on learning in the digitally infused world. Terry Mayes and Chris Fowler set out the evolution of learning theory and its relationship with methods of enabling learning digitally. The key points are that learning is both constructive (based on the development of meaning by the learner) and socially situated (facilitated by the interpersonal situation in which the learner is embedded); and that digital technology can support modes of learning based on this understanding of the nature of learning. This opens up a question of 'learning literacy', which becomes more complex and subtle as our understanding of learning grows. Johannes Cronjé stresses the importance in digitally supported learning of the metaphor of the academy: the arena where learning takes place face-to-face in a real physical setting. One of the results of this is to encourage interaction between learners, leading away from pre-internet conceptions of computer-based learning as a solitary pursuit. But to prosper in this digitally enabled environment for (co-operative) learning, participants need to engage with three literacies: visual literacy, co-operative literacy and academic literacy.

Chapters 4 and 5 by Paul Gilster and Claire Bélisle move from the process of education to the nature of knowledge in a digitally infused society and its implications for notions of literacy. Gilster considers how the capacity and usage of the internet have blurred the distinction between and enabled a convergence of content (information products such as books, papers, web pages) and communication (the interaction between members of communities of interest), a development that opens up opportunities but also presents challenges to scholars. Bélisle discusses the evolution of concepts of literacy, making the point that literacy can only be fully addressed in the contexts of socio-cultural meanings and ways of thinking; and that the emergence and growth of digital knowledge have impacted substantially on both contexts, creating a need for a digital literacy that enables the individual to engage in an informed way with a society imbued with digital knowledge.

The following four chapters explore in some detail the literacies that have become salient in the digitally infused world. In Chapter 6 Maryann Kope takes up the idea of e-literacy, as a convergence of IT literacy and information literacy, and argues that academic literacy should be added to this equation to provide a critical and intellectual integrating context that will enable students to become e-literate in a full and meaningful sense. In Chapter 7 Ola Pilerot focuses on information literacy, showing how the term can be approached from different perspectives, and reveal both tensions and synergies with other literacies, as well as issues arising from the role of librarians as the main torchbearers of information literacy.

These points are true of most putative literacies. In seeking a literacy for the present, David F. Warlick, in Chapter 8, takes the familiar three Rs – reading, writing, arithmetic – and redefines them for the digital environment: reading as accessing, interpreting and evaluating information, arithmetic as deploying and processing information, and writing as presenting information compellingly. But he argues that literacy for the digital environment requires a fourth element, the ethical use of information. Renee Hobbs, in Chapter 9, focuses on media literacy, addressing the way in which digital facilities available to young people have presented challenges to media literacy educators.

The final two chapters in the first part of the book offer perspectives on the digital literacy environment of different student groups in different parts of the world. In Chapter 20 Chris Sutton considers the digital literacy challenge to vocational education in Australia and presents a model which meets the multiliteracy needs of vocational students learning online. And in Chapter 11, Denise and Jeff Haywood and Hamish Macleod report on a major study of student digital skills and their relation to employability across Europe; this underlines the importance, both to students and to those who enable their learning, of awareness of how the use of digital tools in work contexts is changing, and of addressing the e-literacies that will make people more employable.

Conclusion

Literacy and the digital make for a combination of concepts that has spawned a multitude of offspring. Yet there are many ways in which these offspring hang together. Visions of the literacies of the digitally infused society continue to evolve and to find connections and overlaps. All of them, however, seek to make a rapidly changing element of the present world understandable and masterable. If the ability to deal effectively with the digital is no antidote to the uncertainty of the world itself, at least it can make part of that world more amenable.

References

ACRL (2000) *Information Literacy Competency Standards for Higher Education*, Chicago, Association of College and Research Libraries.

AMLA (2005) Media Literacy, Denver, CO, Alliance for a Media Literate America, www.amlainfo.org/home/media-literacy.

Bauman, Z. (2000) *Liquid Modernity*, Cambridge, Polity Press.

Bauman, Z. (2001) *The Individualized Society*, Cambridge, Polity Press.

Bauman, Z. (2005) Education in Liquid Modernity, *Review of Education, Pedagogy, and Cultural Studies*, **27**, 303–17.

Beck, U. (1992) *The Risk Society*, London, Sage.

Breivik, P. S. (1998) *Student Learning in the Information Age*, Phoenix, AZ, Oryx Press for the American Council on Education.

Breivik, P. S. and Wedgeworth, R. (1988) *Libraries and the Search for Academic Excellence*, Metuchen, NJ, Scarecrow Press.

Brzezinski (1970) *Between Two Ages: America's role in the technetronic era*, New York, NY, Viking Press.

Crowther, J., Hamilton, M. and Tett, L. (2001) *Powerful Literacies*, Leicester, NIACE.

Dakers, J. (2006) Towards a Philosophy for Technology Education. In Dakers, J. R. (ed.), *Defining Technological Literacy*, New York, NY, Palgrave Macmillan, 145–58.

Denholm, A. (2005) Hop, Skip and Jump: reviving lost play skills, *The Herald* (Glasgow), (4 June), 7.

Dertouzos, M. L., and Moses, J. (eds) (1979) *The Computer Age: a twenty-year view*, Cambridge, MA, MIT Press.

DfEE (1998) *The Learning Age: a Renaissance for a new Britain*, Cm 3790, London, Stationery Office.

Dondis, D. A. (1973) *A Primer of Visual Literacy*, Cambridge, MA, MIT Press.

ed.gov (1997) *Technological Literacy: President Clinton's call to action for American education in the 21st century*, www.ed.gov/updates/PresEDPlan/part11.html.

ETS (2002) *Digital Transformation: a framework for ICT literacy*, Princeton, NJ, Educational Testing Service.

European Commission (1994) *Europe and the Global Information Society: recommendations to the European Council by the High-level Group on the Information Society* (Bangemann Report), http://europa.eu.int/ISPO/infosoc/backg/bangeman.html.

European Commission (2003) *eLearning: better eLearning for Europe*, Brussels, Directorate-General for Education and Culture.

Forrester, T. (ed.) 1980 *The Microelectronics Revolution*, Oxford, Blackwell.

Freire, P. and Macedo, D. (1987) *Literacy: reading the word and the world*, Westport, CT, Bergin & Garvey.

Gates, B. (1995) *The Road Ahead*, London, Viking Penguin.

Gilster, P. (1997) *Digital Literacy*, New York, NY, John Wiley.

Handel, S. (1967) *The Electronic Revolution*, Harmondsworth, Penguin.

House of Lords (1996) Information Society: agenda for action in the UK Select Committee on Science and Technology Session 1995–96 5th Report, HL Paper 77, London, HMSO.

ITEA (1996) *Technology for All Americans: a rationale and structure for the study of technology*, Reston, VA, International Technology Education Association.

IVLA (2006) *What is 'Visual Literacy'?*, International Visual Literacy Association, www.ivla.org/org_what_vis_lit.htm.

Johnston, B. and Webber, S. (2003) Information Literacy in Higher Education: a review and case study, *Studies in Higher Education*, **28**, 335–52.

Kahn, R. and Kellner, D. (2006) Reconstructing Technoliteracy: a multiple literacies approach. In Dakers, J. (ed.), *Defining Technological Literacy*, New York, NY, Palgrave Macmillan, 253–73.

Kellner, D. (2002) Technological Revolution, Multiple Literacies, and the Restructuring of Education. In Snyder, I., *Silicon Literacies*, London, Routledge, 154–69.

Knobel, M. and Lankshear, C. (2002) What am I bid? Reading, writing and ratings at eBay.com. In Snyder, I., *Silicon Literacies*, London, Routledge, 15–30.

Kress, G. (2003) *Literacy in the New Media Age*, London, Routledge.

LAMP (2004) *International Planning Report*, Montréal, UNESCO, Institute for Statistics.

Lankshear, C. and Knobel, M. (2003) *New Literacies: changing knowledge and classroom learning*, Buckingham, Open University Press.

Large, P. (1980) *The Micro Revolution*, Glasgow, Fontana.

Lyon, D. (1988) *The Information Society: issues and illusions*, Cambridge, Polity Press.

Martin, A. (2001) Concepts of C&IT Literacy in Higher Education. In Martin, A. (ed.), *Final Report of Phase I of the Citscapes Project*, IT Education Unit, University of Glasgow, www.citscapes.ac.uk/products/phase1/ch4.pdf.

Martin, A. (2003) Towards e-literacy. In Martin, A., and Rader, H. (eds), *Information and IT Literacy: enabling learning in the 21st century*, London, Facet Publishing, 3–23.

Martin, A. (2006) A Framework for Digital Literacy, DigEuLit Project working paper, www.digeulit.ec/docs/public.asp.

Mattelart, A. (2003) *The Information Society: an introduction*, London, Sage.

May, C. (2002) *The Information Society: a skeptical view*, Cambridge, Polity Press.

Michael, M. (2006) How to Understand Mundane Technology: new ways of thinking about human–technology relations. In Dakers, J. (ed.), *Defining Technological Literacy*, New York, NY, Palgrave Macmillan, 49–63.

Ministry of Education (2003) *Digital Horizons: learning through ICT*, rev. edn, Wellington, New Zealand Ministry of Education, December, www.minedu.govt.nz/web/downloadable/dl6760_v1/digital-horizons-revision-03.pdf.

NCEE (1983) *A Nation at Risk: the imperative for educational reform*, Washington, DC, National Commission on Excellence in Education.

Nevison, J. M. (1976) Computing in the Liberal Arts College, *Science*, (22 October), 396–402.

Nora, S. and Minc, A. (1981) *The Computerization of Society*, Cambridge, MA, MIT Press [originally published as *L'Informatisation de la Société*, Paris, 1978].

NRC (1999) *Being Fluent with Information Technology*, Committee on Information Technology Literacy, National Research Council, Washington, DC, National Academy Press.

Rader, H. (2003) Information Literacy – a Global Perspective. In Martin, A. and Rader, H. (eds) *Infromation and IT Literacy: enabling learning in the 21st century*, London, Facet Publishing, 24–42.

Samuelson, R. J. (2000) The Internet and Gutenberg, *Newsweek*, (24 January), 2.

SED (1969) *Computers and the Schools: an interim report*, Scottish Education Department, Consultative Committee on the Curriculum Curriculum, Paper 6, Edinburgh, HMSO.

SED (1972) *Computers and the Schools: final report*, Scottish Education Department, Consultative Committee on the Curriculum, Curriculum Paper 11, Edinburgh, HMSO.

Snyder, I. (ed.)(2002) *Silicon Literacies*, London, Routledge.

Søby, M. (2003) *Digital Competence: from ICT skills to digital 'Bildung'*, ITU, University of Oslo.

Street, B. (2001) Contexts for Literacy Work: the 'new orders' and the 'new literacy studies'. In Crowther, J., Hamilton, M. and Tett, L., *Powerful Literacies*, Leicester, NIACE, 13–22.

Toffler, A. (1980) *The Third Wave*, Glasgow, William Collins.

Town, S. (2000) Wisdom or Welfare? The Seven Pillars Model. In Corrall, S. and Hathaway, H., *Seven Pillars of Wisdom? Good practice in information skills development*, London, SCONUL, 11–21.

Tyner, K. (1998) *Literacy in a Digital World*, Mahwah, NJ, Lawrence Erlbaum.

UGC/CBURC (1970) *Teaching Computing in Universities*, London, HMSO.

UNESCO (2003) *Conference Report of the Information Literacy Meeting of Experts Prague, The Czech Republic, September 20–23, 2003,* www.nclis.gov/libinter/infolitconfandmeet/post-infolitconfandmeet/FinalReportPrague.pdf.

UNESCO (2005) *Education for All: literacy for life*, fourth annual Education for All Global Monitoring Report, Paris, UNESCO Publishing.

Van Joolingen, W. (2004) *The PISA Framework for Assessment of ICT Literacy*, PowerPoint presentation, www.ictliteracy.info/rf.pdf/PISA%20framework.ppt.

Waks, L. J. (2006) Rethinking Technological Literacy for the Global Network Era. In Dakers, J. (ed.), *Defining Technological Literacy*, New York, NY, Palgrave Macmillan, 275–95.

Webster, F. (1995) *Theories of the Information Society*, London, Routledge.

Wilde, J. and Wilde, R. (1991) *Visual Literacy*, New York, NY, Watson-Guptill Publications.

2

Learners, learning literacy and the pedagogy of e-learning

Terry Mayes and Chris Fowler

Abstract

This chapter outlines the landscape of e-learning and considers how learners can flourish within it. It traces the development of understanding about pedagogy that underpins technology-enhanced learning, describing the shift in emphasis from the delivery of powerful representations of the subject matter, through the computer as tutor, to the current focus on dialogue in learning communities. Increasingly, the pedagogical focus is on the emergence of tools that support participation in learning groups, and the formation of learning relationships. The chapter describes one approach that attempts to capitalize on a neglected form of learning: 'vicarious' learning, which occurs as a consequence of observing other learners. This leads to consideration of Wenger's recent call for a new discourse based on the 'horizontalization' of learning. The chapter concludes by describing a view of 'learning literacy' that places willingness and confidence to participate in new learning relationships as the key requirements. These characteristics depend not on skill so much as on developing an identity as a learner.

Introduction

In a paper called 'Learning Technology and Groundhog Day' (Mayes, 1995) the author argued that the field of educational technology was locked into a cycle of high expectation followed by disappointment, reminiscent of the protagonist in the film 'Groundhog Day' who wakes up each morning to find that it is the same day, with the same outcomes repeated indefinitely. The moral of the film was that escape would be possible only when the victim acknowledged his true nature. Only when we understand the true nature of learning, the paper argued, could we expect the technology of learning to be applied in a genuinely effective way.

Today we want to point to the first real signs that escape from Groundhog Day is close. It has not happened yet. For a lasting escape it is probably necessary for the policy-makers in education and training to question the assumptions about learning that underpin their role as 'providers'. Nevertheless there is an extraordinary phenomenon under way, in which learners of all kinds are forming spontaneous learning communities, and forming virtual learning relationships; in which the sharing of a learning experience online is, for a significant minority of learners who are social software users, becoming the accepted mode of learning anything; and in which the particular learning group to which you belong can display the characteristics of a genuine community of practice, but might last only a few days before dividing into further more specialist communities. This phenomenon is being driven by a particular kind of learner, characterized less by the nature of the information skills involved, much more by the influence of a culture of sharing which emphasizes a willingness to join others in a virtual experience of learning, involving confidence and sociality rather than skill.

Literacy can be regarded as a learning outcome, which itself then underpins successful learning at a new level. The concept of *digital literacy* can have many shades of meaning, but here we focus our discussion on those aspects of online learning, and those characteristics of online learners, that seem now to be most associated with successful learning. Models of e-learning are, of course, special instances of general models of learning and the achievement of fluency in any medium will depend on first learning how to learn in a generic way. This will itself entail the achievement of a certain level of literacy in a conventional sense, which will provide a baseline for online learning. However, our main point is this: the discourse of literacy, and especially that of digital literacy, has previously been focused on the achievement of skill. We want to move the debate about e-literacy further back, to the question of how learners become learners in the first place. Our proposed concept of *learning literacy* requires a consideration of how ideas about how technology enhances learning have evolved with the e-learning community's increasing understanding of pedagogy. Just as the field of educational technology has matured from a 'delivery of content' model to one that emphasizes the crucial role of dialogue, so the field of digital literacy, we suggest, should shift its emphasis from skill to *identity*.

We argue here that the emergence of what is referred to as *social software* is producing a key advance in the role played by technology in learning. The term is generally used to refer to the way in which the proliferation of personal weblogs have forced the development of subscription tools 'bridging the individual voices of blog authors into wider networks and communities linked by common domains and personal relationships' (Wenger, 2005). Added to this is the phenomenon of social bookmarking, the sharing of personally tagged web pages, allowing the spontaneous formation of learning groups. The implications of this development seem profound for the understanding of how informal internet-based learning is now taking centre stage, and the lesson this conveys for instructional designers and learning technologists, not to mention policy-makers in lifelong learning.

A developing framework for e-learning

We have described elsewhere our own framework for making sense of the confusing world of digital learning (Mayes and Fowler, 1999; Fowler and Mayes, 1999; Mayes, 2002). Here, we attempt to describe the development of e-learning as an interplay between what the technology is capable of achieving and our developing understanding of where it can add most value.

Although there is a long history of educational technology that emphasizes the approach of individualized instruction, there were two main drivers behind the early attempts to enhance learning through the use of computers. First was the power of multimedia to support a transmission-based didactic mode of teaching, for which there is a strong folk tradition that compelling explanations, and vivid representations, will lead to better learning. There is a crucial point here for digital learning: the presentation of subject matter using multimedia is based on a discredited idea – that naturalistic representations of knowledge would lead to better learning. Much of what became known as the computer-aided learning (CAL) tradition was based on this assumption.

A significant proportion of what is termed e-learning is still based in the training departments of organizations within a training philosophy that is traditional instructional design. The intellectual base for instructional systems design (ISD) consists of principles that are derived directly from the associationist tradition, are widely accepted within the organizational training culture, and focus particularly on task analysis. The basic approach of ISD is that competence in advanced and complex tasks is built step by step from simpler units of knowledge or skill, finally adding co-ordination to the whole structure (Gagné, 1985)

Through the 1980s and early 1990s, as technology capabilities advanced, the focus moved towards the design of tutoring environments, and the support that could be offered to learners as they engaged with simulations and problem-solving environments that gave learners rapid feedback on their responses. The underlying view of the learner shifted towards a cognitive model in which learning is represented as a process of interpreting and constructing meaning. The key challenge for the learner viewed through this perspective is the building of a framework for understanding. Both the associationist and cognitive accounts of learning stress the importance of learning through *activity*, though the emphasis differs depending on the kind of learning outcomes intended. The associationist account is easier to apply to skills, the cognitive to conceptual understanding. For the building of skill the focus is on building more complex skills from the practising of sub-tasks. For cognitive learning the activity focuses on problem solving. In both perspectives the availability of feedback about performance is critical.

From the early 1970s a strong research and development effort was mounted to develop intelligent tutoring systems (ITS) (Anderson et al., 1995). These depended on the computational power to match appropriate content, based on a model of the subject matter, to the moment-to-moment needs of the individual learner, based on a model of the learner as a problem-solver. In general, these approaches were based on an assumption that the tutoring process involved identifying the misconceptions or the missing conceptions of the learner and then providing explanations at the right level. As the ITS movement developed, as was the case with other areas of artificial intelligence (AI), our respect for the complex nature of effective tutoring increased.

Vygotsky, the Soviet psychologist, developed the concept of the *zone of proximal development* (ZPD) in 1934; the term has become part of mainstream thinking about tutoring since the translation of his *Mind and Society* in 1978. Vygotsky defined the ZPD as the distance between a learner's current conceptual development (as measured by independent problem solving) and that learner's potential capability, as measured by what can be accomplished, 'under . . . guidance or in collaboration with more capable peers' (Vygotsky, 1978). The concept influenced Lave and Wenger (1991), whose socio-anthropological account of learning communities can be thought of as a kind of description of the ZPD.

The concept of *scaffolding* describes the process of exploiting the ZPD. Typically a tutor will have the main responsibility for providing the guidance, but with the wider learning group itself also playing a role. It is conventionally assumed that to be effective scaffolders, tutors must be sufficiently expert in their domain to judge individual learning needs, and sufficiently skilled as teachers to adjust dynamically, continuously to switch between the novice's and expert's perspectives. In the ZPD learning is distributed, thought and intelligence being 'stretched across' the larger structures of activity (Salomon, Perkins and Globerson, 1991; Pea, 1993). However, through social software we see the emergence of a kind of informal scaffolding, operating spontaneously as a learning community is formed. Indeed, the work of Chi et al. (2001) has shown that experts in the subject matter don't necessarily make effective tutors. Contrary to popular belief, learners will usually benefit from the suppression of tutors' explanations, and peers can be very effective scaffolders if they encourage their fellow learners to engage in self-explanation and reflection (Chi et al., 1994).

During the mid- to late 1990s a consensus emerged in the field, centred around the principles of constructivist pedagogy. This shifted the focus a little away from tutorials, onto the need to give the learners more direct control of their learning, offering them a choice of resources with which to carry out tasks that were meaningful and authentic, as in problem-based learning. This approach is usually assumed to have derived from a cognitive perspective, with the centrality of the search for meaning. However, in its emphasis on learning by doing, and the importance of feedback, constructivist approaches lean partly towards the associationist tradition. In their emphasis on authentic tasks, however, they take on key assumptions from a third broad perspective, known as *situated learning*.

In the mid-1990s came a fundamental advance in technology, the development of the internet, and an accompanying development in understanding of its role in the support of learning. Now that a dialogue model of learning could come fully into focus, both of the earlier pedagogical perspectives became subsumed within this third set of assumptions which positions the learning activity, whether skill-based or conceptual, within the social and cultural setting in which the learning occurs. This setting will also at least partly define the learning outcomes. This situative view of learning focuses on the way knowledge is distributed socially. When knowledge is seen as situated in the practices of communities then the outcomes of learning involve the abilities of individuals to participate in those practices successfully. The patterns of successful practice become seen as the key influence. The essence of a community of practice is that, through joint engagement in some activity, an identified group of people come to develop and share *practices*. This is usually interpreted as a stable and relatively enduring group, librarians for example, whose practices involve the development of a constellation of beliefs, attitudes, values and specific knowledge built up over many years.

Yet a community of practice can be built around a common endeavour which has a much shorter time-span. Greeno et al. (1998) give examples of communities of practice which are shorter-lived and more fragile than the well established communities discussed by Wenger. Some examples are a garage band, an engineering team, a day care co-operative, a research group or a kindergarten class. A characteristic of these groups is that they allow a greater scope for interplay between the psychological (or personal) and the social in determining practice than do the long-established communities. The influence of individuals, and of individual relationships, is likely to be greater. Activity, motivation and learning are all related to a need for a positive sense of identity (or positive self-esteem), shaped by social forces (Ellemers, Spears and Doosje, 1999).

The smaller the group the larger the role played by individual relationships. Many learning groups are quite temporary and fragile, but are characterized by strong relationships and the emergence of a strong peer identity. The virtual computer-mediated discussion group or the year group are examples. The learner will usually express a need to participate as a full member. Such groups can have the characteristics of a community of practice but here the practice is the learning itself, in a particular educational or training setting. Some characteristics of these groups are determinants of the nature of the approach to learning that actually occurs. Successful students are those who learn how to pass assessments, not necessarily those who have the deepest interest in the subject matter, and many aspects of student behaviour are determined by social goals which have little or nothing to do with the curriculum, but everything to do with peer esteem.

We must also view learning as situated within *individual relationships*. Most learning will actually be mediated through relationships with individual members of the communities or groups in question. The social categorization of these individuals will vary according to the context and nature of particular dialogues. Sometimes their membership of a group will be most salient, in other situations their personal characteristics will be perceived as more important. Such relationships will vary according to the characteristics of the groups involved, the context within which they operate, and the strength of the relationships (Fowler and Mayes, 1999).

In our previous work we have explored how vicarious learning can be exploited through technology (Mayes, 2001; Mayes et al., 2001). Vicarious learning refers to the benefits of the observation of other learners engaged in real learning episodes. In real classroom experience the questions asked by other learners, and the resulting discussion, can often articulate and expose shared aspects of conceptual difficulty. Such dialogues can involve discourse between learner and teacher, discussion between peers, or even direct interaction with courseware. Such dialogues may constitute a new kind of 'reusable' learning resource, which we termed tertiary courseware. This idea contrasts with the traditional approach to instructional dialogue by assuming that there is considerable scope for learning without being a direct participant. Underpinning the idea of vicarious learning is an assumption that learners not only *can* learn by observing other learners, but will actively want to do so. But why should a learner find vicarious resources any more motivating than conventional subject matter? In fact much of the potential effectiveness of vicarious resources will depend on the potency of the identification the new learner can develop for the original participants, and on the extent to which the dialogue is considered relevant to the achievement of the learner's goals. For Wenger (1998) this identification and this relevance will be largely determined by the extent to which the original participants in the dialogue are seen as representative members of a target community of practice. This view encourages us to consider vicarious learning not just in terms of techniques for supporting the overhearing of dialogues, but more generally in terms of its effect on the formation of learning identities.

Recently, Wenger (2005) has called for a new discourse on learning based on the concept of learning through participation. This discourse takes learning capability as a consequence of the relationship between individual identities and social systems. Social systems will be experienced at many levels of scale, and constellations of practices. Individuals will navigate through these multiple forms of participation in the ongoing construction of a learning identity. In this discourse learning 'seems increasingly organized as a horizontal process of mutual negotiation, as opposed to the more traditional view of a vertical relationship between a producer and a recipient of knowledge'.

Wenger explores the idea that one important effect of the internet is to enable what he calls the phenomenon of 'horizontalization'. People build blogs, and contribute to wikis, as a way of establishing knowledge sharing and knowledge creating networks. The horizontal connections do not eliminate the idea that some people are more expert than others, but the relationship between them will involve a negotiation of mutual relevance. Wenger offers the example of progressive doctors who are trying to re-conceptualize the medical consultation as the 'meeting of two forms of knowledgeability that have to meet and negotiate how they inform each other'.

Conclusion

The main argument presented here is that, in considering the implications of the kind of informal learning communities that are emerging everywhere we look on the internet, we are seeing the development of a genuinely effective technology-based enhancement. The learning itself is not technology-driven, but the technology is allowing a fundamental principle of how people learn to flourish in a new global setting. Applying this observation to the concept of digital literacy for learning acknowledges that for individuals learning increasingly requires 'learning to participate' in social learning systems. By emphasizing peer-to-peer creating of horizontal connections we bring the focus onto learning identity and learning relationships. What 'literacy' is relevant for successful participation in a learning community? At first the question seems rather self-evident. There is certainly a 'performance imperative' of learning how to put yourself in a position where you can participate at all. So a conventional view of the need for some pre-existing level of knowledge and skill is still lurking somewhere in the question. Yet the message of this chapter is that to conceptualize literacy for learning in those terms is to fail to look in the right place. Just as our understanding of pedagogy for e-learning has moved from information processing and skill to meaning, relationships and identity, so our conceptualization of the characteristics needed by learners should move into the same terrain.

References

Anderson, J. R., Corbett, A. T., Koedinger, K. R. and Pelletier, R. (1995) Cognitive Tutors: lessons learned, *Journal of the Learning Sciences*, 4, 167–207.

Chi, M. T. H., de Leeuw, N., Chiu, M. H. and LaVancher, C. (1994) Eliciting Self-explanations Improves Understanding, *Cognitive Science*, 18, 439–77.

Chi, M. T. H., Siler, S., Jeong, H., Yamauchi, T. and Hausmann, R. (2001) Learning from Human Tutoring, *Cognitive Science*, 25, 471–534.

Ellemers, N., Spears, R. and Doosje, B. (eds) (1999) *Social Identity: context, commitment, content*, Malden, MA, Blackwell.

Fowler, C. J. H. and Mayes, J. T. (1999) Learning Relationships: from theory to design, *Association for Learning Technology Journal*, 7 (3), 6–16.

Gagné, R. (1985) *The Conditions of Learning*, New York, NY, Holt, Rinehart & Winston.

Greeno, J. G., Eckert, P., Stucky, S. U., Sachs, P. and Wenger, E. (1998) *Learning In and For Participation in Work and Society*. International conference (US Dept of Education and OECD) on 'How Adults Learn' April 1998, Washington, DC.

Lave, J. and Wenger, E. (1991) *Situated Learning: legitimate peripheral participation*, Cambridge, Cambridge University Press.

Mayes, J. T. (1995) Learning Technology and Groundhog Day. In Strang et al. (eds), *Hypermedia at Work: practice and theory in education*, Canterbury, University of Kent Press, 21–37.

Mayes, J. T. (2001) Learning Technology and Learning Relationships. In Stephenson, J. (ed.), *Teaching and Learning Online: pedagogies for new technologies*, London, Kogan Page, 16–26.

Mayes, J. T. (2002) The Technology of Learning in a Social World. In Harrison, R., Reeve, F., Hanson, A. and Clarke, J. (eds), *Supporting Lifelong Learning, volume 1: Perspectives on Learning*, London, Routledge, 163–75.

Mayes, J. T. and Fowler, C. J. H. (1999) Learning Technology and Usability: a framework for understanding courseware, *Interacting with Computers*, 11, 485–97.

Mayes, J. T, Dineen, F., McKendree, J. and Lee, J. (2001) Learning from Watching Others Learn. In Steeples, C. and Jones, C. (eds), *Networked Learning: perspectives and issues*, London, Springer, 213–27.

Pea, R. (1993) Practices of Distributed Intelligence and Designs for Education. In Salomon, G. (ed), *Distributed Cognition*, New York, Cambridge University Press, 47–87.

Salomon, G., Perkins, D. and Globerson, T. (1991) Partners in Cognition: extending human intelligence with intelligent technologies, *Educational Researcher*, 4, 2–8.

Vygotsky, L. S. (1978) *Mind and Society: the development of higher psychological processes*, Cambridge, MA. Harvard University Press.

Wenger, E. (1998) *Communities of Practice: learning, meaning, and identity*, Cambridge, Cambridge University Press.

Wenger, E. (2005) *Learning for a Small Planet: a research agenda*, www.ewenger.com/research/.

3

Real learning in virtual environments

Johannes Cronjé

Abstract

Virtual learning environments mirror their physical counterparts in many ways, using metaphorical representations to enable students to understand the interface. Digital campuses share the architectural features exhibited by physical institutions: an entrance, administration block, lecture halls, library, ancillary services and recreation areas. Lectures are replaced by learning tasks that require learners to interact, promoting a feeling of community. Co-operative learning allows us to compensate for the absence of interactivity in web-based learning. While computer literacy is taken for granted, students in digital learning environments require three specific literacies: visual, co-operative and academic literacy.

Introduction

E-learning courses show a distinct advantage over conventional distance education because in a digital environment e-mail and bulletin boards have made it easier and cheaper for messages to be exchanged within a cost-effective learning environment (Woods and Baker, 2004). Nevertheless they lack the personal dimension of contact education. In most cases an instructor cannot see the body language of a student or hear their expressions of joy or disappointment. Neither can you feel the oppressive heat in a desert classroom, or smell the stink bomb from a naughty learner. So, how does one get a taste for e-learning?

The answer seems to lie in the creation of learning communities by using metaphor and collaborative learning tasks. Functioning in online learning communities requires students to be able to decode the metaphors, interact with their peers, and take responsibility for their own learning. Three literacies are required: visual literacy, co-operative literacy and academic literacy.

While McInnerney and Roberts (2004) highlight the importance of social context in determining the success or failure of learning, Jones (1997) shows the relationship between an online community and the internet when he distinguishes between 'a virtual community's cyber-place and the virtual community itself. A virtual community's cyber-place will be termed a virtual settlement.' This chapter considers the architecture and functioning of virtual settlements where communities learn – virtual learning environments and portals – and compares them metaphorically with physical campuses.

Real or virtual

Now that the internet and digital technology have reached into just about every home in the developed world, and even the wealthier parts of the poorest of developing countries, it becomes hard to talk of the internet as a virtual environment. To many users it has become the primary actual means of communication. It is the way we really bank, purchase books, order theatre tickets and book airline tickets. The generation currently entering school does not know about over-the-counter banking, and needs the concept of a telegram to be explained to them.

The blurring of the line between virtual and actual extends to the debate about media and learning generally. Clark (1994) has long argued that the medium through which material is delivered has no greater effect on the quality of learning than a grocery truck has on the nutritional value of the food it delivers. Russell (n.d.) shows that when two media are used to teach the same content the results of pre-tests and post-tests of both groups invariably show no significant difference. Kozma (1994), on the other hand, argues that certain media have certain attributes that allow certain techniques that cannot be achieved by any other medium. For Kozma (1987, 21) 'to be effective, a tool for learning must closely parallel the learning process; and the computer, as an information processor, could hardly be better suited for this'. McInnerney and Roberts (2004) argue that for online social interaction the medium cannot be separated from the social interaction that occurs in the everyday world.

Recognizing the close relationship between media, and considering the pervasiveness of electronic media, this chapter prefers the term 'digital' to 'virtual' in the belief that it is actual learning and actual communication that takes place in a digital environment, and that the concept *virtual* relates to the metaphoric relationship between the digital and physical realm.

The role of metaphor

For Jones (1997) 'the degree to which information technologies can effectively control or aid virtual communities is delimited by the finite capacity of human cognition'. Aspects of learning environments must be transparent to reduce the cognitive load on the learners so that they can decode contextual information more easily.

Metaphor is essential in creating an online learning environment. Branscomb (1996) sees metaphors 'as a map for sorting out what is similar and what is different when confronting a new problem'. Aristotle (s.a.) defines metaphor as 'the application of an alien name by transference' or, calling something by another name. Pacagnella (1997), for instance, refers to the internet as a 'dense *bazaar* inhabited by all kinds of people' (my emphasis).

Graphic user interfaces in digital environments rely heavily on visual metaphors – making something look like something else. 'A visual metaphor helps the course designer establish a "presence" on the screen and simultaneously creates coherence within the course by presenting materials in a consistent manner' (Kies, 1998). Rieber and Noah (1997) claim that visual metaphors 'may help the learner put new concepts together with already understood ideas into a new cognitive synthesis'.

The architecture of digital learning environments

To survive and grow an online community needs a minimum level of interactivity, a variety of communicators, a common public space where a significant portion of interactive group-computer-mediated communication occurs, and a minimum level of sustained membership (Jones, 1997). To sustain a learning community, an online environment requires a number of components.

It would seem that the various digital campuses, e.g. Lotus Learning Space, WebCT, Moodle or Blackboard, all share the architectural features exhibited by physical institutions. These include an entrance, administration block, lecture halls, library, ancillary services and recreation areas.

Entrance

The main entrance serves both to attract visitors (and therefore potential students) and to control access. People who arrive at the entrance are usually categorized as staff, students or visitors, and on that basis gain different levels of access to the campus. Digitally this is achieved with a username and password.

Administration

Two main aspects are administered: finances and student records. A sophisticated system allows these elements to meet, so that a service is provided only to paid-up students. Other aspects that require administration, of course, are the staff, the alumni and the learning materials.

Lecture halls

Digital lecture halls contain much the same elements as physical ones. Staying with the metaphor of the physical classroom, these could be grouped as boards, desks and school bags.

Boards

Classrooms have chalkboards, bulletin boards and posters. Chalkboards are for real-time interaction. Bulletin boards are for asynchronous interaction. Posters are for stable content, and could be commercially produced, or could be the work of students.

Desks

There are two types of desks: teachers' desks and learners' desks. Desks form the principal site of operation. Physical classroom desks have pencils, textbooks and the voice and ears of the student. In a virtual classroom these are word processors, databases, spreadsheets, graphics packages and e-mail.

School bags

School bags contain personal items that do not necessarily support the mainstream activities in the classroom, such as toys, previous work, humorous information as well as trophies of any sort. In an actual classroom, the equipment in the bags could be protractors, stencils, compasses, etc. In a virtual classroom they could be graphic manipulation tools, word processors and website generating tools. Many digital school bags are just repositories of favourite links.

Library

The library or resource centre contains actual documents or links to other sites, which could simply be information sites, or links to online books or journals. The instructor usually provides the resources, although some libraries allow students to add links as the course progresses.

Ancillary services

Ancillary services provide help with academic, social and financial aspects as well as prospective employment agencies, student exchange programmes, etc.

Recreation areas

Recreation areas could be individual and co-operative. In a bricks-and-mortar campus these range from benches under trees to coffee shops and cinemas. In virtual campuses these could be arcade games, chat rooms, etc.

Tasks

Internet-based education differs from conventional education by the absence of physical contact, and from traditional distance education by the increased level of interaction. While interaction in lecture form becomes more difficult online, interaction between learners becomes easier. Lectures are replaced by learning tasks that require learners to interact, promoting a feeling of community (Lipman, 1991; Wenger, 2001) and allowing the exchange of ideas (Jonassen, 1991). Also 'computer-mediated groups can create solidarity through developing interpretive consensus' (Baym, 1995). Group learning tasks require the sending of messages. Cronjé and Clarke (1999) show that lecturers mainly send messages to make suggestions, encourage, explain and to give directives, while students send messages to give information, ask questions, present a problem, initiate or contribute to the discussion; or to express amusement and joke.

Group work can promote interaction and encourage individuals to complete a course, for groups are mutually independent. The entire group depends on the success of all its members (Buher and Walbert, 2004). Conversely, should some members not co-operate, the success of the whole group can be compromised. Woods and Baker (2004) caution that mere interaction is not sufficient to ensure positive social dynamics in an online environment as it may lead to increased competition, distrust and jealousy. Buhler and Walbert (2004) feel that facilitators need to control the dynamics of such interaction to develop a level of intimacy, while Kozar (1995) suggests play as a possible solution. It allows for 'people to renew and strengthen friendships ... [and the] creation of new patterns for the performance of tradition'. Baym (1995) adds that 'humorous performance can be used to create group solidarity, group identity, and individual identity' in computer-mediated communication.

Implications for digital literacy

While computer literacy is taken for granted, students who function in a digital learning environment where they engage in co-operative learning tasks require three specific literacies: visual literacy, co-operative literacy and academic literacy.

Visual literacy

Jones (1997) describes the view of technological determinists that 'the invention and adoption of a particular technology will lead to a particular set of outcomes'. In the same way as the chalkboard in the front of the classroom dictates that learners sit in rows facing it, internet technology creates new requirements both practically and methodologically. Cunningham (1992) points out that 'our knowledge of the things in the world is mediated by signs, that we build up structures of signs through experience and these structures define what we take as reality'. Visual literacy is a prerequisite for operating in digital learning environments, as they combine a number of metaphors. 'Cyberspace is not one distinct place but many cyberspaces with any number of models from the real world that are replicated in computer-mediated communication' (Branscomb, 1996).

Co-operative literacy

Johnson and Johnson (1991) list the prerequisites for effective co-operative learning as a mutual goals, positive interdependence and individual accountability. Students need to learn how to co-operate in achieving those goals, and take responsibility for their learning, while realizing that other students may depend on their output. Collaborative online projects should be preceded with adequate exposure of students to theory and practice of collaborative group work.

Academic literacy

Pacagnella (1997) points out that people and their environment are inseparable, and 'social constructivism claims that the facts of the world are not independent of us as observers and that scientific knowledge is always the result of a situated perspective'. Internet-based learning is most useful for collaborative, self-directed and resource-based approaches with computer-literate students. Students should be aware of online evaluation procedures and criteria, know how to prioritize, stick to deadlines and develop self-motivation skills.

Conclusion

Although superficially it would seem that digital environments provide an entirely new learning experience, the tools and techniques remain essentially the same. The institution still provides access to materials; administers money, staff, students and content; provides structured guidance, resources and opportunities for peer support; and encourages networking and recreational activities.

Within this context it still remains the student's responsibility to make the most of all the learning opportunities. However, because of the distinct lack of face-to-face contact it becomes necessary for students to develop other skills, such as the ability to decode a visual interface; learn from their peers and support their peers; and learn to manage their own learning.

References

Aristotle (s.a.) *Poetics*, tr. S. H. Butcher, *The Internet Classics Archive*, http://classics.mit.edu//Aristotle/poetics.html.

Baym, N. (1995) The Performance of Humor in Computer-mediated Communication, *Journal of Computer-mediated Communication*, **1** (2), http://jcmc.huji.ac.il/vol1/issue2/baym.html.

Branscomb, A. W. (1996) Cyberspaces: familiar territory or lawless frontiers, *Journal of Computer-mediated Communication*, **2** (1), http://jcmc.huji.ac.il/vol2/issue1/introl.html.

Buher, G. and Walbert, D. (2004) *Making Small Groups Work*, www.learnnc.org/index.nsf/doc/buher-classman0701?OpenDocument.

Clark, R. E. (1994) Media will Never Influence Learning, *Educational Technology Research and Development*, **42** (2), 21–30.

Cronjé, J. C. and Clarke, P. A. (1999) Teaching 'Teaching on the Internet' on the Internet, *SA Journal for Higher Education*, **13** (1), 213–26.

Cunningham, D. (1992) *A Brief History of Semiotics*, www.coe.usouthal.edu/semed/brehist.html.

Johnson, D. W. and Johnson, R. T. (1991) *Learning Together and Alone*, Upper Saddle River, NJ, Prentice Hall.

Jonassen, D. H. (1991) Evaluating Constructivist Learning, *Educational Technology*, **31** (10), 28–33.

Jones, Q. (1997) Virtual-communities, Virtual Settlements and Cyber-archaeology: a theoretical outline, *Journal of Computer-Mediated Communication*, **3** (3), http://jcmc.huji.ac.il/vol3/issue3/jones.html.

Kies, D. (1998) *Implementing Online Pedagogy*, www.cod.edu/dept/KiesDan/UWS/.

Kozar, S. (1995) Enduring Traditions, Ethereal Transmissions: recreating Chinese New Year celebrations on the internet, *Journal of Computer-Mediated Communication*, **1** (2), http://jcmc.huji.ac.il/vol1/issue2/kozar.html.

Kozma, R. B. (1987) The Implications of Cognitive Psychology for Computer-based Learning Tools, *Educational Technology*, **27** (11), 20–5.

Kozma, R. B. (1994) Will Media Influence Learning? reframing the debate, *Educational Technology Research and Development*, **42** (2), 7–20.

Lipman, M. (1991) *Thinking in Education*, Cambridge, Cambridge University Press.

McInnerney, J. M. and Roberts, T. S. (2004) Online Learning: social interaction and the creation of a sense of community, *Educational Technology and Society*, **7** (3), 73–81.

Pacagnella, L. (1997) Getting the Seat of Your Pants Dirty: strategies for ethnographic research on virtual communities, *Journal of Computer Mediated-Communication*, **3** (1), http://jcmc.huji.ac.il/vol3/issue1/paccagnella.html.

Rieber, L. P. and Noah, D. (1997) *Effect of Gaming and Visual Metaphors on Reflective Cognition Within Computer-based Simulations*, http://itech1.coe.uga.edu/faculty/lprieber/aera1997/aera1997.html.

Russell, T. R. (n.d.) *The No Significant Difference Phenomenon*, http://cuda.teleeducation.nb.ca/nosignificantdifference/.

Wenger, E. (2001) Supporting Communities of Practice: a survey of community-orientated technologies, www.ewenger.com/tech/.

Woods, R. H. and Baker, J. D. (2004) Interaction and Immediacy in Online Learning, *International Review of Research in Open and Distance Learning*, (August), www.irrodl.org/content/v5.2/woods-baker.html.

4

Digital fusion: defining the intersection of content and communications

Paul Gilster

Abstract

As publishing increasingly becomes an online venture, changes in the nature of information are emerging. 'Content', normally considered to be professionally published material such as books and movies, is merging with 'communications', usually considered to be informal and represented by letters, telephone calls, etc. This chapter analyses trends in digital information and concludes that new research opportunities are evolving from this unusual access to materials. The growth of scholarly preprints to augment traditional peer review and the availability of connected resources including wikis, weblogs, mailing lists and online journals connecting to 'halos' of imagery and data – and perhaps one day to a new form of e-mail archive – are symptomatic of this evolution.

Introduction

The internet's great utility for scholars, educators and lay researchers has been opening access to information in venues outside the traditional library. Those whose lives have revolved around books and journals now find themselves able to work with numerous scholarly materials once restricted to reference departments, and to do so from the office or the home. That this revolution in access is not complete need hardly be reiterated – all too many journals, and all too many useful documents in older issues of available journals, have yet to be placed online.

Here we consider how this extension and transformation of our tools is proceeding, and what will be needed to make it more useful. The boundaries of research are changing to incorporate materials once considered outside the realm of traditional scholarship. The burden is thus placed on the scholarly community – as well as those who toil in our libraries – to master a changing set of skills. There is little help in this, as the technology advances at a rate exceeding the best efforts of educators to revise and reform existing curricula. Today's researcher will be increasingly self-taught or forever toiling to catch up.

Redefining the collection

The evolving resources of the net need not confound us; indeed, they resemble more traditional venues in important respects. 'The Web', says Bonita Wilson in the online *D-Lib Magazine* (2005), 'is enabling the creation of personalized – yet networked – collections of materials and services that in some ways resemble library special collections.' *D-Lib Magazine* cites, for example, the growth of tools like *Connotea*, which creates online collections of bookmarks, a new kind of community allowing scholars to share sources (Hammond et al., 2005). Another type of sharing occurs in the online tools called 'wikis', which allow collaborative editing in ways that can be useful to small, targeted research groups.

But the changes now under full sail go beyond next generation software tools. For something intriguing is occurring as we analyse the *distribution* of such information. Computer people normally distinguish between 'content' – professionally published material such as books and movies – and 'communications' – material exchanged informally through letters, perhaps, telephone calls or instant messaging. The library's focus has fallen largely on the former. Yet the technologies driving the internet are creating vast amounts of new data in which the two become indistinguishable. This trend causes much good information to be hidden in venues outside the web pages and databases we have gradually learned to add to our research arsenal, and the search engines that scan them. The net has changed the rules yet again, by making it possible to store communications that would otherwise be lost, and by encouraging the one-to-one and one-to-selected group formats used in e-mail, mailing lists, hybrid web-based discussion pages and newsgroups.

Let's discuss this first in reference to the past, for we've always had misapprehensions about where the value lies between the printed word vs. the more personal word as found in letters or, today, e-mail or discussion group messages. No one has analysed this transformation more presciently than Andrew Odlzyko, formerly head of cryptography for AT&T Labs, and now director of the University of Minnesota's Digital Technology Center. Dr Odlyzko places the issue of content vs. connectivity in perspective by examining the spread of information in 19th-century America (Odlyzko, 2001). The US government chose early in that century to build a newspaper distribution network as a way of creating national unity. Odlyzko notes that Congress subsidized this distribution system by raising prices on letters; content was subsidized on the back of communications.

The assumption was similar to what we hear about the internet today: content is king. The result of the subsidy for newspaper distribution was that newspapers accounted for no more than 15% of total postal revenues in the 1830s, even as they were responsible for 95% of the total weight of mail carried. But to the pioneers, newspapers – content – were a luxury, whereas letters – communications – were a necessity. The people living in those frontier towns across America objected to this imbalance because it raised the cost of their letters. Popular pressure soon forced a reduction in postal rates.

Most of those 19th-century missives are long gone, while scattered collections of early newspapers survive. But, today, we find ourselves able to do better. Our digital storage means that we can hope to preserve both content and communications and the intersections where the two meet. And that means understanding how many forms of communication have now become archivable, and searchable.

The challenge this offers the research community has already begun to become apparent. To cite just one example, excellent references are being created in the home pages of authors, scientists and scholars. Researchers must learn to navigate this unofficial, non-traditional realm. In a survey in the *Journal of Electronic Publishing* asking scientists how they find information, the most widely used methods were 'references in other publications' and 'web searching using general or topic-specific search engines' (Bjork and Turk, 2000). It gives this researcher pause to report that the least important methods were 'searches in traditional bibliographic databases' and 'browsing in libraries'. The challenge to printed media is also clear. It is a remarkable fact that paper documents of all kinds amount to a mere 0.01% of new information being produced today (Lyman and Varian, 2003). The University of California at Berkeley study behind this number notes that the figure includes not only books and newspapers, but also scholarly periodicals, newsletters and documents printed at home or in offices.

It is clear then that a great deal of research is taking place outside conventionally published venues, around the edges of what we regard as a 'collection'. This research is under-analysed because commentators, in their conviction that 'content is king', have missed the mark. The world wide web, often considered a content-delivery system, is hardly king of the internet; in fact, roughly five times more e-mail is produced per year than the stock of pages on the web, which in 2002 consisted of perhaps 167 terabytes of static HTML pages and a remarkable 91,850 terabytes of 'deep web' data (defined as database-driven sites that produce web pages on demand) (Lyman and Varian, 2003). And it should be added that many communications services are now shoehorned into the web format because of the ubiquity of the browser, leading for example to newsgroup- or mailing-list-style discussion groups implemented in HTML format on websites.

What do we make, for example, of the 'wiki' – a collaborative website that is created through multiple and continuing authorship? The wiki is unlike a conventional website in that anyone is allowed to edit content using a standard browser interface and no other necessary tools. Here is a communications tool to be sure, one with many similarities to both mailing lists (in that messages are readily posted and exchanged with all readers) and weblogs, in that a forum is provided for individual expression to an audience chosen by field of interest. But here, too, is the potential for what we would consider content. The controversial Wikipedia is an attempt to create an open-source encyclopedia, its publication made possible by the software that allows community involvement, with all the questions that raises about editorial control. The Wikipedia relies on a naïve notion of community self-discipline; i.e. each entry is gradually strengthened as specialists find mistakes and correct them, making its status as a reliable source questionable in the extreme. Nonetheless, numerous Wikipedia articles meet high standards; its presence suggests the possibility of high-quality wiki treatments of specialized content, and reinforces the point that the internet has broadened our traditional view of what in communications is searchable (Cedergren, 2003).

Toward a new generation of tools

All this occurs at a time when weblogs – individual websites not changeable by the community, as in wikis, but offering venues for reaching an audience of peers through the web in a daily, diary-like format, are proliferating. Indeed, the aforementioned Berkeley study finds 2.9 million active weblogs housing 81 GB of information as of 2003. It is clear, then, that the modern researcher – and certainly the modern curator of collections – must be aware of the information that is being assembled in these venues, even as we can hope the community of developers will continue to create the requisite tools to provide accurate searching of such archives, especially in terms of adequate filtering.

As a case in point, a new generation of archival tools for one-to-one correspondence is long overdue. At a conference on the impact of electronic publishing, particle physicist Ian Butterworth of Imperial College, London, pointed out that his students no longer look at printed pages. They get all their information from the display screen. 'If they don't know how to do something they mainly contact a colleague' Butterworth said. 'They e-mail colleagues in Bologna, Hamburg or Amsterdam. These young people are … in one of the largest physics departments in a subject involving strong international collaboration, and they can all access powerful workstations' (Butterworth, 1998).

This being the case, what will happen to scientific correspondence that was once preserved in paper form? Unlike the conventional letter, the e-mail missive makes itself readily available to standard indexing. Innovative categories of scholarly information could be created by such materials if appropriate protocols for archiving and examining older correspondence can be established. In his book *God's Equation*, Amir Aczel uses hitherto unpublished letters between Albert Einstein and Austrian astronomer Erwin Freundlich to examine Einstein's search for the so-called 'cosmological constant' (Aczel, 1999). How much of today's scientific correspondence will be saved the way Einstein's letters to Freundlich were? The odds say that most of them will be, at least, if we mean by 'saved' that they are to be found somewhere in magnetic storage media in a computer centre or a personal workstation. We need to develop the tools that allow us to archive such materials, so that they, too, can become part of our future collections. A need is emerging for e-mail repositories into which researchers voluntarily contribute exchanges germane to their work, just as we are now seeing preprints of scholarly articles being made available to a wide audience rather than a small panel of reviewers.

It may seem evident that for subjects like particle physics and deep-space astronomy, which proceed largely through digital methods, we need programmers to develop solutions for maintaining these exchanges. But digital methods now permeate the academy from library to laboratory, in the sciences as well as the humanities. The implications were noted by Steven Harnad as early as 1990:

> On the brink of intellectual perestroika is that vast PREPUBLICATION phase of scientific inquiry in which ideas and findings are discussed informally with colleagues (currently in person, by phone and by regular mail), presented more formally in seminars, conferences and symposia, and distributed still more widely in the form of preprints and tech reports that have undergone various degrees of peer review. It has now become possible to do all of this in a remarkable new way that is not only incomparably more thorough and systematic in its distribution, potentially global in scale, and almost instantaneous in speed, but so unprecedentedly interactive that it will substantially restructure the pursuit of knowledge.
>
> (Harnad, 1990).

Appropriate tools will allow electronic conversations to become both as easy to store and as easy to find again as paper letters in a metal filing cabinet. Secure archival repositories can be created to preserve such materials, academic storehouses whose contributors will understand they are making private correspondence available for future research as and when they see fit.

As we work on these tools, hybrid forms of content continue to evolve. We have seen, in the academic disciplines, traditional paper-based journals and conference proceedings being supplemented by electronic copies of the same, some free of charge, others offered on subscription; even five years ago, 4000 peer-reviewed journal titles and 4600 conferences were available electronically (Association of Research Libraries, 2000). Note the malleability of these journals. Some, like LIBRES, began as electronic discussion areas. The ARL Directory of Electronic Journals, Newsletters and Academic Discussion Lists used the following description when noting LIBRES for the first time: 'LIBRES is an electronic conference designed to foster library and information science research and support the development of our knowledge base. This forum will serve as a professional networking and information source. We will share ideas, solutions and experiences' (Mogge, 1999).

By 1993 LIBRES had evolved into a quarterly, peer-reviewed journal with its own editorial board, now distributed through LISTSERV (mailing list), FTP, Gopher and the web. It had evolved, in other words, from conference (communication of insights among scholars) to content (traditional academic journal now in digital format). Other journals, like *Postmodern Culture*, began their lives on LISTSERVs and became electronic journals on the web; the latter sponsors its own conference areas for discussion of the journal's contents and related issues.

The growth of online scholarship in the direction of self-publishing is an extraordinary phenomenon (Harnad and Hemus, 1998). We can consider such efforts another form of self-archiving, and note the synergy of this notion with the idea of electronic mail archival collections that would track significant research. Self-publishing on individual websites and the growth of free scholarly journals that short-circuit burdensome subscription fees allow for heightened communication between author and audience, in this case, the network of one's peers in a given discipline (Day, 1999). Open scholarly journals in venues like the Public Library of Science (PLOS) and BioMed Central provide unlimited use to third parties (Buckholtz, 2001). Anyone can read, download or distribute any article published by the PLOS journals, for example, spreading research quickly to an audience of peers.

The challenge of peer review

The opening of the scholarly journal occurs as the peer-review process is mutating. One of the successes of digital publishing in this arena is the electronic 'preprint' archive established by Paul Ginsparg at Los Alamos National Laboratory, which now resides at Cornell University. This archive, which became available in the field of high-energy physics in 1991, has expanded to cover a broad swathe of mathematics, physics and computer science. Its broadening domain reflects the archive's wide acceptance in the physics community, allowing scientists to report their work directly to their peers, bypassing the traditional channels of learned societies or commercial publishing houses. The arXiv e-Print Archive site has progressed well beyond its experimental origins to become a leading venue for the publication of scientific papers. As of January 2005, arXiv had received over 300,000 manuscripts in its 13-year history and was receiving new material at the rate of 3300 papers per month (Peet, 2005).

The advantages are many. Immediate access to research is now available. Papers are assessed not by a few editors, but by an audience of fellow physicists as they circulate at zero cost around the internet. The long wait for print publication is erased. Content within a paper is, of course, searchable, and it is easy to move between the article itself and the online references cited within it. A pre-print archive like Ginsparg's also includes the ability to cite going forward, meaning you can quickly retrieve papers that cite the one you have just been reading, but were published at a later date. Many of these advantages have become apparent in other disciplines.

So let us sum up the dilemma of researchers today as we move from informal brainstorming via e-mail and discussion group to the publication of preprints for peer review to fully integrated online journals in a variety of formats. Research publications are available in numerous forms, from traditional paper-based journals and conference proceedings to electronic copies of these, accessible through subscription or other fee services. Electronic-only journals or archives proliferate, some made available free of charge. Web pages created by authors or institutions, often found serendipitously through searching web directories or search engines, provide valuable links to ongoing research, as do pre-print archives like arXiv.

Searchable collections may include all the sources of information mentioned, scattered globally, and accessible only in sporadic form depending upon the whim of publishers and the technological tools that created the information. Moreover, because of the ease with which information links on the net, electronic journals are beginning to connect directly to databases like NASA's archive of images and data, or data sources like ITIS (the Integrated Taxonomic Information System) to form a vast, interconnected archive. Research papers are now filtered through electronic mail exchanges that may one day prove historically valuable but which have no ready means of access or long-term storage. Wikis, weblogs and mailing lists provide information nuggets but lack appropriate tools for discovering them. These too are collections.

Conclusion

The fallacy of the internet as a 'digital library' (it is anything but) has led us to value the world wide web too exclusively as an information source, which has made researchers less effective in working with data sources outside this well publicized path. We should not expect the internet's resources to yield to the same disciplines as the well ordered stacks within our traditional buildings – not, that is, at this early stage in its development.

Until better tools become available, the thorough scholar will supplement conventional library research with the search engines that mine the intersection of content and communications. Where there are archives of personal communications, as in scholarly mailing groups, they may have to be examined on a case-by-case basis. This means downloading list descriptions and learning where the archives are. The art of filtering using available software tools becomes a needed skill whether the target is buried in a mailing list, newsgroup, wiki, weblog or preprint archive. The complex future of the net may well point in the direction of file-sharing, with computers networked not to central servers but to services like the open-source Gnutella project, that allow users to exchange data one to one. Pure communication, it might be argued, yet capable of moving vast amounts of content not through a conventional broadcast model like a publishing house or television station, but through research teams opening their results – and their disks – to the use of others in their field.

Pushing the boundaries of research means adapting our research skills to this communications-rich, not content-driven internet. It is clear that traditional publishing, whether print or electronic in form, is just one component in this evolving space. For better or worse, researchers must track net developments with renewed fervour, hoping to know where the quarry in their various data hunts may best be run to ground while keeping an eye on evolving archival projects that may provide more satisfying solutions. This is a challenge both exasperating and intriguing, but for now, at least, the net has placed us all on *terra incognita*.

References

Aczel, A. (1999) *God's Equation*, New York, NY, Four Walls Eight Windows.

Association of Research Libraries (2000) *A Directory of Scholarly Electronic Journals and Academic Discussion Lists*, www.arl.org/scomm/edir/.

Björk, B.-C. and Turk, Z. (2000) How Scientists Retrieve Publications: an empirical study of how the internet is overtaking paper media, *Journal of Electronic Publishing*, 6, (December), www.press.umich.edu/jep/06-02/bjork.html.

Buckholtz, A. (2001) Returning Scientific Publishing to Scientists, *Journal of Electronic Publishing*, 7 (1), www.press.umich.edu/jep/07-01/index.html.

Butterworth, I. (1998) The Impact of Information Technology and Networks: new perspectives for scientific, technical and medical publishing. In Butterworth, I. (ed.), *The Impact of Electronic Publishing on the Academic Community*, London, Portland Press.

Cedergren, M. (2003) Open Content and Value Creation, *First Monday*, 8 (8), www.firstmonday.org/issues/issue8_8/cedergren/index.html.

Day, M. (1999) The Scholarly Journal in Transition and the PubMed Central Proposal, *Ariadne*, 21, www.ariadne.ac.uk/issue21/pubmed/.

Hammond, T., Hannay, T., Lund, B. et al. (2005) Social Bookmarking Tools: a general review, *D-Lib Magazine*, **11** (4), www.dlib.org/dlib/april05/04contents.html.

Harnad, S. (1990) Scholarly Skywriting and the Prepublication Continuum of Scientific Inquiry, *Psychological Science*, **1**, 342–3, www.ecs.soton.ac.uk/~harnad/Papers/Harnad/harnad90.skywriting.html.

Harnad, S. and Hemus, M. (1998) All or None: no stable hybrid or half-way solutions for launching the learned periodical literature into the post-Gutenberg galaxy. In Butterworth, I. (ed.), *The Impact of Electronic Publishing on the Academic Community*, London, Portland Press.

Lyman, P. and Varian, H. (2003) How Much Information?, www.sims.berkeley.edu/research/projects/how-much-info-2003/.

Mogge, D. (1999) Seven Years of Tracking Electronic Publishing: the ARL directory of electronic journals, newsletters and academic discussion lists, *Library Hi Tech*, **17** (1), 17–25, db.arl.org/dsej/2000/mogge.html.

Odlyzko, A. (2001) Content is not King, *First Monday*, **6** (2), www.firstmonday.org/issues/issue6_2/odlyzko/.

Peet, R. (2005) Crises and Opportunities: a scientist's view of scholarly communication, www.unc.edu/scholcomdig/whitepapers/peet.html.

Wilson, B. (2005) Personalized Information Organization, *D-Lib Magazine*, **11** (4), www.dlib.org/dlib/april05/04editorial.html.

5

Literacy and the digital knowledge revolution

Claire Bélisle

Abstract

Although literacy is based on mastering a series of technical and cultural skills, such as reading, writing, numeracy and media proficiency, these skills do not in themselves amount to literacy. As research increasingly shows, literacy is fundamentally situated and determined by the cultural, political and historical contexts of the communities in which it is activated. However, with the new digital knowledge contexts within which 21st century skills are being deployed, literacy (and therefore education) is facing a major challenge. The evolving digital technologies are not only transforming access, they are also fostering new approaches to knowledge, new knowledge architectures, new knowledge ethics, and new accountability requirements and assessments. These emerging issues for education will be described as part of the ongoing digital knowledge revolution.

Introduction

With the ongoing transition towards the knowledge society, new expectations are challenging educational workers. The methods or ways of learning and acquiring knowledge are changing, the learning environment is changing, the timespan of learning is expanding, and even the aims and content of learning are changing. When confronted with change, it is most important to have identified landmarks. The global socio-economic transformation we are experiencing today has brought information, knowledge and innovation as the main sources of economic growth and employment opportunities. Consequently, education will be increasingly challenged to meet the new requirements of knowledge society workers and citizens. Refocusing on literacy as the programmatic educational goal is presented here as a means to establish landmarks in order to address the 'tectonics of educational change' (Tuomi, 2005) that the knowledge revolution is bringing about.

Rethinking literacy

Although literacy is based on mastering a series of technical and cognitive skills, such as reading, writing, numeracy and media proficiency, these skills in themselves only partly account for literacy. As brought forth more and more by research, literacy is fundamentally situated and determined by the cultural, political and historical contexts of the communities in which it is activated. It is recognized today that literacy not only entails linguistic and social embeddedness, but also that it is a continuum of multiple levels and that, ultimately, it points to one's cultural identity. This deep cultural process is today pressed forward by the growing opportunities that technological tools allow in interacting with information and knowledge. Three complementary approaches to literacy stand out in educational analysis (Bawden, 2001; Varis, 2002; Street, 2003; Leu et al., 2004): an autonomous model of literacy, based on the assumption that reading and writing are simply technical skills; a socio-cultural model, based on the recognition of all literacies as socially and ideologically embedded; and a strong claim model, based on anthropological statements of the revolutionary power of instrumented thinking processes. Reviewing how the concept of literacy has been enriched will provide the background for understanding the challenges of an emerging new epistemological model of knowledge.

The autonomous model or functional literacy

Literacy has long been seen as a set of simple, learned, cognitive and practical skills necessary to deal with written texts and numbers. This functional understanding of literacy has been the basis of most school curricula, which refer to 'the ability to read and use written information, to write appropriately in a range of contexts, and to recognize numbers and basic mathematical signs and symbols' (Langford, 1998). This initial functional approach has become both an academic landmark in linguistic and literacy studies and a political tool in the hands of policy-makers and stakeholders. Thus, UNESCO's 1978 definition of 'functional literacy' holds that 'A person is functionally literate who can engage in all those activities in which literacy is required for effective functioning of his group and community and also for enabling him to continue to use reading, writing and calculation for his own and the community's development' (UNESCO, 2006, 156). However, this initial understanding has also evolved in the international policy community, which has moved 'from viewing literacy as a simple process of acquiring basic cognitive skills, to using these skills in ways that contribute to socio-economic development, to developing the capacity for social awareness and critical reflection as a basis for personal and social change' (UNESCO, 2006). This functional approach is the basis of what can be measured in cultural development, as exemplified by the UNESCO Institute of Statistics when it provides data to show that there are 771 million illiterate adults (15 years and over) in the world, two-thirds of whom are women. This counting of about 10% of the world population as illiterate refers to a spectrum of literacy levels, which have different meanings according to the country they refer to. But, presented globally, it drives home the dramatic need to develop education and overcome this persistent basic illiteracy.

The initial concept of literacy as referring to the acquisition of the three 'Rs', reading, 'riting and 'rithmetic, is still very much alive even though its shortcomings have been labelled by scholars who refer to this approach as the 'autonomous' or the 'literacy per se' vision (cf. a pioneer literacy scholar, Street, 1984). As brought to light by sociological studies, this 'neutral or universal' literacy carries a hidden agenda of values, behaviours and success stories that proponents of functional literacy tend to consider as universal, but that results from the cultural embeddedness of literacy skills. Hence the emergence of a more encompassing approach in terms not only of skills but of competence, as an underlying capacity to know which skills to use in different contexts and to be able to activate instantly the skills pertinent to the task at hand.

Literacy as a socio-cultural practice

The difficulties faced by teachers, in assuring access to literacy by students from all social horizons, has been a powerful incentive to deepen their understanding of literacy. In doing so, they have come to conclusions already reached by anthropologists. The social and historical context of literacy must be taken into account to appreciate what literacy means for a specific social group. As Langford (1998) has specifically underlined, 'the concept of literacy really depends on the information needs of the society of the time'. Presented as the *ideological* model of literacy, the socio-cultural model is based on the recognition that in reality, literacy varies from one social group to another and is largely determined by the cultural, political and historical contexts in which it is developed. Literacy here is to be understood in relation to giving access to, and understanding of, the structures of power and authority through mastery of written texts and numbers.

The model offers a 'culturally sensitive view of literacy practices as they vary from one context to another. . . . It is always embedded in socially constructed epistemological principles.' (Street, 2003) Thus literacy has been associated in the western hemisphere with economic progress, citizenship, and development of social and cognitive skills. With the emergence of mass media, it became obvious that specific competence was needed to deal with the mass of solicitations and persuasive messages that were being sent to listeners and viewers. Media literacy has become an indispensable competence to cope with the universal need to 'understand, produce and negotiate meanings in a culture made up of powerful images, words and sounds. A media literate person – and everyone should have the opportunity to become one – can decode, evaluate, analyze and produce both print and electronic media' (Aufderheide and Firestone, 1993). Several approaches have been pursued to develop media literacy, either through schooling by fostering media competence through analysis of contents and specific formats of each medium; or through the 'learn by doing' approach by having students go through all the production phases; or through media awareness discussion, after having had a personal experience of the expressive and aesthetic dimension by looking at films, programmes or exhibitions.

The New Literacy Studies, initiated by Brian Street's seminal 1984 book, *Literacy in Theory and Practice*, combine the cultural model with a sociolinguistic framework. This approach views literacy as having autonomous as well as ideological dimensions. Street brought into full light the awareness that literacy is not simply a set of skills or competences in mastering graphemes, phonemes and written and spoken texts. The cultural dimensions of literacy involve attitudes, values, practices and conventions. Being competent implies one knows which practices, attitudes and values are adequate in a given situation. While education is often focused on mastering the autonomous dimensions of a given literacy, the 'ideological' dimensions can present much more compelling and in depth challenges.

The 1990 International Literacy Year marked an important step with the broadening of the concept of literacy which came to be understood as including more complex skills such as 'speaking, listening and critical thinking [skills] within reading and writing' (Langford, 1998). Three main characteristics are associated with literacy: to be literate is to think critically, to be a lifelong learner and to master interaction with technologically based information. Literacy has now come to be seen in a more encompassing approach as knowledge acquisition: to be literate is not only to identify and satisfy information needs through mastery of print, but involves the capacity and the inclination constantly to continue constructing one's own knowledge, as learning is a lifelong learning endeavour, never fully attained.

The strong claim of literacy as an intellectual empowerment

Literacy not only provides means and skills to deal with written texts and numbers within specific cultural and ideological contexts, but it brings a profound enrichment and eventually entails a transformation of human thinking capacities. This intellectual empowerment happens whenever humankind endows itself with new cognitive tools, such as writing, or with new technical instruments, such as those that digital technology has made possible. Scholars such as the historian Elisabeth Eisenstein and the media specialist Marshall McLuhan have, by focusing on periods distinguished by important technological changes such as the advent of printing or the development of radio and television, sparked controversial discussions on the interactions between culture and technology. Does human understanding evolve with the advent of empowering technology? The English anthropologist Goody (1977) has studied more specifically the cognitive processes of serialized categorizing, stimulated by the use of writing and the intellectual development that ensued. Professor Ong (1982) has shown how writing has transformed human consciousness. Probably initially 'invented largely to make something like lists' and assist the failures of human memory, writing has introduced 'division and alienation, but a higher unity as well. It intensifies the sense of self and fosters more conscious interaction between persons. Writing is consciousness raising.'

This does not necessarily argue for an evolutionary approach to human reasoning capacities, as David Olson demonstrates in his quest to identify the cognitive implications of writing and reading (Olson, 1994). But it does point to the emergence of innovative cognitive activities, which have led to the development of new cognitive tools, from consciousness of thinking activities to concepts, from the logic of rhetorical disputation (the art of discourse) to the logic of critical enquiry (the art of thinking) (Ong, 1982).

William St Clair, author of an important scholarly book on the history of the English book trade, discerns 'recognisable correspondence between historic reading patterns and consequent mentalities' (St Clair, 2005). He builds the case for a political economy of reading through inquiries on the processes by which the texts reached the hands, and therefore potentially the minds, of different constituencies of readers. His findings show that the governing economic structures and business practices help 'to determine society itself, affecting every stage of cultural formation from textual production through the choice, production, and distribution of print, to readerly access, readerly horizons, choice of reading, reception, and consequent mentalities' (ibid., 17).

These historical inquiries, into the consequences that reading and writing entail for the art of thinking, provide stimulating perspectives to understand the digital literacy landscape. Important avenues for intellectual development have been opened with the exponential growth of information[1] and with the availability of powerful visual and multimedia tools.[2] By recording, extracting or constructing visual and oral accounts of reality (events, people, situations, etc.), movies, tapes, photographs, virtual reality and cyberspace provide the mind with genuinely new raw materials to think with and to produce knowledge. Will the challenges emerging with digital knowledge contexts, for which digital literacy is being deployed, open new horizons for the human art of thinking and creating knowledge?

Contextualizing digital knowledge[3]

Changes in the understanding of literacy are part of the significant evolutions that have brought information and knowledge to the forefront of societies today. Work is more and more characterized by the effective use of information tools to produce, distribute and sell goods and services in a global and competitive economy. Digital literacy has its origin in the need to develop 'information-seeking' competence within an emerging context of technology-based information needs. After the introduction of mass production and automation in agriculture and then in industry, the change towards standardized production is now happening in services and mainly in communication, information and knowledge professions. Organizations see themselves pushed into more productive ways of performing and producing information and knowledge in order to survive the competition. Those professions that work primarily with information and knowledge – such as researchers, teachers, trainers or journalists – are having difficulty to cope with the changes already disrupting their daily practices. Governments all around the world, aware of the consequences of the developing global information economy, are implementing important public policies to integrate digital information and communication (IC) tools in all daily activities. The investment is not only in deploying information and communication infrastructure, software and cultural content but, more fundamentally, in training people. As digital technology mediates more and more all accesses to information, and a majority of people are now working primarily with information and knowledge, it is becoming crucial to assess what are the challenges that emerge with digital knowledge.

Digital literacy has initially been understood as equivalent to technological literacy, in a technologically centred approach. The implicit assumption was that technology is introducing change in society and that individuals need to master the technological tools in order to be able to adjust to these changes. Going from literacy as basic skills to literacy as mind empowerment has generally been possible without reassessing the common understanding of what is knowledge. Even when digital literacy integrates an in-depth understanding of literacy, with what it implies in terms of competences, empowerment and critical reflection, it is still considering information as it has been produced within the culture of print: basically stabilized and structured representations of reality, accessible through texts (alphabetical and numerical) read, interpreted and endowed with meaning by actors, validated by recognized academic institutions and professions, and with media and multimedia representations for leisure, distraction or practical use.

The nature of digital knowledge

What one means by knowledge is a very complex epistemological question. Knowledge is much more than transmitted or acquired information. It is the awareness and understanding of facts, truths or beliefs resulting from perception, learning and reasoning, and can be understood as resulting from the integrated experience of four basic cognitive processes:

1 The organization of information units into coherent wholes or the construction of facts, stories, reasonings, rendering the units intelligible.
2 The contextualizing of these facts, by referring them to previous experience and existing knowledge.
3 The semantic interpretation or the invention of meaning or deciding what the facts, stories, reasonings, are about.
4 The awareness by the knower that he or she has understood, or consciousness of his or her new resulting knowledge.[4]

When the fourth process is taken into account, knowledge can only happen within a human mind, considering that consciousness is a characteristic of living beings. But it has now become commonplace to work with knowledge tools that can, by resorting, for example, to pattern-matching, accomplish certain semantic tasks.

Digital knowledge is knowledge not only accessed through digital tools, but also partially processed through digital tools. The use of technological tools to access information (such as databases, digital libraries, or simply the web) has resulted in the need to cope with information of immeasurable quantities, with great levels of complexity, accessible at unconceivable speeds. This needs to be done with data dispatched in picoseconds and gigabits. Knowledge skills needed include knowing how to be able to gather vast amounts of information from varied sources, knowing how to select and synthesize it, how to interpret it and evaluate it taking into account diverse cultural context and formatting. Because the human mind cannot deal with great quantities of symbols simultaneously, technological tools become absolutely necessary to organize such complex information in readable patterns. Designing tools to process information data in order to extract significant elements required the description of usually implicit knowledge construction processes.

Knowledge results from the development and use of a number of cognitive skills such as:

• locating and identifying pertinent information
• becoming aware of contexts
• assessing the origin, the reliability and the accuracy of information
• discerning, choosing and organizing relevant information
• discriminating, interpreting, critically analysing
• condensing, summarizing

- modelling and structuring
- critically evaluating, putting in perspective, comparing and pointing to specific characteristics.

Many of these skills have already been transposed in tools that allow clustering, summarizing, simulation, translation, data mining, pattern detection, etc. These tools work on knowledge bases, which are organized and structured collections of facts, rules, schemas or statements, represented in machine-interpretable form, about a knowledge domain. As everyday knowledge becomes more and more multicultural, multilingual and multimodal, as the sources of academic knowledge change, as new knowledge-legitimizing authorities emerge, as working knowledge becomes an economic commodity, one has good grounds for beginning to think that a knowledge revolution is undoubtedly on the move.

The digital knowledge revolution

Knowledge is today very often associated with the notion of revolution.[5] Revolutions are not necessarily bloody, chaotic and destructive. But revolutions are always disruptive, severing links that hold institutions together, toppling established assumptions about reality and delegitimizing dominant power structures. It will be argued here that such a revolution is happening in the knowledge landscape and that becoming digitally literate involves dealing with the fundamental changes developing in the way people relate to knowledge. Three dimensions can be distinguished and depending on the type of knowledge considered, each one of these dimensions is more or less dominant.

Tool-based knowledge processing

Digital knowledge refers to a new condition of knowledge which can be processed and transformed by technological tools. The first, most visible aspect is instantaneous access to outstanding sources of information. But a more important change is under way with the provision of tools capable of content categorizing, semantic marking, allowing knowledge foraging and mining by machines. What this implies is still debatable, but already standardization and tokenization of knowledge are developing rapidly. Knowledge processes, such as searching texts for words, summarizing texts and pictures, customizing information, translating within specific contexts, clustering large quantities of information, searching for labelled contents, are being taken over by technological tools. Important quantities of knowledge can be handled, taking into consideration not only the way knowledge is produced and its epistemological context (for example scientific or religious knowledge) but also the way it is structured and represented. Knowledge can be managed through the descriptors of its semantic content as well as its form. This implies a machine-interpretable description of the knowledge units that correspond to the information needed to apply specific processes to it.

Knowledge work itself is rapidly undergoing basic changes. Knowledge workers such as documentalists, librarians and researchers typically gather information, organize it, search it, analyse it, synthesize solutions, share and distribute them. With the emerging digital tools, documents can be automatically gathered by the system, registered, sorted and analysed. Digital knowledge tools will extract document features, textual features and metadata features (information about creation, date, author, type of document, origin, etc.). Use of linguistic analysis techniques in the case of texts will allow instrumented grasping of the conceptual content of the document, identifying entities and finding both statistical and lexical relations between the domain entities. Using digital tools implies procedural competency, as these tools are characterized by their symbolic manipulation of information through procedures and representations. These tools act on other tools or on information; they materialize mental processes such as selecting, comparing, summarizing and translating – activities more or less supported by the software devices.

According to Edward K. Owusu-Ansah (2005), 'Education is a process by which the existing knowledge of a society is transferred from one generation to another, and a process in which the tools and aptitudes for generating new knowledge are developed.' That is why the educational and academic world is so concerned and questioned by this transformation of information.

A new emerging paradigm is working with technologically based knowledge and knowledge work. Mack, Ravin and Byrd (2001) define it as 'solving problems and accomplishing goals by gathering, organising and analyzing, creating and synthesizing information and expertise'. Knowledge work tasks require specific expertise. Categories, taxonomies, models, all need to be mastered or familiarized when looking for information. Performing knowledge work typically results in the production of a document. Knowledge available is not just printed text any more. Rather it is information digitally stored available through a series of entries produced by document analysis operation such as text analysis, feature extraction, clustering, categorization, searching, navigation and visualization, summarization, glossary extraction classification and question answering. Visual techniques allow a better grasp by humans and much human reasoning and problem solving is facilitated by visual metaphors and techniques. Digital information can also be much more easily customized and personalized.

Multiple representational schemas

In this revolution, one of the main assumptions being challenged is the dominance of textual knowledge over other forms of representation. Text in schools and academic circles is basically assumed to be the most articulated expression of knowledge. This is true up to a certain level. But, when one takes into consideration exploring huge amounts of data, or the infinitely small or the cosmos, or the inside of living organisms, then forms other than textual propositions for representing knowledge have to be taken into account with cognitive and technological tools such as conceptual maps, Petri nets, visualization with NMR (nuclear magnetic resonance) techniques, geospatial equipment or statistical tools. Elisabeth Daley (2003), of the Annenberg Center for Communication, has aptly argued for 'an expanded concept of literacy' that would include media literacy.

But with digital knowledge there is a general need to study the changes happening in the way people relate to knowledge. One cannot avoid the evidence of a greater use of diverse symbolic systems in interacting with society and with reality, as the information society develops. Literary practices are being redefined with chats, blogs and self-publication. Identity changes are a mouse click away, with MOOs (multi-user role-playing environments, or text-based online virtual reality systems), forums and group games. New language forms are emerging with SMS (short message service). Collective authorship, made possible through wikis, peer-to-peer exchanges and open-source software, is but the emerging tip of a looming iceberg of information. With the internet, whole virtual libraries, streamed media programs, terabytes of climatic change data, personal blogs and hundreds of heterogeneous sources are becoming instantly accessible to people sitting in front of a networked screen at home or in the office. Still, this information explosion is only part of the changes that the use of digital technology generates.

New legitimizing sources

This revolution is also undermining existing power structures. For example, new information sources such as blogs or RSS (really simple syndication) are gradually replacing newspapers. Established legitimating procedures, such as those of the standard paper publishing circuit, are being toppled by self-publishing facilities and immediate online access to articles as soon as they are produced, thus bypassing the long wait for official publication. The monopoly of recognized national academic institutions over diplomas, qualifying and certifying training, is ending with the establishment of European certifying networks, with the development of multicultural and multilingual university training and diplomas. Networks of power are emerging, with seminal associations of public and private institutions, and with international links being established between local institutions, bypassing the national levels.

Copyright laws are perceived as preposterous and outdated. Peer-to-peer technology has popularized exchanges of music and film files. Copying is widespread, yet officially illegal. Universities are setting up defence structures, investing in spyware to identify copying from the web in student essays. Meanwhile surveys attest to the change of mentality in students who in great majority (70%) think that at least 25% of a typical student paper is copied from the internet and 73% acknowledge that the papers they produce for their professors contain at least one fully copied piece from the internet.[6] An intense debate is going on about the values on which to build in the future and the ways to solve the present dilemmas without ending up with half of the population behaving illegally.

One thing that is now known about information is that it is very much culturally sensitive. The basic social character of knowledge and information has implications for the way the information society will develop. How do knowledge workers find relevant information, how does one see implications and connections in seemingly unrelated facts? What are the knowledge needs and challenges in an information society? What are the new categories used to circumscribe the kind of competences and proficiencies needed? Will traditional knowledge professionals such as teachers master the digital knowledge tools? Or will specific digital educational knowledge tools become standard in academic institutions?

Extending knowledge processes

Knowledge expertise today is not only knowing facts and figures, basic logical and mathematical processes, but it is also understanding and mastering the basic software-processing techniques and the knowledge processing tools. In order to be accessible to the users, documents are gathered by the system, registered, managed and analysed. Content analysers will extract text and metadata, and format information, making it available for subsequent indexing and analysis processes. The knowledge tools will assist in analysing information or synthesizing information depending on the task under way, generating graphic visualizations, expressing organizational structures, discovering new potential relationships.

Clustering tools gather similar documents into smaller groups and label the groups. Document-categorization tools assign documents to categories. Here what is decisive is the type of features used to compare and classify, the way in which features associated with categories are represented and the way in which document features are compared with category features. Taxonomy generation allows labelling hierarchically organized clusters of documents. One might want to assign documents accurately to taxonomy nodes whether through an automatically generated taxonomy or one built by the management. Document experts might need to review and change decisions made by automatic clustering and labelling machinery.

Text-mining involves correlating typical textual features extracted from documents with meta-data features, the results being presented with visualization techniques which allow the discovery of new facts or relationships. Already the conceptual structures generated by standard office tools can be perceived as very complicated if not properly understood and mastered. An application will typically allow creation of model files, document files, annotated files and collaboratively produced files. Saving, retrieval and visualization of the different states of a document can become tricky if the user does not master the logic behind the tools. Keeping track of the multiple contributions in a document or merging the multiple variations by keeping private or public record of these changes can also result in a very complex task.

All these techniques need domain expertise and some degree of management and administrative skill in addition to a mastery of the software tool itself. Many aspects of tasks assumed by knowledge workers are progressively being transferred to automated systems. How can knowledge tools better assist and help knowledge workers so that their work can be alleviated of routine tasks and enriched towards more meaningful work practices in an effective and productive knowledge workplace? While some tasks will be more and more automated, others will need user involvement and expertise for a long time ahead – tasks such as developing and maintaining taxonomies, assessing the quality of search and categorization and maintaining news channels and highly dynamic sources of information.

The internet culture is already here

This rapid increase in digital technology access and availability of information has in some way changed the nature of the school or college experience. Students today generally interact with academic, disciplinary information through electronic technology, most of it becoming more and more digital. However, their teachers interact with information for their professional experience or practice almost exclusively through print technology. Many teachers are still dictating to frustrated classes of youngsters their 'personal' version of some geography, history, biology or literature contents, while it has been possible for some time now to imagine that such texts or data could be made available online, and that the teachers could spend their educational time teaching students how to think about these contents from a geographical, historical, biological or literary point of view. Yet this change is not happening in most schools and universities. Similar remarks concern grading and evaluation activities. When evaluating tools are developed, the criteria and grading techniques need to be presented explicitly in order to be used by the learners for attaining success. Not only do the evaluation procedures need then to be much more formative than selective, they can also be more adapted to the kind of knowledge and competence aimed at, through the use of simulations and multimedia contexts.

Students who enter classrooms today do not come to discover the world, to enter the mysterious realms of science and technology. They come to meet their class-mates and to obtain a diploma, the necessary asset for entering society today. During the school hours, they have to interrupt the constant connectivity most of them have with their friends and family through mobile phones and internet connec-tions. Many are more at ease with a keyboard than with a pen and notebook. They often have no idea of the traditional values of schools and universities, such as the sacredness of knowledge, the universality of humanism, the objectivity of scien-tific investigation. Knowledge is closer to a commodity than to a personal life quest.

University students, recently asked to carry out an information search task as part of research on the use of online encyclopedias, were interviewed on how they made their choices. For the greater majority, up-to-date information, which they could find on the web, was more pertinent than legitimized information that they could find in official encyclopedias such as Britannica or Universalis. Their way of working and their expectations were very much reliant on search engine pro-cedures. They were much more familiar with browser categories than with the vocabulary of their discipline. They also showed immediate impatience with time lags and lack of instantaneous response from a program. Although they had received specific training on dedicated websites dealing with their discipline, almost all of them preferred to let 'Google' do the work. One of the conclusions that came out of this research was the already intrusive research procedures with which young people had become familiar for their daily interaction with knowl-edge and that were superseding the more sophisticated procedures that the uni-versity would have wanted them to apply in an academic task. One other observation is their significant interest in seeing all the different opinions, all the points of view on an issue, stating that for them there was no 'best' answer, only a more adequate answer depending on the context. What can be identified here is the emergence of another way of relating to information and knowledge with a different set of values.

Conclusion: knowledge and digital literacy

Computers have forever changed our conception of ourselves, of the human mind, of what thinking involves and what is a human mind. Bruner (1990) has aptly pointed out how we have receded from the construction of meaning to the processing of information with computers. Computation has tended to replace interpretation. One is based on applying algorithms and rules, the other on cul-turally embedded and socially negotiated meanings. Will digital knowledge follow the same path, or will the knowledge tools provide knowledge professionals with more time for deep thinking processes?

In oral cultures, listening had been the main access to existing knowledge with the dominant associated cognitive activity being the *memorizing process*. With the advent of writing, a new access to knowledge became possible through reading, and this gave way to a more complex concomitant *cognitive activity*, which involves not only memorizing processes, but also organizing and interpreting text into meaningful units. With digital technology, which provides access through search engines, but also information-processing tools, data-mining tools and knowledge-discovery tools, the dominant cognitive activities solicited are *information structuring*, *knowledge processing* and construction of meaning. While machines will deal more and more directly with structured information and data bases, knowledge workers will be applying to knowledge the cognitive processes previously applied to information: organizing and interpreting taxonomies, clusters and patterns produced with digital tools. Today knowledge-management systems are being developed for use in the corporate world where they can be linked with other tools for project management, collaboration support, information analysis, data management, etc. They are entering academic circles and will soon be household commodities. More and more time will be spent on knowledge management, not only by managers and document specialists, but by anyone and everyone, as digital tools become omnipresent. Taking time for basic text reading will become a rare, still very enjoyable, but probably more leisure than work activity.

Information is travelling through new routes today. In the 18th and 19th centuries postal correspondence was an important vector of new ideas, as we are discovering with the publication of volumes of correspondence of 18th and 19th century authors. In much the same way today, syndicated information and blogs (weblogs) have become important trend-setting avenues, mind openers and 'must-reads' in the information world.

There is one knowledge worker who does not seem eager to take over these tools, and that is the teacher or professor. These knowledge workers live on a more and more uncomfortable contradiction. They are trained to become knowledge 'experts' in a scientific domain but their work is basically communication of a specific sort. Pedagogy is influential communication, providing children and young people with the information and the tools to successfully integrate into society as concerned, autonomous and fulfilled actors.

Today we are setting up more and more procedures in order to circumscribe the work of knowledge workers, thus allowing organizations to function at more complex levels. But there is at this point very little knowledge about how to prepare workers to interact with knowledge systems and applications beyond their technical manipulation. In the same way that the teaching and learning of reading was linked in the 18th century to basic humanistic values brought forth in the

16th century, we need today to develop teachers' and professors' awareness of these systems and the new frontiers that they open up for relating to knowledge. Important issues need to be tackled by research and by informed pedagogues.

Interacting with digital knowledge introduces basic changes in the way we relate to knowledge. Fragmented and tokenized, knowledge has lost part of its mystique. But actors are now endowed with new capacities to process knowledge, to generate deeper understanding of complex realities and to communicate worldwide and locally. Digital literacy is needed as an empowerment to become literate for the information age and for the knowledge society, which means mastering digital knowledge and new metacognitive processes; and also as a socio-cultural practice, which means, for educationalists, not only coping with knowledge as a commodity, but also re-entrenching meaningful production processes, values and beliefs into emerging educational experiences.

Notes

1   For example, 'Print, film, magnetic, and optical storage media produced about 5 exabytes of new information in 2002. . . . *How big is five exabytes?* If digitized with full formatting, the seventeen million books in the Library of Congress contain about 136 terabytes of information; five exabytes of information is equivalent in size to the information contained in 37,000 new libraries the size of the Library of Congress book collections.' Extracted from the report of project *How Much Information 2003?* by Professors Peter Lyman, Hal R. Varian et al., School of Information Management and Systems at the University of California at Berkeley, www.sims.berkeley.edu/research/projects/how-much-info-2003.

2   See, e.g. the *Visual Complexity* website, a unified resource space for anyone interested in the visualization of complex networks, www.visualcomplexity.com/vc/index.cfm.

3   Knowledge and information are sometimes used interchangeably, especially when associated with society: knowledge society or information society. A distinction is made here between the two concepts. Information refers to physical forms or supports (words, numbers, icons, signals, etc.) that lead to semantic contents through interpretive acts. By knowledge is meant the representations of organized facts and concepts believed to be true or highly reliable, and recognized as such. Knowledge is structured and enriched information integrated within an epistemological approach.

4   The description of the knowledge processes is partly inspired by the analysis made by Northrop Frye of 'mimesis' (representation) in his *Anatomy of Criticism* (1957).

5   See the January 2006 issue of *Newsweek*, titled 'The Knowledge Revolution'.

6   Les usages d'Internet dans l'enseignement supérieur, 'De la documentation … au plagiat', report of a survey, involving 975 students and 191 teachers, conducted in

partnership by Le Sphinx Développement and Six Degrées, February 2006,
www.compilatio.net.

References and further reading

Aufderheide, P. and Firestone, C. M. (1993) *Media Literacy: a report of the national leadership conference on media literacy*, Washington, DC, Aspen Institute.

Bawden, D. (2001) Information and Digital Literacies; a review of concepts, *Journal of Documentation*, **57** (2), 218–59.

Bruner, J. (1990) *Acts of Meaning*, Cambridge, MA, Harvard University Press.

Daley, E. (2003) Expanding the Concept of Literacy, *Educause Review*, (March/April).

Goody, J. (1977) *The Domestication of the Savage Mind*, Cambridge, Cambridge University Press.

Grey, W. S. (1956) *The Teaching of Reading and Writing*, Paris, Unesco.

Langford, L. (1998) Information Literacy? seeking clarification, *School Libraries Worldwide*, **4** (1), 59–72.

Leu Jr, D. J., Kinzer, C. K., Coiro, J. and Cammack, D. (2004) Towards a Theory of new Literacies Emerging from the Internet and other ICT. In Ruddell, R. B. and Unrau, N. J. *Theoretical Models and Processes of Reading*, 5th edn, Newark, DE, International Reading Association, 1570–613.

Mack, R., Ravin, Y. and Byrd, R. J. (2001) Knowledge Portals and the Emerging Digital Knowledge Workplace, *Knowledge Management*, **40** (4).

Olson, D. R. (1994) *The World on Paper: the conceptual and cognitive implications of writing and reading*, Cambridge, Cambridge University Press.

Ong, W. J. (1982) *Orality and Literacy: the technologizing of the word*, London, Routledge.

Owusu-Ansah, Edward K. (2005) Knowledge Organization and Dissemination, and Knowledge Navigation and Application: where the classroom and the library meet in higher education, *Designs for Learning*, 12th International Conference on Learning, Granada.

St Clair, W. (2004) *The Reading Nation in the Romantic Period*, Cambridge, Cambridge University Press.

St Clair, W. (2005) *The Political Economy of Reading*, John Coffin Memorial Lecture in the History of the Book, University of London, School of Advanced Study.

Street, B. (1984) *Literacy in Theory and Practice*, Cambridge, Cambridge University Press.

Street, B. (2003) What's New in New Literacy Studies? critical approaches to literacy in theory and practice, *Current Issues in Comparative Education*, **5** (2).

Tuomi, I. (2005) *The Future of Learning in the Knowledge Society: disruptive changes for Europe by 2020*, Report for DG JRC–IPTS and DG EAC.

UNESCO (2006) *Education for All, Global Monitoring Report 2006*,
www.unesco.org/education/GMR2006/full/chapt6_eng.pdf.
Varis, T. (2002) *New Literacies and e-Learning Competences*,
www.elearningeuropa.info/index.php?page=docanddoc_id=595anddocIng=
6andmenuzone=1.

6

Understanding e-literacy

Maryann Kope

Abstract

The technological changes which have infused almost every aspect of our lives have raised new questions and issues about what it means to be literate. 'E-literacy' is a relatively new term, created to attempt to capture the converging and emerging literacies necessary to function in the digital age, including, in particular, information and computer literacy. In this chapter, the author proposes that academic literacy be included in the definition of e-literacy and discusses some key components of the three literacies that e-literacy would then incorporate. By examining areas of convergence between academic literacy and information and computer literacy, some previously unrecognized commonalities are illuminated. The implications of these commonalities for learning support in a higher education context are discussed.

Introduction

'E-literacy' is a relatively new term, created to attempt to capture the converging and emerging literacies necessary to function in the digital age. The organizers of the eLit2003 Conference defined e-literacy as a combination of information and computer literacy (eLit, 2003). This chapter unravels some of the concepts incorporated by the term e-literacy and proposes that, to achieve a more comprehensive understanding of e-literacy, an additional skill set needs to be considered as part of the e-literacy equation – academic literacy.

The first part of this chapter examines the meanings of the three literacies of which e-literacy is comprised in order to arrive at the definitions which underpin the rest of the chapter. The second part explores some of the key connections between academic literacy and information and computer literacy. This approach is more focused than the work of Bawden (2001), to which readers can refer for a detailed review of information and digital literacies. My perspective is also different. Although I work in a university library, I am not a librarian; but as a learning professional, I have an interest in the evolution and merging of literacies relevant to student learning.

The connections between academic literacy and computer and information literacy have received little recognition from researchers or university professionals. Because this recognition has been lacking, the links and overlaps between academic literacy and information and computer literacy have not been exploited to the mutual benefit of staff, faculty and students. By exploring some of these commonalities, this chapter aims to promote a richer understanding of e-literacy. By recognizing points of connection, university professionals can establish a foundation on which to build new collaborative services that address the merging of literacies and provide a more seamless approach to supporting and developing student learning.

Information literacy

The term 'information literacy' has been called an 'often-used but dangerously ambiguous concept' (Shapiro and Hughes, 1996). It has had varied connotations and has evolved over time, absorbing other concepts along the way (Bawden, 2001). Controversies surrounding a precise definition of information literacy have been attributed to the fact that it is multi-faceted and a combination of knowledge and skills (Bawden, 2001), and that it includes the controversial term 'literacy' (Robson, 1998). The American Library Association's (1989) definition of information literacy as 'a set of abilities requiring individuals to recognize when information is needed and have the ability to locate, evaluate and use effectively the needed information' has received wide acceptance and will be used for this chapter.

Information literacy is perhaps the first example of how, despite some controversy over terminology, the merging of skill sets can create new competencies. Information literacy has itself been described as the merging of library literacy and media literacy (Aufderheide and Firestone, 1993) and as a combination of library skills and computer literacy (Kuhlthau, 1987). However, in a 1985 definition of information literacy that has acquired significance (Bawden, 2001), information literacy was considered to be distinct from computer literacy.

Kuhlthau (1987) further demonstrates that traditional library skills are themselves a merging of 'location' and 'interpretation' skills. She describes location skills as involving 'a knowledge of the sources and tools in libraries'. Interpretation skills involve the next step after information is located and include a broad range of cognitive skills. Interpretation skills overlap the skill set for academic literacy; this area of convergence will be explored in more detail in the section on academic literacy and information literacy.

Computer literacy

Computer literacy has evolved into a broad term that encompasses a range of related literacies, including digital, network, IT, electronic, internet and hyper-literacy (Bawden, 2001). It also appears to have a dual meaning. The common understanding of the term seems to be 'competence in the use of computers' but, in the literature on rhetoric and composition, computer literacy refers to the particular skills needed for reading and writing with computers (Selfe, 1989; Cesarini, 2002). For the purposes of this chapter, the former meaning is used.

Many definitions of computer literacy emphasize the notion of skills, both general and specific, usually the ability to use software applications. As the term has evolved, it has deepened to include an understanding of what computers 'can and cannot do' (Tuckett, 1989, Brouwer, 1997) as well as 'self-reliance' and the ability to use computers 'in a social context' (Brouwer, 1997). The social context is defined as what a user needs to function in a specific role or society as well as the 'social-political dimensions of understanding information technology use' (Brouwer, 1997). Further, there is an appreciation of the interactive nature of the internet, so the user can communicate and publish as well as access information (Bawden, 2001).

The comprehensive nature of computer literacy was addressed in the report *Being Fluent with Information Technology* (American National Research Council, 1999). The report reiterates the points made by Tuckett (1989) and Brouwer (1997) that people need a deeper understanding of computers to enable them to adapt to changes in technology.

The report identifies three kinds of knowledge needed to be information fluent: contemporary skills, foundational concepts and, most relevant to this chapter and discussed further below, intellectual capabilities. In a similar vein, Gilster (1997) claims that digital literacy is 'about mastering ideas, not keystrokes' and that the most essential of the core competencies needed for digital literacy is 'the art of critical thinking' or, more specifically, 'the ability to make informed judgements about what you find on-line'. The significance of intellectual capabilities was also recognized by Brouwer (1997), who noted the importance of 'empowering . . . users to become more critical and proactive in considering the tools at their disposal as well as making appropriate use of those tools'. He further emphasized the need for students to develop a 'conceptual model' of how software operates as a basis for understanding and learning new technologies.

The continuum we see in computer literacy, ranging from 'technical' skills to critical and conceptual thinking, parallels the evolution of library skills to the more complex construct of information literacy. The same higher-order thinking skills are a key component of academic literacy.

Academic literacy

The term 'academic literacy' is used to describe the skills students need to succeed in a higher education environment, and more specifically as 'a set of behaviours peculiar to the formally educated' (Williams and Snipper, 1990) and 'the ability to operate within the texts and genres of Western traditions, and to engage in certain reading and writing processes reflective of these texts and genres' (Pugh, Pawan, and Antommarchi, 2000).

Academic literacy, as used in this chapter, includes a broad range of learning skills and strategies, including:

- critical and analytical thinking
- problem solving
- discipline-specific study strategies
- active listening and learning from lectures
- advanced reading skills
- learning from visuals (graphs, diagrams, animations, etc.)
- exam preparation and writing strategies
- presentation skills
- concentration and memory
- time, workload and self-management
- group skills
- and perhaps the newest area – learning with and from technology.

Though not as common as information or computer literacy either as a term, concept or discipline, academic literacy has an important role to play in understanding e-literacy. The list of skills above suggests important points of connection with both information and computer literacy. However, there has been little recognition of these connections among researchers or professionals in these fields.

Part of the reason for this lack of recognition may be the specialization and separation of staff and services in academic, information and computer literacy into different administrative divisions, units and buildings in the university system. Information literacy is clearly the bailiwick of the academic library. Responsibility for computer literacy is more diverse, ranging from academic computer science departments, to computing support services, to libraries or some combination of these. The development of students' academic literacy skills is shared by curricular systems (programmes, courses, faculty) and extra-curricular services, particularly learning support programmes.

In North American university systems, extra-curricular services in academic literacy (though not usually described as such) are frequently congregated with other student services and administered by student affairs. There are many such services on a university campus that contribute to the development of academic literacy. However, because the mandate of most learning service units is specifically to support the development of the academic literacy skill set, this chapter considers learning support services as playing a central role and makes them the focus of discussion.

The separation of staff and services as described above can create barriers to communication and the sharing of expertise. How many librarians, systems analysts or learning professionals are aware of what they have in common? How many have regular contact, share expertise or collaborate on joint projects? Opportunities for collaboration for the mutual benefit of faculty, librarians, staff and students can be challenging to explore or develop. The result may be a fragmented, incoherent system of support to clients, particularly students. A recognition of the connections between academic literacy and information and computer literacy can suggest ways to address these issues.

Academic literacy and information literacy

What do these fields have in common and why haven't the commonalities been recognized? As mentioned above, the learning professionals who provide academic literacy support in North American universities often work within student service units, in isolation physically and administratively from the library. Though the spectrum of issues they address is broad, learning professionals typically have little involvement in research skills, and see a distinction between their role and that of the library. Simply put, the library's role is to help students find information, and the learning centre's role is to help students to 'know it and show it' – to attend, take in, process, integrate and reproduce information, with a focus on listening, reading, note taking, concentrating, recalling, presenting and taking exams. Where the learning centre integrates writing support services, writing and referencing are also included. The learning centre helps students not only with research material obtained from or through the library, but with all sources of course-related information – lectures, textbooks, readings, in-class presentations, etc.

Though information literacy professionals may be surprised by or disagree with this division between finding information and what one does with it, the difference has been well documented by Kuhlthau (1987). She defines library skills as having two components – location skills and interpretation skills.

Location skills are described as the 'ability to find specific information within sources' but 'stop short of using the information once it's found'. Interpretation skills involve the next step after information is located and include 'thinking about information, seeking further information based on expanding thoughts, and preparing to present information to others'. Kuhlthau (1987) also lists recalling, summarizing, paraphrasing, extending, critical thinking and 'meaningfully processing information and making it one's own' as examples of interpretation skills. Others reviewed by Bawden (2001) (though not identified specifically as interpretation skills) include:

- 'the integration of new information into an existing body of knowledge' (Doyle, 1994)
- the ability to 'deal with information sources including those outside of the library' (Dupuis, 1997)
- the ability to apply principles (Snavely and Cooper, 1997)
- the ability to communicate the information which has been found (Shapiro and Hughes, 1996).

Kuhlthau (1987) cautions that location skills and interpretation skills 'cannot be artificially divided into separate activities', yet interpretation skills in another academic context are the same capabilities that learning specialists claim as key parts of the cognitive and metacognitive skill set they address. Broader educational goals such as active learning, learning how to learn, self-reliant learning and lifelong learning have been claimed by libraries (Doyle, 1994) and learning centres both. Thus we see a major overlap between information literacy and academic literacy – one which clearly connects academic literacy into the e-literacy equation.

A further commonality between information literacy and academic literacy goes beyond 'content' to the approach taken in providing services to students. Both libraries and learning centres have typically provided generic, skill-development workshops for students. Both have realized that transferability is a key issue their programmes must address (Kuhlthau, 1987). There has been a parallel call for the embedding of skill development into the curriculum by both library and learning specialists. Librarians have been far more vocal than learning specialists on this issue, but it has been for years and remains a priority today for learning professionals as well (Gibbs, 1988). Both have recognized that collaboration with faculty and the integration of skill development within a course and curricular context is one of the most effective ways for students to develop either academic or information skills.

The trend to embedding skill development in course curricula and, along with it, closer collaboration with faculty, reflects another similarity between information literacy and academic literacy programmes. Both are shifting emphasis from content-based instruction (with its prescriptive 'how to' methods) to a process-based focus which takes a more holistic approach to supporting student learning (Kuhlthau, 1987).

These important commonalities between information literacy and academic literacy prompt the question: if libraries and learning centres have so much in common, why isn't there more connection or collaboration between them? One possible answer is that, relative to the central role played by academic libraries on campus, learning centres and services (key providers of support for academic literacy) do not typically enjoy a high profile, particularly at selective admission or research universities. Perhaps because of the strong influence of developmental education in the USA, in North America there may be an assumption that learning support services are remedial. Although this is often not the case, particularly in selective admission institutions (the norm in Canada), faculty and librarian accessibility (in the broad sense of a recognition of legitimacy and relevance) to learning support services may be limited by this assumption of remediation.

Moreover, in contrast to a research library's mandate to serve faculty, in North America there is often a separation between learning-related services for students and teaching-related services for faculty which tends to limit the interaction of learning professionals with course instructors. Student learning support may be further distanced from other academic services when located, and therefore associated, with less academically oriented services for students. This can affect not only the profile of learning services, but also the inclination of librarians, other campus educationalists (such as curriculum and instructional development staff) and faculty to recognize learning specialists as partners in the enterprise of teaching and learning and to collaborate with them. As a result, their expertise may be unacknowledged and untapped by campus colleagues.

On the library side, opportunities for collaboration may be on the upswing due to the broadening of the library's role, described as 'a transition to being an intellectual center for students' (Marcum, 2001). This transition is reflected in the growing number of information or computer 'commons' sprouting up on campuses across North America, and, along with them, an increase in collaboration between the library and other services or departments, such as computing support and instructional development (see, for example, Chapter 16 in this volume).

With a greater focus on the student learning experience in the university system (Barr and Tagg, 1995) the connections between learning-related services that overlap in content, goals or approach are beginning to receive more attention. My own institution, the University of Guelph in Ontario, Canada, has taken an innovative approach by grouping support services for learning, writing, research (through the library's reference services and information literacy programme) and technology (in partnership with our computing department) together in a consortium located in the main library. The consortium is called the 'Learning Commons' and was created in 1999 to enhance student learning by recognizing, supporting and capitalizing on the connections between learning, writing, research and technology. The physical proximity of services has enhanced student access to them and created synergy and opportunities for information sharing and collaboration among staff.

In Guelph's case, an institution-level initiative created a space for a closer connection of information literacy and academic literacy. But a change at this level may not be necessary if university professionals recognize their common interests and goals, share expertise and work towards exploiting what they have in common for the benefit of their institutions and the students they serve.

Academic literacy and computer literacy

Technology improves physical access to information but does not necessarily improve intellectual access.

(Ford, 1994).

Similar to information literacy, the connections between academic literacy and computer literacy usually are not identified as such. Even when they are recognized, aspects of academic literacy such as intellectual skills and learning strategies needed for computer literacy are typically considered part of the computer literacy skill set. For example, in his list of skills for digital literacy, Gilster (1997) identifies 'reading and understanding in a dynamic and non-sequential hypertext environment'. He calls digital literacy 'a way of reading and understanding information that differs from what we do when we sit down to read a book or a newspaper. The differences are inherent in the medium itself, and digital literacy involves mastering them.' Brouwer (1997) mentions several learning-with-computer issues, including problems with anonymity in faculty–student electronic communication and the impact of following hypertext links on the linear development of an argument.

The report *Being Fluent with Information Technology* (American National Research Council, 1999) was among the first to specifically identify the intellectual capabilities needed for competence with information technology. The report describes these intellectual capabilities as the ability to:

- apply information technology in complex and sustained situations and understand the consequences of doing so
- encapsulate higher-level thinking in the context of information technology
- manipulate the medium to advantage
- handle unintended and unexpected problems.

Though it does not connect these capabilities with academic literacy, the report does recognize their general applicability to many domains, notes the issue of transferability (a common concern for learning specialists) and suggests that the capabilities be regarded as '"life skills" that are formulated in the context of information technology' (American National Research Council, 1999). The report further defines intellectual capabilities as the ability to:

- engage in sustained reasoning
- manage complexity
- test a solution
- manage problems in faulty solutions
- organize and navigate information structures and evaluate information
- collaborate
- communicate to other audiences
- expect the unexpected
- anticipate changing technologies
- think about information technology abstractly.

It also identifies critical thinking as an important skill.

Though Gilster (1997) and the authors of *Being Fluent with Information Technology* (American National Research Council, 1999) include particular intellectual skills and capabilities as aspects of computer literacy, the same skills and capabilities can also be considered as learning issues specific to the use of computers and thus part of the academic literacy skill set. This overlap parallels the one between information and academic literacy. However, the difference here is that the literature on computer literacy has paid relatively little attention to the importance of learning issues, despite the growing recognition among learning specialists of the specific skills and strategies necessary to use computers effectively as a tool and medium for learning.

Because learning specialists tend to be practitioners more than theorists, these skills and issues are conceptualized in concrete and practical terms which can be translated into deliverable services for students. They include:

- reading from hypertext
- note taking from a screen
- avoiding plagiarism from online documents
- visual literacy
- word processing as a composing and editing tool
- self-management issues when using computers such as concentration, procrastination and addiction
- presentation skills using software such as PowerPoint

- academic communication with faculty and classmates through e-mail, discussion and chat
- working in online groups and online group dynamics
- gender differences in using and learning with computers
- lack of computer experience and skills in particular student groups (adult students, international students).

The challenge to learning service providers is to raise awareness of the importance of these learning issues, and the role that learning specialists can play in helping to address them, when there may be little or no history of contact with those responsible for computer literacy. As with information literacy, without a recognition of the importance of the learning issues in computer literacy and a collaborative response, institutional efforts to address computer literacy may be incomplete.

Towards an understanding of e-literacy

This chapter has argued that an understanding of e-literacy must include more than information and computer literacy. By exploring the relationships between academic literacy and information and computer literacy, I have attempted to demonstrate the important, though largely unrecognized, connections and commonalities. The cognitive skills, learning strategies and intellectual goals which characterize academic literacy need to be recognized as a critical component of e-literacy if a complete understanding is to be achieved now, and if a solid foundation for future development of the concept is to be built for the future.

References

American Library Association (1989) *Presidential Committee on Information Literacy: final report*, Chicago, American Library Association, www.ala.org/ala/acrl/acrl-standards/informationliteracycompetency.htm.

American National Research Council Committee on Information Technology Literacy (1999) *Being Fluent with Information Technology*, Washington, DC, National Academy Press.

Aufderheide, P. and Firestone, C. M. (1993) *Media Literacy: a report of the national leadership conference on media literacy*, ERIC Clearinghouse on Educational Resources, ED 365 294.

Barr, R. B. and Tagg, J. (1995) From Teaching to Learning: a new paradigm for undergraduate education, *Change*, (November/December), 13–25.

Bawden, D. (2001) *Information and Digital Literacies: a review of concepts*, London, Department of Information Science, City University, http://gti1.edu.um.es:8080/jgomez/hei/intranet/bawden.pdf.

Brouwer, P. S. (1997) Critical Thinking in the Information Age, *Journal of Educational Technology Systems*, **25** (2), 189–97.

Cesarini, P. (2002) *Computers, Technology, and Literacies*, www.literacyandtechnology.org/v4/cesarini.htm.

Doyle, C. S. (1994) *Information Literacy in an Information Society: a concept for the information age*, ERIC Clearinghouse on Educational Resources, ED 372 763.

Dupuis, E. A. (1997) The Information Literacy Challenge: addressing the changing needs of our students through our programs, *Internet Reference Services Quarterly*, **2** (2/3), 93–111.

eLit (2003) Second International Conference on Information and IT Literacy, Glasgow Caledonian University, Themes page, www.elit-conf.org/elit2003/themes/.

Ford, B. J. (1994) Information Literacy as a Barrier, *IFLA Journal*, **21** (2), 99–101.

Gibbs, G. (1988) An Antidote to Study Skills: developing awareness, purpose and flexibility, presentation at the Eighth Annual Conference on Teaching and Learning in Higher Education, McMaster University, Hamilton, Ontario, Canada.

Gilster, P. (1997) *Digital Literacy*, New York, NY, Wiley.

Kuhlthau, C. C. (1987) *Information Skills for an Information Society*, ERIC Clearinghouse on Educational Resources, ED 297 740.

Marcum, D. (2001) Presentation notes from 'Virtual Place, Virtuous Space: College Libraries in the 21st Century'. In American Library Association Annual Convention, San Francisco, California. American Library Association, Association of College and Research Libraries, College Libraries Section, www.ala.org/ala/acrlbucket/cls/acrlpresentation/deannamarcum.htm.

Pugh, S. L., Pawan, F. and Antommarchi, C. (2000) Academic Literacy and the New College Learner. In Flippo, R. F. and Caverly, D. C. (eds), *Handbook of College Reading and Study Strategy Research*, Mahwah, NJ, Lawrence Erlbaum.

Robson, J. (1998) Say Informacy, *Library Journal*, **123** (18), 8.

Selfe, C. (1989) Redefining Literacy: the multilayered grammars of computers. In Hawisher, G. E. and Selfe, C. (eds), *Critical Perspectives on Computers and Composition Instruction*, New York, NY, Teachers College Press.

Shapiro, J. J. and Hughes, S. K. (1996) Information Literacy as a Liberal Art: enlightenment proposals for a new curriculum, *Educom Review*, **31** (2), www.educause.edu/apps/er/review/reviewArticles/31231.html.

Snavely, L. and Cooper, N. (1997) The Information Literacy Debate, *Journal of Academic Librarianship*, **23** (1), 9–20.

Tuckett, H. W. (1989) Computer Literacy, Information Literacy and the Role of the Instruction Librarian. In Mensching, G. E. and Mensching, T. B. (eds), *Coping with Information Illiteracy: bibliographic instruction for the information age*, Ann Arbor, MI, Pieran Press.

Williams, J. D. and Snipper, G. C. (1990) *Literacy and Bilingualism*, New York, NY, Longman.

7

Information literacy – an overview

Ola Pilerot

Abstract

This chapter aims to present an overview of the multifaceted concept of information literacy. It should be seen as an exploration of ways of comprehending information literacy. The main questions are: what are the dominating ways of seeing information literacy and why is there an information-literacy initiative? Many authors rightly claim that the task of educating information-literate students and people is not the responsibility of one single group or profession, and consequently this chapter also looks at collaborative aspects of information-literacy education. In accordance with the scope of this book the chapter also presents information literacy in the light of other literacies.

Introduction

That information literacy is of great interest to many is evident by the amount of publications that relate to the concept (see Rader, 2002). Among its advocates one group dominates, namely librarians, which is apparent by the number of contributions to the literature made by library professionals. Despite the fact that the term 'information literacy' is said to have been coined in the early 1970s (Carbo, 1997), it is evident that the pedagogical ambition which goes along with information literacy education was recognized by librarians long before that:

> A librarian should be more than a keeper of books; he should be an educator. . . . All that is taught in college amounts to very little; but if we can send students out self-reliant in their investigations, we have accomplished very much.
>
> (Robinson, 1876)

Ways of comprehending information literacy

When reviewing a number of documents with the common aim of defining or presenting an overview of the concept of information literacy (see e.g. Owusu-Ansah, 2003; Kapitzke, 2003) it becomes apparent that it is a concept that is often similarly regarded. Definitions and models, with slight variations, continuously appear, often in the form of lists that easily remind the reader of recipes or panaceas. The most widely spread of them all is formulated by the American Library Association (1989, 1):

> To be information literate, a person must be able to recognise when information is needed and have the ability to locate, evaluate, and use effectively the needed information.

Seemingly stemming from the above definition, lists of desired attributes and standardized descriptions of how an information-literate student (or person) should behave or function have been developed.

Taken together a majority of the lists and models seem to have some prominent but also problematic features: to a critical extent they lack consideration of contextual factors; they concentrate on skills presented as generic and easily transferable between sectors and disciplines; they imply in accordance with a behaviourist standpoint that information literacy consists of individual attributes and characteristics that should be conquered; and they are to a large extent presenting the phenomenon from a librarian's point of view.

So, perhaps it is not surprising that voices have been raised to suggest that 'the literature on information literacy reveals the presence of a consensual core' (Owusu-Ansah, 2003, 220). However, as suggested by Lupton this consensus might be due to a prevalence of librarian-centric views. She refers to an exploration of the information literacy discourse and concludes that 'it became clear that information literacy education was indeed primarily based on the practice of librarians rather than in the experiences of students' (Lupton, 2004, 9).

Until the late 1990s there were two ways of viewing information literacy that dominated and competed with each other: the behavioural and information-processing approach, and the constructivist approach (Bruce, 1997b, 2). According to the former view the information-literate person should be able to demonstrate certain skills that can be used in a linear process to solve information-related problems. Bruce (ibid., 2) suggests that this might depend on the fact that this approach 'represents the organisational view of learning in many learning-institutions'. Since then two highly important works for the information literacy movement have been published: Christine Bruce's PhD thesis from 1997, *The Seven Faces of Information Literacy*, and Louise Limberg's dissertation *Experiencing Information Seeking and Learning: a study of the interaction between two phenomena*, originally published in Swedish in 1998. These two books have had an enormous impact on how the view of information literacy has evolved in the library world and elsewhere. Both are well grounded in comprehensive empirical studies, and challenge the dominating view as described above. Bruce describes her model as the relational view of information literacy:

> This involved a change from describing information literacy in terms of attributes (skills, knowledge and attitudes) to describing it in terms of varying conceptions of experiences which are defined in terms of relations between people and aspects of the world.
>
> (Bruce, 1997a, 16)

Limberg, who, like Bruce, carried out a study with a phenomenographic approach with the aim of revealing varying conceptions of information seeking and use, reached the important conclusion, 'that the description of variation in information seeking and use contributes to a deeper, richer and more complex understanding of information literacy' (Limberg, 2000, 204). Within the area of information literacy research the relational model has gained a strong position, but it seems as if a similar response within the field of practitioners is still to be awaited, a matter that mirrors the sometimes all too large gap between research and practice.

Why is there an information literacy initiative?

Why is information literacy such an important issue for so many? One reason mentioned by numerous authors is the increase of easily available information. It could also easily be claimed that there has been a shift of paradigms in the educational context which has fuelled the initiative. On all educational levels there is an ambition to move away from the teacher-centred education in favour of student-centred pedagogy (Martin, 2003, 4); a pedagogy that naturally involves problem- and inquiry-based learning. Students are supposed to use information that they are required to identify, locate and access to solve problems. This development functions as a strong argument for developing information-literate students. A third important factor is the globally spread ideological and political idea of life long learning; if citizens are supposed to subscribe to life-long learning, they need to know not only how to locate and access information, but also how to evaluate and thereby be able to make use of the information. The individual citizen has been given a greater responsibility for his or her own learning and therefore needs to develop information literacy; or, as stated in the Prague Declaration (2003), formulated at the Information Literacy Meeting of Experts (2003): information literacy 'is a prerequisite for participating effectively in the Information Society'.

Information literacy in relation to other literacies

Bawden (2001) concludes that information literacy and digital literacy are associated with issues as varied as information overload, lifelong learning, knowledge management and the growth of the information society, and that they are central topics for the information sciences, but, as he continues:

> To deal with the complexities of the current information environment, a complex and broad form of literacy is required. It must subsume all the skill based literacies, but cannot be restricted to them, nor can it be restricted to any particular technology or set of technologies. Understanding, meaning and context must be central to it.
>
> (Bawden, 2001, 251)

These three latter terms – understanding, meaning and context – are not seldom pinpointed as central to the concept of information literacy. Klaus (2000, 209) has stated that the 'very words – information and literacy – call upon us to be concerned with meaning and interpretation that is inherent in what people do and think'. In a similar way Kuhlthau (2001) has claimed that, 'students need to learn to construct meaning from vast, disparate sources of information through an inquiry process approach to learning'. To construct meaning can also be seen as a need to create coherence in a more diversified and incoherent world of information, and the prime tool to fulfil this need may be seen as information literacy.

Bruce (2003, 261) asserts that information literacy is often seen as the 'overarching literacy essential for twenty-first-century living'. In another paper by Bawden (with Robinson, 2001) the terms information literacy and digital literacy are used almost interchangeably. After referring to a general definition of information literacy as the 'ability to make effective use of information sources, including analyzing and evaluating information, and organizing and using it in an individual or group context', the authors continue:

> The term 'digital literacy' has been used more recently to encompass the situation where networked resources are a significant part of those available and includes such skills as 'hypertextual navigation' and 'knowledge assembly'.
>
> (Robinson and Bawden, 2001, 172)

Their conclusion is that, 'From what has been said above, it will be clear that the promotion of information, or digital, literacy will be a necessary function of any library service aspiring to promote open society' (ibid.).

It seems to be easier for authorities and politicians, on all levels, to comprehend and identify a need for IT skills than for the broader and more complex concept of information literacy. Thus it is not surprising that information literacy education is sometimes contrasted and profiled against information technology training. It may be in response to this that Johnston and Webber (2003, 335) state:

> the scale and connectedness of the global information society demands an educational response that focuses on information use as distinct from use of information technology (IT): education for information literacy rather than IT literacy.

Collaboration and obstacles for collaboration

A key factor for successful implementation of high-quality information literacy education identified by several authors is collaborative efforts. The project of developing information-literate individuals and organizations must be seen as a joint venture (Bruce, 2004, 17).

Even though the literature provides evidence of examples of successful implementations these collaborative efforts are still seen as innovative practices (ibid., 11). Within the field of library research there is a fairly large number of published articles dealing with different aspects of librarian–faculty relations. Among the few that have studied this area from a different angle is a report on librarian–faculty relations from a sociological perspective, conducted by Christiansen, Stombler and Thaxton (2004). They identify a number of obstacles that have to be eliminated before fruitful collaboration can start to be developed on a wider range. They confirm that there is an asymmetrical disconnection between librarians and faculty which is evident in several ways (Christiansen, Stombler and Thaxton, 2004, 118). Librarians show a great interest in, and knowledge about, faculty and the work they do, and they are also eager to increase contact with faculty. On the other hand, faculty is not as well informed and knowledgeable about librarians' work and is not seeking similar contact (ibid.). The main explanation for this disconnection, according to Christiansen, Stombler and Thaxton, has two dimensions: an organizational and a social status dimension. Simply speaking, few, if any, universities or educational institutions are designed, either physically or organizationally, in a way that stimulates collaboration between the two groups. The root of the social status dimension is to be found in the way the two groups' work is perceived (by themselves and by contemporary society):

> The perception among faculty is that librarians' work is service-oriented – their primary duties are the organization and facilitation of access to knowledge and other resources. By contrast, faculty sees their own work as focusing on the production and dissemination of knowledge. As many sociologists have discussed in numerous contexts, contemporary society generally views service-oriented work as being of lesser importance than production ...
>
> (Christiansen , Stombler and Thaxton, 2004, 119).

As pointed out by McGuinness (2003), the status issue is not new. McGuinness's work explores the status of information literacy education within the context of third-level, undergraduate education in the Irish Republic and has shown that collaboration between librarians and faculty, when it comes to teaching, does not exist in the way it is advocated in the literature (McGuinness, 2003, 249). The reason for this seems to be very similar to the reasons identified by Christensen, Stombler and Thaxton. McGuinness notes that 'librarians appear as service-providers to the academics, principally concerned with the management of information resources' (249).

These obvious obstacles in this brief account may be perceived as problems that are difficult to solve, and that is probably true. But there are suggestions as to how these problems can be dealt with. Bruce has identified some keys to implement information literacy education (2004, 15ff.). She brings up the need for a cultural change and a change in educational values, for example, the shift from a teacher-centred to a learner-centred view of learning. She also highlights the need for guidelines and policies that can direct and support the adoption and implementation of information literacy education. Finally, she emphasizes the role of education for teachers, information specialists and managers as being critical to global information literacy education initiatives.

Embedment, integration and stand alone

There is a widespread belief that the most successful way to teach information literacy is to teach it in connection with other subjects (see, for example, Hepworth, 1999). A majority of authors state that embedment, integration or incorporation is the sole key to a successful implementation of information literacy education. The author agrees that these strategies are of great importance but is of the belief that it is also quite reasonable to both teach and treat information literacy as a subject in its own right. Webber and Johnston have given numerous accounts of their successful work with credit-bearing courses for business students at Strathclyde university. Pilerot (2003a, 2003b) provides examples of well functioning credit-bearing information literacy courses for doctoral students, and for graduate students. Webber and Johnston (2005) identify a tension between the different approaches to course design as they argue that regarding information literacy as a subject in its own right can actually provide a more holistic approach covering aspects of information literacy, such as the importance of information literacy for citizenship, economic growth and employability, which may not be covered by a discipline-specific approach.

Conclusion

The concept of information literacy is understood in a range of ways. However, two main approaches to the phenomenon are discernible. One view is based on the idea that the information-literate person can be characterized by certain attributes, a view which has been claimed to be library-oriented and thus widely spread among librarians. The other approach has developed from research on information literacy and is recognized by its focus on variations in ways that the phenomenon can be understood and conceptualized. The latter approach clearly advocates that information literacy education always should focus on the user (or users), the individual and the student, as opposed to the former view that has been traditionally shaped by the way librarians experience the concept.

The way the concept has been dealt with in this chapter mirrors the way it is most often dealt with in general: as a process closely connected to formal (higher) education. There is a need for future research to focus on information literacy in other settings, such as the workplace and in the context of citizenship. The concept is still often experienced as an elusive phenomenon difficult to capture, but with more research – and by lessening the gap between research and practice – information literacy will be more comprehensible and thereby applicable for more people.

References

American Library Association (ALA) (1989) *Presidential Committee on Information Literacy: final report*, Chicago, IL, American Association of School Librarians, American Library Association.

Bawden, D. (2001) Information and Digital Literacies: a review of concepts, *Journal of Documentation*, **57** (2), 218–59.

Bruce, C. (1997a) *The Seven Faces of Information Literacy*, Adelaide, Auslib Press.

Bruce, C. (1997b) The Relational Approach: a new model for information literacy, *New Review of Information and Library Research*, **3**, 1–22.

Bruce, C. (2003) Information Literacy. In Feather, J. and Sturges, P. (eds), *International Encyclopedia of Information and Library Science*, 2nd edn, London, Routledge.

Bruce, C. (2004) Information Literacy as a Catalyst for Educational Change. In Danaher, P. A., MacPherson, C., Nouwens, F. and Orr, D. (eds), *3rd International Lifelong Learning Conference, Yeppoon, Central Queensland, Australia*, Central Queensland University.

Carbo, T. (1997) Mediacy: knowledge and skills to navigate the information highway, *International Information and Library Review*, **29** (3/4), 393–401.

Christiansen, L., Stombler. M. and Thaxton, L. (2004) A Report on Librarian–Faculty Relations from a Sociological Perspective, *Journal of Academic Librarianship*, **30** (2), 116–21.

Hepworth, M. (1999) A Study of Undergraduate Information Literacy and Skills: the inclusion of information literacy and skills in the undergraduate curriculum, *65th IFLA Council and General Conference, Bangkok, Thailand, August 20–28, 1999*, www.ifla.org/IV/ifla65/papers/107-124e.htm.

Information Literacy Meeting of Experts (2003) *The Prague Declaration: towards an information literate society*, National Commission on Library and Information Science; National Forum on Information Literacy and UNESCO, www.infolit.org/International_Conference/PragueDeclaration.pdf.

Johnston, B. and Webber, S. (2003) Information Literacy in Higher Education: a review and case study, *Studies in Higher Education*, **28** (3), 335–52.

Kapitzke, C. (2003) Information Literacy: a positivist epistemology and a politics of outformation, *Educational Theory*, **53** (1), 37–53.

Klaus, H. (2000) Understanding Scholarly and Professional Communication: thesauri and database searching. In Bruce, C. and Candy, P. (eds), *Information Literacy Around the World: advances in programs and research*, Wagga Wagga, Centre for Information Studies, Charles Stuart University.

Kuhlthau, C. (2001) Rethinking Libraries for the Information Age School: vital roles in inquiry learning, Keynote paper, *2001 IASL Conference Auckland, New Zealand 9–12 July*, www.iasl-slo.org/keynote-kuhlthau2001.html.

Limberg, L. (1998) *Att Söka Information för att Lära: en studie av samspel mellan informationssökning och lärande Borås*, VALFRID.

Limberg, L. (2000) Is There a Relation Between Information Seeking and Learning Outcomes? In Bruce, C. and Candy, P. (eds), *Information Literacy Around the World: advances in programs and research*, Wagga Wagga, Centre for Information Studies, Charles Sturt University.

Lupton, M. (2004) *The Learning Connection: information literacy and the student experience*, Adelaide, Auslib Press.

McGuinness, C. (2003) Attitudes of Academics to the Library's Role in Information Literacy Education. In Martin, A. and Rader, H. (eds), *Information and IT Literacy: enabling learning in the 21st century*, London, Facet Publishing.

Martin, A. (2003) Towards E-literacy. In Martin, A. and Rader, H. (eds), *Information and IT Literacy: enabling learning in the 21st century*, London, Facet Publishing.

Owusu-Ansah, E. K. (2003) Information Literacy and the Academic Library: a critical look at a concept and the controversies surrounding it, *Journal of Academic Librarianship*, **29** (4), 219–30.

Pilerot, O. (2003a) Information Literacy at a Distance – collaboration between a university library and two public libraries, paper presented at the *Second International Conference on Information and IT Literacy, eLit 2003, Glasgow Caledonian University, 11–13 June 2003*, www.iteu.gla.ac.uk/elit/elit2003/papers/ppt/pilerot.pdf.

Pilerot, O. (2003b) Information Literacy Education – a case study. In Hummelshoj, M. (ed.), *Nord I&D, Knowledge and Change. Proceedings of the 12th Nordic conference for information and documentation, September 1–3, 2004, Aalborg, Denmark*, Aalborg, Royal School of Library and Information Science.

Rader, H. B. (2002) Information Literacy 1973–2002: a selected literature review, *Library Trends*, **51** (2), 242–59.

Robinson, L. and Bawden, D. (2001) Libraries and Open Society: Popper, Soros and digital information, *Aslib Proceedings*, **53** (5), 167–78.

Robinson, O. H. (1876) Proceedings, *American Library Journal*, **1**, 123–4.

Webber, S. and Johnston, B. (2005) Partnerships for Curriculum Change and Course Design, PowerPoint presentation at an information literacy seminar, 31 March, at Skövde University, Sweden, unpublished.

8

Contemporary literacy – the three Es

David F. Warlick

Abstract

Retooling classrooms for 21st-century teaching and learning will not be served by completely reinventing literacy. It is important to acknowledge the continuing value of reading, arithmetic and writing, as basic skills, and to build on that foundation and expanded model of contemporary literacy. This chapter seeks to start with the three Rs, and grow them into three Es, an expanded model for being proficient and efficient users of information.

Introduction

Before we begin a discussion of contemporary literacy, it is important to settle on a definition for 'literacy' that can serve as a framework. This is no small task, considering that the word has been used in a wide variety of contexts, addressing a broad range of skill sets. But, for the sake of this chapter, I want to suggest a consensus around the following definition:

> Literacy comprises those essential information skills required to accomplish goals within one's contemporary information environment.

The only part of this definition that might seem out of place to most 21st-century inhabitants is the last part, 'within one's contemporary information environment'. During most of the last two centuries, that environment changed very little. It was at the beginning of the 19th century that Sir William Curtis, Lord Mayor of London, coined the phrase, 'the three Rs'. Not an extraordinarily literate man, as evidenced by his spelling, Curtis did effectively define an effective literacy framework for a *published-print* information environment.

Today, however, that environment has changed, and it has happened in just 30 years – mostly in the last ten years. Information has changed in what it looks like, what we look at to view it, where and how we find it, what we can do with it, and how we communicate it.

Any effort to effectively define a new literacy model that reflects this new information environment effectively requires us to drill down into the roots of how information has changed. Factoring all aspects of information reveals three new characteristics of the contemporary information environment that are fundamental to using this environment to accomplish goals: information is networked; information is digital; and information is in abundance.

Information is networked

Information in the published-print environment was networked. But it was a network based on transporting paper and other printed materials across oceans, rivers, mountains, towns and across the classroom. Today, information is transported through a well greased electronic conduit that sends content across the classroom only slightly faster than it can be sent around the world. This new ease of information transportation has profound implications not only for its availability and access, but also for the very nature of the information and how we use it.

Information is digital

Most recorded information, until recently, consisted of symbols scratched or stamped on paper. At best it was magnetically encoded on thin plastic tape to be watched or listened to later. Today, however, all information (images, sound, animation, video) is communicated in the same language, the binary code of ones and zeros – that is, digital. When every medium expresses itself in the same language, then information can be made, mixed, assembled, manipulated and communicated in ways that would have seemed magical only a couple of decades ago.

Information is in abundance

During much of the last two centuries, information was a scarcity for most people, and it was purchased largely from a few publishers. Today, information pervades our daily lives, and we use information to make hundreds of daily decisions. We depend on information like no society before us. It is the infrastructure on which our economy and culture rides.

Contemporary literacy

With these three fundamental characteristics in mind, we can begin to shape a literacy model. But it is also essential to set out a framework of two guidelines that can be easily integrated into children's learning in our classrooms.

1 The structure of our classrooms and schools and the governance of education, along with the momentum behind our existing curriculum, results in a system that resists change. Therefore, it is critical that our definition of literacy not be reinvented. Instead it must evolve out of the published-print environment that addresses the networked digital environment.

2 In addition, education remains, on almost every surface, a community endeavour. Therefore, any model for integrating contemporary literacy into standard classroom instruction must be simple enough that it can be convincingly expressed in three or four sentences. There is a need for detailed hierarchies of literacy skills to be used to guide professional educators in their instructional planning. However, the model must also be reducible to three (or four) bullet points that can be explained to the community during short conversations.

With these two constraints in mind, the three Rs make an appropriate place to start. All things considered, reading, arithmetic and writing convey a useful progression of the information process. This is shown in Figure 8.1.

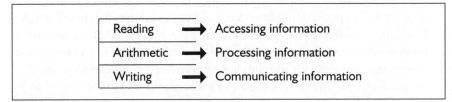

Figure 8.1   *Development of the three Rs*

Reading

What does it mean to be a reader in the 21st century? Networked digital information has enormous implications for acquiring knowledge. Consider the machinery and expense involved in printing a book or even a newspaper. Producing information involved an investment of capital, so decisions had to be made about the value of the content compared with the cost of producing it. So there was an editorial process built into the process of generating information.

Also, since information had to be physically transported, and physically stored, we built libraries to house information and hired librarians who selected the information appropriate to the community. Add in teachers, parents, religious institutions, service clubs and many others, and the information that we and our students encountered had been substantially filtered for reliability, credibility and appropriateness. This served as no guarantee that information was reliable, credible or appropriate. But it was relatively safe.

From a literacy standpoint, we were taught to read what somebody handed to us. We read information, which people in authority and people we trusted approved. If you could read and understand the text, then you were literate.

Today, nearly anyone can produce and publish almost any information and for almost any reason, and, through the networks, that information is available directly to the information consumer, right down to our children. For this reason, reading, as a literacy, should be expanded to include skills that involve not only decoding text, but also deal with an open communication environment and the new authors. These skills include four major categories: finding information, decoding information, critically evaluating information and organizing information.

- *Finding information*. During the last two centuries, most collections of information were small enough that they could be organized alphabetically or by general subject area. At the book level, skills in using a table of contents and index were sufficient for locating the information we needed. Today, information is global and it consists of billions of pages of content, interconnected logically through producer-installed hyperlinks – the world wide web. Using this logically interconnected information environment becomes the prime skill in locating information. It involves a wide range of idea- and content-processing skills as well as background knowledge about the information being sought. In addition, information users must be able to pose Boolean questions resourcefully to search engines, and to refine search strategies in an investigative process that addresses the unique characteristics of each research problem. As the contemporary information environment continues to evolve, new techniques and new literacy skills evolve. Emerging techniques such as RSS (really simple syndication) and other protocols that will likely rise out of the XML (extensible markup language)/metadata environment will increasingly become critical to the information navigator of the 21st century.
- *Decoding information*. We have long taught students to decode text, and this skill is more critical today than ever before. We also know that images, sound, animation and video often communicate more effectively than text. With the growing availability of information, the even more rapidly growing availability of information production technologies, and the rising sense that success in almost any endeavour depends on communication, we must expand the range of information media that students can decode and understand.
- *Critically evaluating information*. In the published-print information environment, information came from trusted sources, almost exclusively. We were

taught, implicitly, to assume the authority of the information that we encountered. Therefore, if you could read the text, you were literate. Today, information is available from a global information web, and the authority and reliability of the source can no longer be assumed. Rather than teaching students to assume the authority of information, we must teach them to prove the authority. More than any other aspect of contemporary literacy, this element must weave its way into every nook and cranny of the teaching and learning process. Teachers by nature present information from authority. We work from authority. Our students learn from our authority. But this is the wrong lesson to be teaching if we seek to make our students literate in the new information environment.

Serious journalism is a very good example. When a news story puts forward an idea, it precedes the statement with 'According to …'. All facets of the story are corroborated by sources and other supporting information. As teachers, we must practise the same process of validating what we present with supporting evidence of its accuracy, reliability and relevance. In an open and potent information environment, information must support itself. Often the evidence that proves the accuracy of information is not immediately apparent. Therefore, it is critical that students be taught a range of investigative techniques for digging into the information, its sources and its intent. This involves higher order thinking skills as well as more precise techniques in order to trace the information's ownership and context.

- *Organizing information*. With a growing and evolving global library, one strategy for making sense from (and use of) the information environment is to create and cultivate personal digital libraries. We have long kept bookmarks or favourites with our web browsers. Many of us have organized our bookmarks into what might be called a personal library. Our bookmarks, along with emerging RSS aggregators that help us subscribe to our favourite weblogs, news sources, ongoing web searches, multimedia programming (podcasts), book and movie lists and each other's bookmarks (and the information sources that we haven't imagined yet), all point to a growing need that information-literate people should not only know how to use a library, but also how to build one. It is critical that students learn how large amounts of selected information can be organized in order to help their owners to solve problems, answer questions and accomplish goals. Adding value to information by organizing it into a functional context is no long the exclusive skill domain of web designers or librarians. It is a basic skill.

Reading has not changed, and its importance as a basic literacy skill has increased dramatically. However, in order to acquire knowledge within a globally networked information environment where authors, editors and publishers are our neighbours (or on the other side of the tracks of our belief systems), it is critical that students be taught to *expose the truth*, not just read it.

Arithmetic

Numbers help us to describe precisely our environment and the laws that affect our environment. Mathematics helps us to make those numbers tell their story, and enables us to change the story in order to add value to our environment. Knowing how to add, subtract, count, measure and calculate remains a prerequisite to being literate in the new information environment. Today, however, as we use mathematics to solve problems, we are not addressing a dozen numbers on a piece of paper, but thousands of numbers, and they are digital.

Being able to process information in the new information environment will require a practical understanding of the language of numbers. It will also require a range of technical skills involved in working the digital numbers that are all around us. Students must learn how to:

1 capture digital information and import the data into the appropriate information processing tool (i.e. statistical software, spreadsheet)
2 use information-processing software to analyse the information (i.e. statistical functions, graphing), and
3 have an adequate understanding of their environment (physical, historical, cultural and economic) in order to apply the conclusions in a way that solves problems, answers questions and accomplishes goals.

The core of mathematics, in the curriculum, is for students to understand the language of numbers, and the process (paper-based, digital and in-your-head) for using numbers to achieve an end. New formats of information must also be factored into information-processing skills. Historically, numbers were the only style of information that we were thoroughly taught to process. Even though we were taught some writing, text was for reading, pictures were for looking at, audio was for listening to, and video was for watching. Processing these other media required technology that was prohibitively expensive and required training that was not available to most people.

In the new information environment, all information is made of numbers. Binary ones and zeros now convey our text, our pictures, our music and other audio, animation and video. Since information is now carried on the digital number streams, it no longer requires specialized and expensive tools to produce and edit the content. With a reasonably powerful laptop computer we can write a book, enhance photos and draw graphs, produce music, create animation, and capture and edit video. It is all mathematics, because it is all the act of adding value to information by processing that information, through its numbers.

Like reading, being able to use the new information environment to accomplish goals requires us to expand our notions of what it means to be literate. Students must learn not only how to add and subtract on paper, but how to *employ information*.

Writing

One of the characteristics of the new information environment is the degree to which information has come to influence and describe our daily lives. Only a very few generations ago, the typical home was completely devoid of information. Life was ruled by habit and reacting to current conditions. Today, we are swimming in information. It is on our walls, in our cars, in our pockets, playing into our ears, and bombarding our eyes. Information is in the air that we breathe. There is so much information around us that we must increasingly choose the information that we use, among a dizzying array of options.

In the information age, information must compete for attention in the same way that products on a store shelf competed for attention in the industrial age. This means that communicating not only requires us to write a coherent paragraph, but also to write convincingly. In addition, being able to communicate with images, sound and motion has become a basic skill for a future that is driven by information.

At the same time that students are learning to write, they must learn to express ideas using the full range of information. This involves being able to identify the most effective medium, and the skills to:

1 find and organize
2 evaluate and select
3 process and adapt
4 even produce original information products (images, audio and video).

Effective communication must be learned as a goal-oriented endeavour, and not as discrete skills. When students communicate in order to accomplish goals, using an entire range of media, then they are learning not only writing, but how to *express ideas compellingly*.

Expanding the literacy model

Even though reading, arithmetic and writing, in their historic sense, are no longer adequate to empower success in an information-driven world, the model remains effective. Living and accomplishing goals with information require us to access, process and communicate knowledge (see Figure 8.2). The information environment has simply become much richer than that of the industrial age.

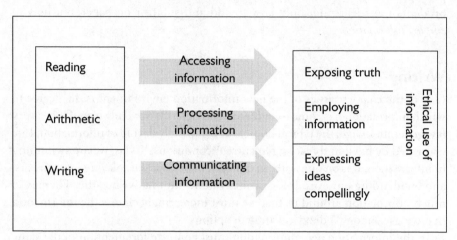

Figure 8.2   *Expanding the literacy model*

We must add, however, an additional component to our literacy model, because the information environment has become so important to our society's success. In the same fashion that information can cure disease, feed the hungry, empower people with skills, increase productivity and entertain millions, its abuse can topple economies and even nations. Information is the power behind modern society and it is crucial that students be taught its ethical use, as they are being taught to expose, employ and express knowledge. They must learn to love and protect the truth. Three aspects of information ethics combine to describe practices that must become a part of school curriculum: information property, information reliability and information infrastructure.

Information property

According to an October 2004 article in *WIRED Magazine* (Anderson, 2004), 57% of Amazon.com's total sales come from products that will never appear in a bookstore because they do not appeal to a large enough audience. Niche products account for 22% of Rhapsody's downloads and 20% of Netflix's rentals. Drawing income by producing content is no longer the exclusive endeavour of best-selling authors, blockbuster movie producers or top-40 musicians. Because of a new digital bazaar, where content can be sold globally, our neighbours are now producing and earning income by writing books, composing music and producing independent videos. When the authors of the information we use are our neigh-bours, and when we, as information producers, understand the time and effort that goes into its production, then we should become more willing and eager to cred-it content producers. In the classroom, we should make our students information property owners. As students produce reports, multimedia presentations, web pages and other information products, their ownership and responsibility for the work should be integrated into the discussions and assessment of their work.

Information reliability

The reliability of information is addressed in exposing the truth of the informa-tion that we encounter. But the other side of this coin is our responsibility to assure that the information we produce is accurate and reliable. This is one reason why it is important to credit or cite the sources of information that are included not only in student products but also in our teaching resources. Beyond citations, it has become important to include with our messages, information about the infor-mation. As before, a good model to follow is *responsible* journalism. A good news story does not merely report the facts, but it attributes the facts of the story to reli-able sources that readers will trust. This is a practice that all information producers should adopt, especially teachers as they present material in the classroom. We must teach students, by example, that it is not only important to prove the authority of the information that they use, but to prove the authority of the information that we present.

Information infrastructure

In a sophisticated society with almost unlimited options, information is critical to success in almost any endeavour. The wires on which this information rides are as important as our roads, bridges, railways, airports and seaports. We live on the networks today, and we live in a time when planting a virus on a network is no different from planting a bomb under a bridge. Students must learn that the infor-mation infrastructure of our society is a crucial part of what makes us successful, and they must learn this in the earliest years. As young children learn about communities and the people who help us in our communities, they should learn the role that networked digital information plays in our success. When inviting nurses, fire fighters, truck drivers and other community helpers into the classroom, ask them how they use the internet, e-mail and other network services to help peo-ple. The internet is no longer a toy – it is a big part of where we live. We must teach people that it cannot be treated as a toy.

Conclusion

We straddle two worlds. Most of the teachers in our classrooms today grew up and attended schools with books and paper, pens and pencils, and no world wide web. Our students have grown up with a global library of digital information that can be found and accessed almost at will and an information environment that is rapidly becoming more conversation than library. Teaching students *about* the new information environment requires us to teach them from the new information environment, where content becomes more raw material than answers to questions.

Reference

Anderson, C. (2004) The Long Tail, *Wired Magazine*, **12** (10), www.wired.com/wired/archive/12.10/tail_pr.html.

9

Reconceptualizing media literacy for the digital age

Renee Hobbs

Abstract

This chapter identifies how media literacy education must adapt to accommodate the changing nature of young people's experience with digital media and new communication technologies. Teachers who traditionally emphasize the processes of analysing news, advertising and entertainment media must expand their focus to include new media (like cellphones and handheld devices), new message forms (like search engines, instant messaging, blogs and online entertainment) and new social issues (including identity and anonymity, privacy and surveillance). By examining certain conceptual principles and instructional practices which may (or may not) support this shift in focus, this chapter examines the process that teachers will experience as they aim to strengthen students' communication and critical thinking skills as full participants in the digital age.

Introduction

One September morning in a high school just outside Washington DC, Mr Smith, a social studies teacher, started his semester standing at the front of the room full of somewhat sleepy students aged 15–17. The elective course was entitled 'Media Literacy' and, as he passed out the course syllabus, he previewed some of the topics and issues that would be explored over the coming months: analysing news media, learning how news is constructed, and understanding media's function in society; analysing advertising including reflections on the processes of consumer socialization and the manufacture of desire; examining patterns of representation of race, gender and class in mass media messages; and understanding the psychological impact of media violence and the role of entertainment violence in contemporary culture. Through a series of readings, screenings, discussion and writing activities, this teacher's aim was to help students to become critical thinkers in responding to media messages, to understand the social, political and economic contexts in which messages are constructed and disseminated, and to reflect on and examine their own behaviours as consumers and citizens. During the semester-long course, Mr Smith made active use of newspapers, magazines, television news and entertainment programmes, documentaries and curriculum materials he found online and at the Center for Media Literacy's website in Los Angeles.

While still a novelty in most US public schools, media literacy is now beginning to acquire some status within the K-12 content areas of English language arts, social studies and health education (Hobbs, 2004). As a result of advocacy by educators in the State of Texas, the concept 'viewing and representing' can now be found in American textbooks, for example, where students are led through activities demonstrating the importance of 'reading' a film, documentary or television programme and 'writing' using electronic and digital tools including publishing and presentation software (Odell et al., 2000). In the USA, media literacy is increasingly being used as a means to introduce students to cultural studies, in contrast to more vocationally oriented courses in media and communications at many high schools, universities and colleges which may emphasize the acquisition of production skills (Potter, 1998). Others view it as an innovative approach to education that synthesizes advances in interpretive and semiotic theory in the specific context of educational practices with children and young people (Buckingham, 2003). After nearly 20 years of work by practitioners and scholars, some topics and issues have emerged as focal points for media literacy: news, advertising, issues of representation and media violence (Considine and Haley, 1999; Thoman, 2001). Key concepts have also emerged (albeit somewhat differentially formulated in Canada, the UK and the USA) that emphasize the constructedness of media messages, an appreciation of both the artistic and the economic function of messages, sensitivity towards the processes involved in the creation of meaning through interpretation, and understanding the ways in which media representations shape our sense of ourselves, our communities, and the world (British Film Institute, 2000).

In this chapter, I suggest some ways that media literacy education must adapt to accommodate the changing nature of young people's experience with digital media and new communication technologies. Teachers who traditionally emphasize the processes of analysing news, advertising and entertainment media should consider expanding their focus to include new media (like the internet, cellphones, videogames and handheld devices), new message forms (like search engines, instant messaging and blogs) and new social and economic issues (including identity and anonymity, privacy and surveillance). In this chapter I focus particularly on the exploration of interpersonal mediated communication as an arena for reconceptualizing media literacy for the digital age so that it continues to be relevant to the lived experiences of youth in contemporary society.

Adolescent life online

Rapidly changing media create new opportunities and challenges for children and young people. The internet has become the primary communication tool for teens, surpassing even the telephone among some groups. In a 2002 survey of more than 6700 teens and parents, 81% of teens between the ages of 12 and 17 use the internet to e-mail friends or relatives while 70% use it for instant messaging to send instant text messages both from their computer and via wireless devices; 56% of teens aged 18–19 prefer the internet to the telephone. Teens also depend on the internet as an educational resource: 56% of younger teens (12–17) consult online resources for guidance on their homework assignments, while 61% of older teens (18–19 years) turn to the internet for help completing their schoolwork. More than one-quarter (26%) of younger teens go online to access news and information about current events while 61% of older teens do the same (Pastore, 2002). Stern (2005, 55) writes, 'It should come as little surprise to us that the Internet is so seamlessly interwoven into most teenagers' lives that it is difficult for them to pinpoint the role it plays.'

As Marshall McLuhan has suggested, for many young people, schools are now much more impoverished in terms of access to information than the home environment (1964). At the turn of the 21st century, we see another kind of digital divide opening up, in addition to the well known and significant digital divide that results from limited access to technology among youth living in poverty. This new divide is between what children are doing with computers and with new media outside school and what they're doing inside school (Buckingham, 2004). My own two teenagers, ages 16 and 17, are chatting online, playing online games, writing and reading blogs created by themselves and their friends, downloading and listening to music, seeking out information on the internet about hobbies and enthusiasms, and reading web comics. Most of the time, when seated at the computer, they are doing three or four of these activities at the same time, often while supposedly writing a paper for English class.

The significant gap between young people's experience of new media outside school and what they're doing in school means that students in contemporary society continue to encounter the challenges of online media and mediated social communication without the benefit of the support, sharing and insights of caring, knowledgeable adults (Buckingham, 2004). Such experiences may heighten the perception that adults are disconnected and unavailable when it comes to digital media and their shifting and increasingly complex social roles in the lives of young people.

Arising from recent scholarship on fan communities, some scholars are exploring how media literacy skills connect to videogames. At the college level, Jenkins developed a simulation 'games workshop' that involves teams of students creating a proposal for a videogame adapted from a pre-existing popular media text, aiming to strengthen students' communication and collaborative skills, gain an understanding of the basic processes and issues involved in game design and planning, and appreciating the process of adaptation from one medium to another (Jenkins, 2005). Others have used media literacy concepts in approaching the study of historical videogames through educational activities that allow young people to learn more about the roles involved in videogame production, the process of game development and the work environments of the videogame industry. In these activities, students also examined how realism and historical accuracy are manipulated in games to see how stereotypes and mythic elements are used (Squire, 2005). Such work underlines the importance of building learning experiences that enable students to analyse critically and reflect on their actual day-to-day media consumption experiences and to examine the constructedness of media messages. Let us turn to consider how media literacy education might be expanded to address the changing nature of mediated interpersonal communication, enabling high-school teachers like Mr Smith to incorporate an exploration of digital relationships in his media literacy class.

Critically analysing digital relationships

Scholarship on the communicative dimensions of online behaviour has grown tremendously in the past ten years (Lievrouw and Livingstone, 2002), but educators and scholars are only just beginning to develop instructional approaches that encourage reflective, critical examination of the complex positive and negative ways that digital media shape and structure interpersonal behaviour. In this section, I consider the emerging literature on adolescents' use of instant messaging (IM), blogs and chat rooms and show how these practices may help extend and magnify concepts central to media literacy education.

Identity development

Media play an important role in how adolescents construct their own configurations of social identity (Fisherkeller, 2002). Young people themselves recognize some of the positive social dimensions of life online even while they are aware that their parents and teachers have concerns about these experiences and relationships. The constant contact that is enabled by IM/chat means that teens can feel 'in touch' with their peers while at home. It is common for teens to carry on multiple interpersonal conversations simultaneously online and the fact that none of these conversations is very deep is perceived as an asset – small talk and the creative exchange of ideas creates a comfortable, low-pressure social experience (Stern, 2005). Young people may also experience more intimate interpersonal exchanges that can progress from small talk to genuine dialogue on issues of importance. Often, this more intimate and personal communication occurs through e-mail exchanges – teens may feel they can focus more on constructing and developing a message and get a sense that their message will receive the more undivided attention of their friends. By contrast, IM/chat is perceived as a medium of social small talk as only one of many online activities being undertaken simultaneously.

Interactive online communication satisfies two major needs for adolescent development: maintaining friendships and belonging to peer groups. In the social world of adolescence where one must look, dress and act a certain way to be accepted by peers, many teens appreciate the chance to communicate their identity only through words. For some teens, online mediated communication is a primary way to satisfy their need to belong to a social group. Online and offline, peer communication provides teens with the opportunity to learn a host of social lessons about power, co-operation and competition, trust, intimacy and respect. In the busy lives of adolescents who are trying to manage academics, sports, social activities and family life, it seems teens are simply taking advantage of internet technologies to meet their essential developmental needs to communicate with others in order to learn about themselves (Stern, 2005).

The opportunities for socialization afforded by the internet can support the development of interpersonal communication skills, enabling otherwise shy, unpopular children or those with disabilities to form friendships with others (Hasselbring and Glaser, 2000). In a study of adolescents aged 13–19, researchers found that 18% of teens used the internet to seek help when they felt very upset, sad, stressed or angry. The most common reasons for seeking help included romantic problems and problems with friendships. Family problems and academic/school problems were less frequently mentioned as issues addressed via internet help (Gould et al., 2002).

In order to increase the perceived relevance of his media literacy class, educators like Mr Smith should consider introducing concepts and instructional strategies building on basic concepts in interpersonal communication in order to explore aspects of online communication as they relate to relationships and identity development. The US National Communication Association has developed instructional standards for teaching speaking, listening and media literacy that provides a framework for introducing such ideas (National Communication Association, 2003). Mr Smith's media literacy class might explore concepts such as feedback, self-disclosure, reciprocity, confirmation and disconfirmation, inclusion, control and affection. These concepts, which are central to the study of interpersonal communication, could meaningfully be introduced to students in order to promote reflection and dialogue on the ways in which e-mail and IM/chat experiences are similar and different from face-to-face interaction. They also connect to the media literacy concepts centred on exploring the relationship between the author and the audience. Students might keep a journal reflecting on their online communication, develop extemporaneous role plays, write scripts to demonstrate their understanding of these ideas, or develop an oral presentation that explains concepts to others.

Blogs and literacy learning

More and more teens are making use of weblogs, or 'blogs'. Blogs are personal journals made up of chronological entries, not unlike a paper diary. The features of a blog include instant publishing of text or graphics to the web without sophisticated technical knowledge, ways for people to read and provide feedback to various blog posts, and hyperlinks to other bloggers. Adolescents make up a large part of the community of bloggers (Huffaker, 2004), but only a tiny fraction of teachers have yet begun to incorporate blogs as a tool for language and literacy education. One interesting example comes from the work of a teacher at Hunterdon High School in New Jersey who uses weblogs in his Journalism 2 class. On his class website, Will Richardson carries on an online conversation with students, encourages them to maintain blogs, to publish and respond to each other's work, and even uses the interactivity and recursiveness of the weblog to support the development of students' editing skills (Richardson, 2005). Blogs can support the development of critical analysis skills, as students ask questions about authors' motives and purposes or examine the rhetorical and visual construction techniques which may be used to make a blog attractive or enhance its readability.

As literacy scholars and educators continue to experiment with this new medium, we can expect to see a growth in the development of theory that examines the benefits and drawbacks associated with the interactivity and immediate gratification provided by new digital publishing tools like weblogs. But, at the present time, many school blogs seem intensely teacher-centred and do not show clear evidence of genuine student investment in online communication. Many school blogs 'typically present themselves as earnest attempts to meld new technology use, student interest, and school work in ways that risk "killing" the medium by reducing its potential scope and vitality to menial school tasks in which students seemingly lack any genuine purpose' (Lankshear and Knobel, 2003, 16). Without authentic problems and questions to investigate, blogs used in the classroom may be just another technology toy. But, because weblogs can function as a kind of diary of one's own process of learning, reflection and growth, they may be able to document (to self and others) the processes involved in building knowledge structures and encourage the kind of meta-analytic thinking that media literacy educators emphasize.

Dependence and addiction

Little is known about the impact of frequent online communication on human development. Rapid increases in adolescents' online behaviour plus the dynamic environment of the internet make it difficult to document the diversity of encounters that young people are actually experiencing in their social interactions online. In research conducted with 208 11–13-year-old students in a private school in North Carolina in 2004, IM/chat use was measured through an anonymous online survey, with 31% of students reporting one to three hours of IM/chat weekly, 26% spending four to seven hours weekly, and 10% using it for more than eight hours per week; 81% of students said IM/chat use was 'somewhat addicting' or 'very addicting'.

Some teachers, ever fearful of new media, may either ignore this issue completely or tackle this topic with too much gusto and inadvertently silence student response. But instructional strategies that relate the concept of media addiction/dependence to online social communication may be effective in increasing young people's metacognitive skills in reflecting on their own behaviour that results from the media choices in the online environment. For example, students may consider IM/chat use in relation to the seven criteria for *dependence* identified by the therapeutic community: tolerance; withdrawal; using larger amounts or over a longer period than was intended; unsuccessful efforts to cut down or control usage; a great deal of time spent in usage; social, occupational or recreational activities curtailed by usage; and continuing use in spite of negative effects (American Psychiatric Association, 1994). Students might keep a journal or take a survey to reflect on their own dependence on online communication or stage a mock debate concerning whether IM/chat creates dependence or addiction, gathering evidence to develop arguments based on these seven criteria. This approach would be consistent with the paradigm used by media literacy educators, based on the work of Paulo Freire, which emphasizes the cycle of *awareness*, *analysis*, *reflection* and *action* that encourages students to reflect on their personal media use choices and habits as a key step in awareness-building.

Harassment and online strangers

More than any other topic, educators and parents are concerned about cyberbullying, online strangers and the grooming of young people for work in the online or real-world sex trade. By early adolescence, in both online and face-to-face experiences, young people are engaging in and encountering social interactions with peers that sometimes feature raunchy language, gossip and harassment. This behaviour generally begins in late elementary grades and peaks in middle school. In a study of North Carolina middle-schoolers, 46% of students have received messages containing profanity and 16% messages that they considered 'threatening or harassing'. Males were nearly twice as likely to have received these kinds of messages as females (11% versus 20%, respectively). Seventh and eighth graders were at least twice as likely to receive 'threatening or harassing' messages compared with sixth graders (Todd, 2005). A survey conducted by the National Children's Home in the UK reported that of 856 children and adolescents (aged 11–19) surveyed, 4% had been the victims of electronic mail bullying and 7% reported being the victim of chat room bullying. Text messaging via cellphones was the most commonly used method of electronic bullying, with 16% of students reporting being victimized through this method (BBC, 2002).

Despite the plethora of news reports about the dangers of such behaviour, children and adolescents continue to communicate with strangers online. In a survey of 213 11–16 year-olds, 74% of participants reported contact with a stranger via e-mail or a chat room, and 25% of these students admitted that they shared identifying information about themselves with these strangers (Stahl and Fritz, 2002). While parents and teachers often react in horror when they learn about online harassment and communicating with strangers, most young people are well aware of the wide range of negative communication behaviour that can occur in interpersonal behaviour online. The thrill of presenting oneself to a stranger (and the power dynamic that is activated by such anonymity) invites opportunities for fantasy and role-playing that young people may use to experiment with their developing social and sexual identities.

There are a number of existing curricular materials that help teachers and parents introduce basic concepts of online safety to children. For example, the 'I-safe America' programme has created curriculum materials for K-12 students with informational mini-lectures, often introduced by law enforcement personnel in a local community, to show children how to recognize dangers and danger signs in online communication. Students are told how to respond assertively to a variety of dangerous situations, learn how to report online incidents and are told that activities in chat rooms are not anonymous and do result in tangible, real-world consequences. Students learn how to understand the techniques used by cyber-predators to contact, communicate, entice and lure, entrap and exploit victims (I-Safe America, 2004).

Beyond such informational efforts, media literacy educators like Mr Smith may want to promote critical thinking skills about online communication by introducing students to some basic psychological concepts that may enable young people to reflect on, discuss and understand the patterns of social power that are embedded in their online social relationships. Much online communication is altered by *disinhibition* effects, the tendency of people to say and do things in cyberspace that they wouldn't ordinarily say or do in the face-to-face world (Suler, 2004). For online communicators, the lack of *social context cues* (normally obtained from the time, place and physical location of an interaction and by the non-verbal and visual cues from others) may obscure the boundaries that would generally separate acceptable and unacceptable forms of behaviour. In addition, IM/chat users perceive that they are alone and may presume other users are also alone, which may release users from the social expectations incurred in group interaction. Educators like Mr Smith may consider using dramatic activities and role-playing to introduce the concepts of *anonymity*, *invisibility* and *surveillance* and discuss the role of disinhibition in students' experiences with online communication.

Conclusion

Media literacy educators generally encourage reflective examination of one's own communication behaviours as part of the process of developing critical analysis skills, even though this generally has focused on media consumption behaviours. More emphasis on incorporating concepts from interpersonal communication would ensure that media literacy stays relevant to young people's lived experience with digital media. From the point of view of educators, the primary challenge associated with reconceptualizing media literacy in a digital age comes from the atomization and overspecialization now endemic in the academic world, which has long separated scholarship in technology and media from studies of social interaction and human relationships. Practitioners and scholars in these areas need continued opportunities for collaboration in order to promote the cross-fertilization of ideas that will enable educators like Mr Smith to empower his students with critical thinking skills in responding to life online.

References

American Psychiatric Association (1994) *Diagnostic and Statistical Manual of Mental Disorders* (Vol. 4) Washington DC, American Psychiatric Association.

British Broadcasting Corporation (2002, April 15), Youngsters Targeted by Digital Bullying, http://news.bbc.co.uk/1/hi/uk/1929944.stm.

British Film Institute (2000) *Moving Images in the Classroom*, London, British Film Institute.

Buckingham, D. (2003) *Media Education: literacy, learning, and contemporary culture*, Cambridge, Polity.

Buckingham, D. (2004), The Other Teachers: how do children learn from TV and other media? Paper presented at the *Beyond the Blackboard Conference*, Robinson College, Cambridge, 3–4 November.

Considine, D. and Haley, G. (1999) *Visual Messages: integrating imagery into instruction*, 2nd edn, Englewood, CO, Teacher Ideas Press.

Fisherkeller, J. (2002) Growing Up with Television: everyday learning among young adolescents, Philadelphia, PA, Temple University Press.

Gould, M., Munfakh, J., Lunbell, K., Kleinman, M. and Parker, S. (2002) Seeking Help from the Internet During Adolescence, *Journal of the American Academy of Child and Adolescent Psychiatry*, **41**, 1182–9.

Hasselbring, T. G. and Glaser, C. (2000) Use of Computer Technology to Help Students with Special Needs, *Future of Children: Children and Computer Technology*, **10** (2), 102–2.

Hobbs, R. (2004) A Review of School-based Initiatives in Media Literacy, *American Behavioral Scientist*, **48** (1), 48–59.

Huffaker, D. (2004) The Educated Blogger: using weblogs to promote literacy in the classroom, *First Monday*, **9** (6), http://firstmonday.org/issues/issue9_6/huffaker/index.html.

I-Safe America (2004) *I-safe America*, www.isafe.org/.

Jenkins, H. (2005) The MIT Games Literacy Workshop, *Journal of Media Literacy*, **52** (1–2), 37–40.

Lankshear, C. and Knobel, M. (2003) Do-it-yourself Broadcasting: writing weblogs in a knowledge society, paper presented to the 84th American Educational Research Association, 21–25 April, Chicago, IL.

Lievrouw, L. A. and Livingstone, S. M. (2002) *Handbook of New Media: social shaping and consequences of ICTs*, Thousand Oaks, CA, Sage.

McLuhan, M. (1964) *Understanding Media: the extensions of man*, 1st edn, New York, NY, McGraw-Hill.

National Communication Association (2003) *Creating Competent Communicators: activities for teaching speaking, listening, and media literacy in K-6 classrooms*, Scottsdale, AZ, Holcomb Hathaway.

Odell, L., Vacca, R., Hobbs, R., Irvin, J. and Warriner, J. (2000) *Elements of Language*, Austin, TX, Holt Rinehart Winston.

Pastore, M. (2002) Internet Key to Communication among Youth, *Click Z Stats Demographics*, www.clickz.com/stats/sectors/demographics/article.php/5901_961881.

Potter, W. J. (1998) *Media Literacy*, Thousand Oaks, CA, Sage.

Richardson, W. (2005) *Welcome to Journalism 2*, Hunterdon County High School, http://central.hcrhs.k12.nj.us/journ2/discuss/msgReader$2.

Squire, K. D. (2005) Toward a Media Literacy for Games, *Journal of Media Literacy*, **52** (1–2), 9–15.

Stahl, C. and Fritz, N. (2002), Internet Safety: adolescents, self report, *Journal of Adolescent Health*, **31** (1), 7–10.

Stern, S. (2005) Growing Up Online, *Journal of Media Literacy*, **52** (1–2), 55–8.

Suler, J. (2004) The Online Disinhibition Effect, *Cyberpsychology and Behavior*, 7, 321–6.

Thoman, E. (2001) *Skills and Strategies for Media Education*, Los Angeles, CA, Center for Media Literacy.

Todd, J. (2005) The Benefits and Risks Associated with Teen Instant Message/Chat, Durham, NC, Cary Academy, http://web1.caryacademy.org/technology/Newsletter/2004-2005/Jan/im_chat_final_web.htm.

10

Literacy, e-literacy and multiliteracies: meeting the challenges of teaching online

Chris Sutton

Abstract

Online teaching and learning are challenging for both teacher and student. There are differences to be negotiated in the modes of learning and communicating and in the language of the technology, the language of the learning environment and the context-specific language of the subject/vocation. It is estimated that there are at least seven literacies involved in teaching and learning in the online environment. Online learners in Australia are predominately middle-aged women; this is the group that is most likely to have problems with multiliteracies and particularly e-literacy. Even more concerning, this is the group in vocational education and training (VET) that is also likely to be asked to teach online. When both teacher *and* learner have difficulties with multiliteracies and e-literacy, there is a detrimental effect on the e-learning experience. This may contribute to the high attrition rates experienced in online courses and the reluctance of teachers to take up flexible-learning options. The Australian VET sector has taken some innovative approaches to materials development that are successfully meeting the challenges of multiliteracies.

Introduction

The Australian vocational education and training (VET) sector gives Australians the opportunity to gain the skills they need to enter the workforce for the first time, to re-enter the workforce, to retrain for a new job or to upgrade their skills for an existing job. More than 1.7 million students or about 13% of the working-age population take part in VET each year. In order to support and encourage a growing demand by learners for more flexible learning in VET, the Australian Flexible Learning Framework (AFLF) 2000–2004 invested millions of dollars in professional development for early adopters and in the production of high-quality e-learning materials to support the sets of Australian quality framework competencies known as training packages. However, despite the availability of such wonderful resources, e-learning has not been taken up on the scale that was expected.

Problems with e-learners and e-learning

I believe that one of the reasons for this is the lack of digital competence and multiliteracies among both learners and teachers in all sectors of education in general and in VET in particular. Traditionally, learners in the VET sector were apprentices and trainees in industry. They were most likely to be 15–18-year-old school-leavers, going straight from secondary education to trade training. However, the profile of students in the VET sector in Australia has changed over the past ten years. No longer are learners drawn predominantly from young, school-leaver populations. The majority of VET students are drawn from those looking to a career change, upskilling to meet new workplace demands or seeking a move into self- employment. This was first mooted by Australian research carried out by the National Council for Vocational Education Research (NCVER) in 2002.

In September 2004 a survey of people within the VET sector who had completed a course online was carried out; 250 people were sent the survey, 123 responded. The results of the survey were as follows:

- 79.7% were women
- 53% were aged between 41 and 60 when they undertook their first online course
- 2% had never even turned on a computer
- 5% could not explain the terms 'icon', 'menu', 'window', 'click', 'select' or 'drag'
- 5% could not log on to a site using a username and password
- 6% could not use scroll bars, resize, move or close windows
- 10% did not know how to use Help screens
- 12% could not install or copy files from a disk or CD-ROM
- 27% did not understand what a .pdf file is, and 23% still do not
- 30% could not save to a CD-ROM
- 30% could not download files
- 40% could not upload files
- 45% had no experience of Webcams
- 52% had no experience of instant messaging, and 48% still have no understanding of it at all.

If this profile is any indicator, the implications for e-learning in the VET sector are that a teacher is likely to have a significant proportion of learners who may not have the basic skills necessary to operate effectively as a learner in the digital environment. They may not be able to carry out such basic tasks as:

- logging on to the learning management system
- navigating the materials
- downloading readings and resources
- uploading assignments to a drop box or filing system
- saving work to a CD-ROM
- installing required applications from a disk or CD or from the web
- using the basic applications of e-learning – e-mail and word processing
- identifying the problem if a basic plug-in such as Adobe Acrobat or Flash Reader is not installed on their PC, or knowing how to install it if necessary.

Not only this, but the teachers themselves may not be digitally competent or e-literate. Yet it is of these teachers that e-teaching is increasingly demanded.

It is from these students that the demand is growing for more flexible choices in how, when and where they will learn. These students do not match the traditional 'rural and remote' profile of distance learners. They are learners who, for many reasons, find it essential to learn at home or within the confines of the workplace. They may live in close proximity to a training organization. Their employers may not wish them to leave the workplace for training. They are demanding e-learning or blended learning options to keep their employees on site.

Online teaching and learning are challenging for both teacher and student. There are differences to be negotiated in the modes of learning and communicating and in the language of the technology, the language of the learning environment and the context specific language of the subject/vocation being studied.

> Implementing digital pedagogies means understanding the ways in which multiple literacies come to bear on the teaching and learning process, as well as within culture in general. These multiple modalities of learning must be encouraged and embraced in order to pedagogically engage within the lived and mediated relations that we are part of each day. It also means that we encourage accessible media design so that all people can be producers of information, and not just passive consumers.
>
> (Lave and Wenger, 1991)

The New London Group (1996) coined the term 'multiliteracies'. It considered two major challenges for language learning in the 21st century:

- the increasing multiplicity and integration of significant modes of meaning-making, where the textual is also related to the visual, the audio, the spatial,

the behavioural and so on, whereby the new communications media are reshaping the way we use language
- the linguistic and cultural differences that have now become central to our working, civic and private lives causing the very nature of language learning to change.

Multiliteracies challenge us to think of literacy in a new way, of a complex and interwoven set of multiple 'languages' that allow us to make meaning and produce in different modes. To be literate in the digital age is to make meaning from sound, signs and symbols in many modes of publication.

A framework for e-learning design

We know from research (Cashion and Palmiera, 2002) that student satisfaction with e-learning is very much influenced by the quality of the teacher and the teaching. Nowhere is this quality of instructional design more important to learners than in the design of the e-learning experience.

Richard Caladine (1997) proposes a Model of Learning and Teaching Activities (MOLTA), intended as 'a categorisation of teaching and learning activities designed to assist in focussing thinking'. Caladine puts forward five categories of activity that can be used in deciding which technology tool is appropriate for certain types of learning delivery. He classifies activities into:

- delivery of material (by the teacher)
- interaction with materials (by students)
- interaction with the teacher (by students)
- interaction between students
- intra-action (by students).

I have taken Caladine's classification and, in the light of the research of Ron Oliver, Jan Herrington, Tom Reeves and other contemporary educators, built a pedagogical framework for instructional design of e-learning that takes into account the challenges of multiliteracies and the varying characteristics of learners in the digital environment. This framework is built on the Six Elements of a Quality Learning Experience (SEQLE) that ensure that the learning experience will be engaging, authentic and supportive of independent knowledge construction and lifelong learning (see Figure 10.1).

In designing learner-centred experiences it is important to ensure that we first consider three characteristics that the learner brings to the online and flexible learning environment: multiliteracies, learning styles and digital competence (see Figure 10.2).

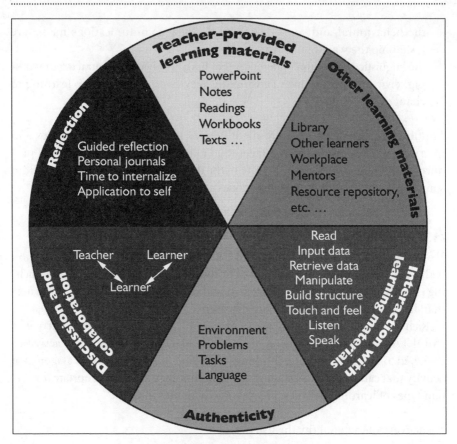

Figure 10.1 *The SEQLE framework*

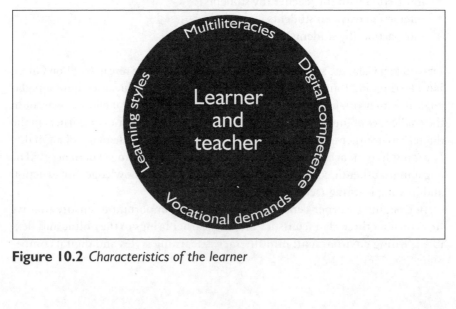

Figure 10.2 *Characteristics of the learner*

Multiliteracies

The implications of multiliteracies for quality learning experiences are enormous. We estimate that there are at least seven literacies that are inherent in the VET e-learning environment:

- English – as the language most commonly used on the web
- the first language if the learner is from non-English speaking background
- PC – the language that deals with the hardware and its manipulation
- internet – the language of browsers and websites
- workplace – the language that is specific to the learner's job
- information – the language that allows us to search and retrieve
- learning – the language specific to being a student.

It is tempting to look at each of these as discrete literacies to be 'learned', but in terms of making meaning they do not operate alone. They are complex and interwoven. They are learned in concert, used in concert and make meaning in concert and through multiple modes. For example, in sending an e-mail, it is difficult to produce the written message without using most or all of the above literacies together.

When you consider these factors and add to them the issues that learners have to deal with in terms of the demands of work, family and time management, it is little wonder that the drop-out rate in online courses in the first few weeks is so high.

Learning styles

In the same way that we are changing our view of literacy and developing an understanding of multiliteracies, we are also changing our view of learning styles. There are those who believe that new learning styles are emerging from the use of new technologies. These emerging learning styles include:

- Fluency in multiple media and in simulation-based virtual settings;
- Communal learning involving diverse, tacit, situated experience, with knowledge distributed across a community and a context as well as within an individual;
- A balance between experiential learning, guided mentoring, and collective reflection;
- Expression through nonlinear, associational webs of representations;
- Co-design of learning experiences personalized to individual needs and preferences.

(Dede, 2005)

The use of modern communications technologies to support learning and the development of multimodal delivery strategies has seen the evolution of new ways of learning. If we are to avoid disadvantaging large numbers of learners we need to encourage the development of new, multiple learning styles.

These changes affect not only the learners, but also the teachers, who must master digital literacy and the literacy of the new media. They must develop the pedagogical understanding to take into account the digital, linguistic and cultural diversity of their students. They need to understand the shift in focus to multiple styles of learning and new ways of learning. If they do not, then the learning experience that is offered to online students will be far from positive and the attrition rate from e-learning, which is already unacceptable, will rise even higher.

Digital competence

We know from the research that in each group of learners the digital competence of both teacher and learner may vary from very poor to extremely proficient. It is essential to find a way of detecting those learners in the group that lack competence and confidence in 'driving' the technology as early as possible, preferably before the course begins. The other consideration here of course is, if I, as the teacher/facilitator, do not have that level of competency, how am I going to support and facilitate the learners? We need to take into account the characteristics of learners and teachers and build into each of the elements teaching practice that builds on prior knowledge, recognizes the challenges of the online environment, provides a constructive approach to the learning and fosters the development of multiliteracies.

Addressing the issues

In terms of pedagogy, there are two areas, among others, in which the implications regarding multiliteracies (Cope and Kalantzis, 1996) need to be carefully considered:

- the literacy needs and pedagogical understanding of online teachers/facilitators
- the pedagogical soundness of the learning materials.

A number of practical steps can be taken:

1　We make sure our teachers are digitally competent and multiliterate *before* we throw them in at the deep end to teach online. Professional education is the most important part of building capability.

2   We find out *before* enrolling learners what their levels of digital competence and multiliteracies are.
3   We ensure that the learning materials and the learning environment encourage the development of multiliteracies, new and multiple learning styles and digital competence. It is in this step that we overlay the characteristics of teachers and learners with the Six Elements of a Quality Learning Experience (see Figure 10.3).

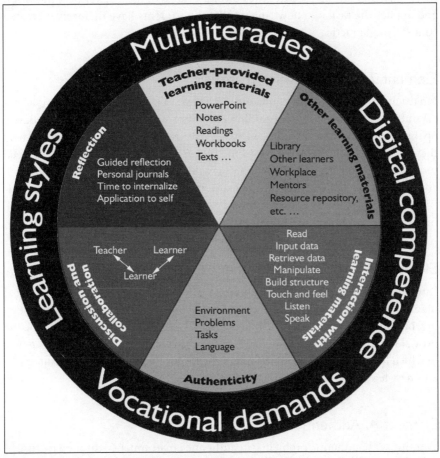

Figure 10.3 *Learner–teacher characteristics and SEQLE*

It is vital that all six elements are present with equal emphasis. No element can be seen as less important and no element should be missing. We can now look more closely at each element.

Element 1. Learning materials provided by the teacher

The first element relies on teachers being aware of the learner issues and developing their materials to take account of learner characteristics. Learning materials that are provided by teachers ought to be designed to encourage exploration, research and risk taking. They also need to take into account the multiliteracies of their learners and ensure that the learning is based in the students' own experience (situated practice); explicitly teaches a metalanguage that describes the task (overt instruction); investigates the cultural context of the task (critical framing); and applies the task in a new context that the students have themselves created (transformed practice) (New London Group, 1996).

Element 2. Other learning materials

No teacher holds all of the knowledge or has all of the literacies. Sending learners out to seek knowledge by building on other sources ensures that they develop those workplace and discipline literacies that are current for the industry or field they are working in. It also develops the lifelong learning skills that people need today to keep up with a rapidly changing world of working in a knowledge society. We need to teach learners how to learn. It is within this element that the multiliteracies necessary for search and retrieval of information, knowledge management and meaning making through multimedia are catered for.

Element 3. Interaction with the learning materials

Interaction is highly essential to good learning design. It includes physical manipulation of resources, entering and retrieving data, interviewing and reporting, building structures, tactile exploration and other similar activities. While the provision of content by teachers and from other sources is vital, it is in the way in which learners interact with these that the multimodal aspects of multiliteracies and new learning styles are practised and strengthened.

Element 4. Authenticity

Working with authentic problems, in authentic environments, through the use of the authentic language of the discipline of the workplace is essential to good learning. Brown, Collins and Duguid (1989) argue that meaningful learning will occur only if it is embedded in the context in which it will be used. Jan Herrington and Ron Oliver of the University of Wollongong (2001) use the term 'Learning Designs' to describe various frameworks that can be used to develop online courses. In later works, with Tom Reeves (Herrington, Oliver and Reeves, 2003), they describe the characteristics of authentic activities in online learning as follows:

- Authentic activities have real-world relevance. Activities match as nearly as possible the real-world tasks in practice rather than decontextualized or classroom-based tasks.
- Authentic activities are ill defined, requiring students to define the tasks and sub-tasks needed to complete the activity. Learners must identify their own unique tasks in order to complete the major task.
- Authentic activities comprise complex tasks to be investigated by students over a sustained period of time. They require significant investment of time and intellectual resources.
- Authentic activities provide the opportunity for students to examine the task from different perspectives, using a variety of resources. They require students to detect relevant from irrelevant information.
- Authentic activities provide the opportunity to collaborate. Collaboration is integral to the task.
- Authentic activities provide the opportunity to reflect. They enable learners to make choices and reflect on their learning both individually and socially.
- Authentic activities can be integrated and applied across different subject areas and lead beyond domain specific outcomes. Activities encourage interdisciplinary perspectives and enable students to play diverse roles thus building robust expertise rather than being limited to a single, well defined field.
- Authentic activities are seamlessly integrated with assessment. They are integrated with the major task in a manner that reflects real-world assessment, rather than removed from the nature of the task.
- Authentic activities create polished products valuable in their own right rather than as preparation for something else. Activities culminate in the creation of a whole product.
- Authentic activities allow competing solutions and diversity of outcome. Authentic activities allow a range and diversity of outcomes rather than a single correct response.

Designing learning to sit in the 'real world' meets the needs of the learners and encourages constant learning and problem solving and the development of workplace literacy.

Element 5. Collaboration

Collaborative learning, involving the teacher working with learners and learners working with each other, assists with multiliteracies and digital competence. In this mode, peer-to-peer support and group knowledge construction come into their own. However, at the core of collaboration is teacher presence; we know our learners want responsive teachers who are present at the locus of learning (Cashion and

Palmiera 2002). There are tools that enhance presence: Instant Messenger, Elluminate Live™, the addition of a photograph to the top of every e-mail. Presence in the discussion and chat spaces and active participation is very important. Teachers need to model the multiliteracies, empathize with digital non-competence, encourage and support, constantly.

Element 6. Reflection

Reflection is the cornerstone of teaching the learner how to learn. Reflection, when it becomes inculcated into the learners' normal practice, gives them the ability to keep up to date in their vocation by reflecting on situations, seeking resources and applying situated learning techniques. The work of Donald Schon (1983) gave us the notions of reflection-in-action and reflection-on-action. Reflection-in-action is 'thinking on our feet'; it involves looking to our experiences, connecting with our feelings, and attending to our theories in use. It helps us build new understandings to inform our actions in the situation that is unfolding. It is an essential part of the development of multiliteracies. Both reflection-in-action and reflection-on-action are valuable tools in detecting those learners that are having difficulty with the technology and are challenged by the multiliteracies and multimodes involved. When a learner completes and submits a weekly learning journal the teacher is given tremendous insight into what is going on in the learning process at the individual level.

Building capability

While SEQLE ensures the development of high-quality, effective online learning experiences, unless there is the capability to deliver them, they are worthless. Capability for e-learning consists of:

- Sound teaching and learning practice. I have found that few, if any, teachers have come into my online facilitator courses with an understanding of what they were being asked to undertake. Almost without exception, the digital competence of those asked to teach online has been affected by:
  — lack of access to technology – many teachers share a computer with six or more colleagues in the workplace and do not have access to PC/internet at home
  — lack of professional development in either ICT literacy or current e-learning pedagogy
  — lack of time to learn new skills and new ways of teaching and learning.
- Strong learner and teacher support. The support that is needed is the support that offers teachers time and resources to develop their skills and be present

for the learner, and support for learners' multiliteracies, for learning how to learn.
- Reliable and consistent business processes and systems.
- Financial sustainability.
- Reliable technical infrastructure. The technical infrastructure needs to be robust, current and adequately resourced for the numbers of students and teachers in order to ensure that the multiliteracies that it supports are appropriate to the ICT environment in which they operate. If an organization has not the resources to maintain the appropriate technical infrastructure for today's learners and teachers, it will fail.

Over the past five years we have developed a large bank of e-learning resources that meet the multiliteracies and multimodal needs of our learners in a wide range of industries. The 'Toolboxes' have been developed under strict quality guidelines with input from Australia's leading e-learning researchers, based on current pedagogical research (Australian Qualifications Framework Advisory Board, 2002). They are interactive. They are authentic. They foster multiliteracies. They are multimodal and encourage the development of new learning styles. However, they are not yet being used to the extent that it was believed they should because we have not developed the required capability.

Conclusion

E-learning and, in particular, online learning have the potential to engage and excite or conversely to frustrate, isolate and alienate learners. The challenge for Australia in the next five years, I believe, is to encourage the implementation of e-learning through a programme of professional development that ensures teachers and trainers are aware of and catering for the multiliteracy needs of their students. Once this is achieved, if learning experiences are built on the SEQLE framework, e-learning will reach its potential to meet the challenges of today's online learner.

References

Australian Qualifications Framework Advisory Board (2002) *Australian Qualifications Framework Implementation Handbook*, 3rd edn, Carlton Vic., www.aqf.edu.au/implem.htm.

Brown, J. S., Collins, A. and Duguid, P. (1989) Situated Cognition and the Culture of Learning, *Educational Researcher*, **18** (1), 32–42.

Caladine, R. (1997) MOLTA – A Model of Teaching and Learning Activities, *Overview*, **3** (1), 45–8, Centre for Education, Development, Innovation and

Research (CEDIR), University of Wollongong,
http://ultibase.rmit.edu.au/Articles/june97/calad1.htm#MOLTA.

Cashion, J. and Palmiera, P. (2002) *The Secret is the Teacher: the learner's view of online learning*, National Centre for Vocational Education Research (NCVER), Australia, www.ncver.edu.au/teaching/publications/906.html.

Cope, B. and Kalantzis, M. (1996) *Putting Multiliteracies to the Test*, www.alea.edu.au/multilit.htm.

Cumming, J., Wyatt-Smith, C. M., Ryan, J. and Doig, S. M. (1998) *The Literacy–Curriculum Interface: the literacy demands of the curriculum in post-compulsory schooling*, www.gu.edu.au/school/cls/clearinghouse/content_1998_interface.html.

Dede, C. (2005) Planning for Neomillennial Learning Styles, *Educause Quarterly*, **28** (1), 7–12, www.educause.edu/apps/eq/eqm05/eqm051.asp.

Herrington, J. and Oliver, R. (2001) *Teaching and Learning Online: a beginner's guide to e-learning and e-teaching in higher education*, Centre for Research in Information Technology and Communications, Edith Cowan University, WA.

Herrington, J., Oliver, R. and Reeves, T. C. (2003) Patterns of Engagement in Authentic Online Learning Environments, *Australian Journal of Educational Technology*, **19** (1), 59–71.

Lave, J. and Wenger, E. (1991) *Situated Learning: legitimate peripheral participation*, New York, NY, Cambridge University Press.

New London Group (1996) A Pedagogy of Multiliteracies: designing social features, *Harvard Educational Review*, **66** (1), 60–92.

Schon, D. A. (1983) *The Reflective Practitioner: how professionals think in action*, London, Temple Smith.

11

Graduate e-literacies and employability

Denise Haywood, Jeff Haywood and Hamish Macleod

Abstract

Graduate employability has become a major concern of politicians, government and state funding agencies, and universities ever since the expansion of higher education began in the 1960s. In this chapter we review recent developments in thinking about graduate skills, focusing particularly on e-literacies and their relationship to the wider employability agenda. We base our analysis on data that we gathered during a European Commission funded project in seven universities across Europe. Our study explored the work universities have been doing in developing undergraduate e-literacies, the skills and attitudes of their undergraduate students, employers' perspectives on graduate skills, and likely directions for graduate e-literacy development in the future.

Background
Recent trends in graduate employability thinking

Governments of all persuasions and worldwide regard education as the foundation on which they will build successful economies that are able to withstand the buffeting of changes in the global marketplace in which they exist. This concern with education as a key ingredient in prosperity is reflected in their interest in expanding and improving education, by whatever means is open to them politically. The European Union (EU) expresses this interest openly in its various policy and strategy documents, for example, 'becoming the most competitive and dynamic knowledge-based economy in the world, capable of sustainable economic growth with more and better jobs and greater social cohesion' (EU, 2000, 2003a, 2005). Remaining, or becoming, one of the most advanced and developed states or super-states is seen to be closely linked to the 'knowledge economy' where intellectual, rather than physical, resources are key to wealth-generation. Information and communications technology (ICT) is a vital part of the knowledge economy, providing the automation, the creativity tools, the local and global communications and part of the support for mass post-compulsory education. A population that is e-literate and confident is a *sine qua non* for success in the modern world. All governments look to their education systems to ensure that those who 'graduate' from them are competent at relevant skill levels.

EU member states make similar pronouncements (UK, 1998; Finland, 1999), and these are mirrored by government agencies in the USA and Australasia (US, 2002; US, 2005a, 2005b). Worldwide, developed and developing countries seek to raise e-literacy to raise prosperity (Kerala, 2005; UNESCO, 2005; NZ, 2005). Much of this interest in e-literacy focuses on higher education, the expansion of which has been rapid in developed countries, and continues to increase (EURYDICE, 2002).

Industry and commerce, whether huge, small, local or global, are dependent on ICT-based high productivity, communications and knowledge management. To have a workforce with low ICT skills is to be severely hindered in the marketplace. The large volume of ICT training materials now available is testimony to the need to enhance employees' ICT skills. Employers increasingly expect their recruits, at whatever level, to come adequately skilled.

For individuals, looking at almost any aspect of modern life, urban or rural, to see ICT present in some form or another and to lack the skills to manage ICT to best personal advantage is to be excluded from development paths and from opportunities for self-improvement. One route to these skills is as part of the education process, and learners expect to be taught in settings where they can acquire the skills they need, whether in the period of compulsory education, at university or college, or in lifelong learning.

So far we have considered a view of ICT and e-literacy skills that assumes individuals are largely living and working within single countries. However, within the European Union in particular, and with respect to its interactions with the rest of the developed world, a further aspect of e-literacies emerges, namely their role in the *mobility* of workers and learners (EU, 2003b). Individuals who wish to be able to move freely and to take up employment or study in other countries need to be assured that their skills and knowledge are comparable to those required elsewhere, that is, they need to know that they are able to meet *standards*, and possibly to have suitable accreditation as proof. In the area of ICT skills, the European Computer Driving Licence (ECDL) provides one such accredited standard (ECDL, 2005), and some are being developed within some countries' education systems. Standards for other e-literacies are much less well developed.

On a day-to-day basis, employers seek graduate recruits for varied reasons: they have (up-to-date) specialist knowledge of subject matter; they have gained matu-

rity since leaving school; they have learned how to cope with advanced and largely independent study; they can think flexibly, creatively and into the future, etc.
For example, a typical list of graduate competences is given by the Council for
Industry and Higher Education in the UK, which offers a set of ten employability skills that graduates should possess (CIHE, 2003), including:

- cognitive skills: 'the ability to identify, analyse and solve problems, work with
  information and handle a mass of diverse data …'
- generic competencies: 'high level and transferable key skills such as the ability to work with others in a team, communication skills, listening & questioning,
  written communication …'
- technical ability: 'having the knowledge and experience of working with relevant modern technology. The ability to apply and exploit information technology.'

What sorts of skills are we talking about?

Many employability skills are couched in high-level language, but in reality are
demonstrated by recruits through their ability to carry out specific tasks, using tools
and sources provided by the employer or available freely outside. For example, 'working with relevant modern technology' may equate to use of Microsoft Office applications, a web browser, an authenticated intranet, a company knowledge base or
staying connected while on the move, some elements of which graduate recruits
will have experienced in the course of their studies, and others of which they may
not have seen, or even be aware of. Ideally the match between university experiences and employer expectations will be close, or at least will be easily bridged.

Some skills are assumed to be possessed by all graduates, or at least are not specifically expressed by employers as a need, and among these are often the 'e-literacies', broadly consisting of the 'ability to work and live in a changing digital
world'. Thus the e-literacies for employability will be particularly focused on: ICT
basics (productivity tools), information management (search, retrieval, storage),
problem-solving using these e-literacies, digital communications, digital presentations, data handling and assessment of quality of information.

What have universities been doing?

E-literacies are gained in a complex context, where home, friends, educational
establishments, special courses and self-tuition all play a part. Thus for many individuals the sources of training and support on which they draw for their skills development and maintenance will be complex, and consist, in varying amounts, of:

- formal training courses within formal education (e.g. e-literacy skills classes)

- informal training within formal education (e.g. as part of subject-specific classes)
- formal training courses outside formal education (e.g. commercial ICT skills courses)
- formal training in the workplace
- informal training in the workplace by colleagues (e.g. mentoring or spontaneous)
- self-tuition by exploration or with manuals, help-files, etc.
- informal tuition from friends, family or colleagues.

Universities have sought effective methods to develop e-literacy skills and knowledge in their graduates to enable them to be better fitted for employment, both as they begin their careers and also in the longer term. Some have adopted an identifiable 'accreditation approach' with specific courses, whereas others have adopted an 'embedded' approach where skills development is integrated into the curriculum and accredited as part of the degree award. Recent developments from around the world in this area can be found in the proceedings of conferences on e-literacy, for example eLit 2005 (www.elit-conf.org/elit2005/). Increasingly these skills development programmes are seen as part of an employability agenda within the university as much as within an academic skills agenda.

Some universities monitor aspects of student e-literacy and attitudes, as part of institutional research that underpins strategy. The University of Edinburgh has been collecting data on the ICT skills, knowledge and attitudes of newly arriving students since 1990 (Macleod et al., 2002; Haywood et al., 2004). There has been a steady rise in PC ownership, in the range of ICT applications that new students feel comfortable using, a view of the increasing importance of ICT in studies and careers, and the disappearance of gender as a factor. These e-literacies appear to be international, as similar skills and attitudes were found across Europe (SEUSISS, 2001; SPOT-PLUS, 2003) and in the USA (ECAR, 2004).

Exploring employer perspectives on graduate ICT skills

The SEUSISS project (Studies of European Universities Skills for ICT in Staff and Students) was a two-year, EC-funded, collaborative activity of seven universities in seven countries, designed to provide European universities with some of the information and tools necessary for them to address current issues in e-literacy, specifically ICT skills. Students were surveyed at these universities regarding their ICT skills, experiences and attitudes; senior staff were asked about ICT skills training; and, to discover how well student ICT skills and attitudes matched employers' needs and wishes, a representative sample of employers in each country (40 in total) was interviewed. In addition, statements about ICT skills by employer and professional organizations were researched. Employers were asked what use their organizations made of ICT, what their experiences were of the skills of graduate recruits and finally their expectations for the future in terms of changes in ICT which would impact on them as employers and graduates as recruits.

In general it was found that employers felt most graduates were adequately skilled in use of ICT, although there were gaps (presentation software, databases and information management), with some disparity between what graduates thought they could do and the reality once in the workplace. Many employers did not even bother to emphasize ICT skills: 'We don't even talk about that, neither do we mention it in the recruiting ads. We take it for granted that people, when they come here, are able to work with the normal software; that is, Microsoft Office, e-mail, and the web. We don't even ask them about it. We consider it self-evident.' This did vary to some degree between different European countries, probably reflecting the extent to which ICT skills development was embedded in education. In reality, many employers seemed to seek little beyond fluency with MS Office and comfort with using the internet. Larger companies had extensive training schemes, but those graduates entering small to medium enterprises (SMEs) would largely have to self-train, and even in large companies there was an expectation that graduates would work out what they needed: 'Graduates are expected to be proactive in determining any training needs they have, including IT skills.' Only a minority of employers were seeking certification of skills (e.g. ECDL) beyond the possession of a degree.

The publications and websites of professional associations and commercial organizations were searched for evidence of their views on educational needs of recruits, in particular ICT skills, but very little information was available on this subject, despite their widespread use of the web for publicity. It would appear that in some countries, perhaps most, these bodies look to universities to define what skills they need.

Examining the short-term horizon with employers, it seems that graduates will need greater skills in:

- web publishing: many companies said that this was an expanding area for them
- mobile working: 'more networking, both as "culture" and in terms of software and hardware'
- knowledge/information management: 'Graduates have good ICT skills and learn fast, although there is a lack of "knowledge management" thinking'
- security: 'a greater emphasis on security – documents, viruses, encryption'.

Futures
What new skills?

Technology does not stand still and so the range of e-literacies will expand and deepen steadily with time. Some of these will quickly become standard, indeed dominant, features at most universities, for example the virtual learning environment, online assessment, the hybrid or digital library, and the e-portfolio. Although primarily viewed as tools for the educational institution, many large companies are developing in-house training and professional development systems that make use of these same tools, and so fluency with them is an advantage for the lifelong learner. Similarly, the educational environment will increasingly expect students to be able to present work in an internet-ready form, through the use of personal websites for example, and companies now routinely also use intranet or internet media to supply and share documentation in HTML or PDF format.

The distinction between secure and open is of much greater significance to the employees of most commercial organizations than it is to the majority of students, who may not perceive, or appreciate, the security concerns of their university, and the processes that it puts in place to ensure security where it is needed. By tradition, many universities have a policy of 'openness wherever possible', whereas commercial organizations often take a diametrically opposed position. Thus new graduate recruits will need to learn quickly about firewalls, virtual private networks, divisions between intranet/extranet/internet, password renewal, digital signatures and so on. Those employees who are mobile workers or travel regularly will find that they are expected to stay online to a substantial degree, even though the mobile phone is still dominant in the area of commercial communications. Laptops, wireless connections, handheld devices, remote access to the company systems, transfer of digital documents, information search and retrieval *en route* will become a normal part of life for some graduate recruits. In both universities and commerce, knowledge management is fast becoming a major concern and so students should acquire an understanding of how information and knowledge can be systematized and shared through knowledge bases. Alongside this lies an even greater pressure to find, assess and convert data gained through information search, retrieval, storage and re-retrieval processes.

In the research areas of higher education, groupware and social networking applications have become frequent, and the R & D side of commercial organizations uses similar tools, sometimes in collaboration with universities. For meetings that require voice or sight, voice-over-IP and desktop videoconferencing are the norm in many large organizations, and are being adopted rapidly by small companies too as they reduce travel and telecommunications costs dramatically. Thus graduates entering these technology-rich working environments will be expected quickly to take up use of these e-tools too.

What new jobs?

The traditional pattern of graduate recruitment has changed in many developed countries as the university participation rate for 17–21-year-olds has expanded to reach 50% or more, and as more non-traditional entrants join universities. Graduates are now taking employment in a wider range of industries, especially in the service sector. Employment is less stable, with a greater element of short contract, freelance and self-employment options than in the past. Thus graduates need to be able to respond quickly and appropriately to the job market, and to shape their skills to demand. All large organizations are now international in reach, often global in location and composition, and so graduate employees may find themselves working and travelling across countries and continents. Thus ability to review their e-literacies in this global context is essential.

What future training?

The key to the successful graduate in their career will be self-development, assessing their own needs and acquiring new skills or updating old ones. The roots of this self-appraisal process lie in the training given at university (and before). In addition to skills development, there needs to be an awareness in the learner regarding their strengths and weaknesses in these skills, and also of their time-limited nature, and hence an awareness of the need for constant reappraisal. Universities themselves play a role in future skills development for graduates by ensuring that these are explicitly updated in continuing professional development courses offered to alumni.

What do universities do about all this?

Universities must recognize that skills are acquired formally and informally, and support both routes. They need to choose whether to adopt a 'training and accreditation' or an 'integration and self-certification' route, or a hybrid of the two. As undergraduates will often have been exposed to only part of the set of e-literacy skills that they might find useful, some approach is needed that ensures all have access to skills development independently of curriculum taken, that offers a self-development route. One way of dealing with this is by embedding employability perspectives in e-literacy skills development and (self-)assessment offerings. To do this effectively means keeping abreast of employers' needs, thereby identifying gaps in university provision and filling these quickly. It also involves giving guidance to students on the skills (types and levels) they ought to be acquiring during their studies, enabling them to check their competence by self-testing, and perhaps offering self- or external accreditation as seems most appropriate.

What can employers do?

Employers can make the task of universities less uncertain by defining more clearly what graduate e-literacy skills are needed. What do they value? How do they rank the importance of different skills both now and for the future? We recognize that this is not easy, but the employers we spoke to in the course of the SEUSISS project did have expectations and made assumptions about what graduates should be able to do that could be translated into clear descriptions to guide universities. To make this as public as possible, employers could ensure that their expectations are made explicit through networks and associations as much as through direct contacts. Creating scenarios of the working day of their graduate recruits would enable students to assess the skills they will need, and reduce uncertainty.

Finally, employers emphasized to us the need for transferability of skills, of generic understanding not blind following, and of generative uses of e-literacy skills rather than simple training. To quote one employer who summed up neatly what others had implied: 'Universities are there to educate and not to train – I want people who can think and learn.'

Conclusions

The e-literacy skill set of graduates across the European universities in our study appeared to be at a level generally acceptable to employers. Skills were broadly similar in each university (country), suggesting that mobility of graduates seeking employment would not be impeded in this respect. However, it was clear that undergraduates bring many of their skills with them to university on arrival, often quite well developed, and some universities do rather little to systematically develop them further. It was also clear that, as employers expand the range of new technologies in everyday use by employees, for example mobile learning, universities may need to review and revise their definitions of their graduates' skill sets.

References

CIHE (2003) *Student Employability Profiles: a guide for employers*, Council for Industry and Higher Education,
www.cihe-uk.com/docs/PUBS/0503SEPEmployers.pdf.
ECAR (2004) *ECAR Study of Students and Information Technology 2004*,
www.educause.edu/ir/library/pdf/ecar_so/ers/ERS0405/ekf0405.pdf.
ECDL (2005) *European Computer Driving Licence Foundation*,
www.ecdl.com/publisher/index.jsp.
EU (2000) *Presidency Conclusions – Lisbon European Council: 23 and 24 March 2000, Lisbon Strategy*,

www.consilium.europa.eu/ueDocs/cms_Data/docs/pressData/en/ec/
00100-r1.en0.htm.

EU (2003a) *The Role of the Universities in the Europe of Knowledge*, COM (2003) 58,
http://europa.eu/eur-lex/en/com/cnc/2003/com2003_0058en01.pdf.

EU (2003b) *Report of Working Group 'Mobility and European Co-operation'*,
www.eu.int/comm/education/policies/2010/doc/mobility_en.pdf.

EU (2005) *Working Together for Growth and Jobs: a new start for the Lisbon Strategy*,
http://ec.europa.eu/growthandjobs/pdf/COM2005_024_en.pdf.

EURYDICE (2002) *Key Data on Education in Europe 2005*,
http://oraprod.eurydice.org/portal/
page?_pageid=196,160677&_dad=portal&_schema=PORTAL&pubid=052EN.

Finland (1999) *Finnish National Strategy for Education, Training and Research in the
Information Society*,
www.minedu.fi/.

Haywood, J., Haywood, D., Macleod, H., Baggetun, R., Baldry, A. P., Harskamp, E.,
Teira, J. and Tenhonen, P. (2004) A Comparison of ICT Skills of Students Across
Europe, *Journal of eLiteracy*, **1** (2), 69–81, www.jelit.org.

Kerala, (2005) *Akshaya Project in the News*,
www.akshaya.net/akshaya/innews/default.asp.

Macleod H., Haywood, D., Haywood, J. and Anderson C. (2002) Gender and
Information and Communications Technology – a 10-year study of new undergraduates, *TechTrends*, **46** (6).

NZ (2005) *New Zealand Literacy Portal: e-literacy*,
www.nzliteracyportal.org.nz/e-Literacy/.

SEUSISS (2001) *SEUSISS Project*, www.intermedia.uib.no/seusiss/.

SPOT-PLUS (2003) *Spot+ Project*, www.spotplus.odl.org/.

UK (1998) *The Learning Age*, www.lifelonglearning.co.uk/greenpaper/.

UNESCO (2005) *Observatory Portal Monitoring the Development of the Information
Society towards Knowledge Societies*,
www.unesco.org/webworld/portal_observatory/pages/Capacity_Building/
E-Literacy/index.shtml.

US (2002) *2020 Visions, Transforming Education and Training through Advanced
Technologies*, www.ta.doc.gov/reports/TechPolicy/2020Visions.pdf.

US (2005a) *21st Century Workforce*, www.dol.gov/21cw/.

US (2005b) *No Child Left Behind Program*, www.ed.gov/nclb/landing.jhtml?src=pb.

Part 2
Enabling and supporting digital literacies

12

Supporting and enabling digital literacy in a global environment: preview of Part 2

Dan Madigan

Abstract

We have learned in the previous section that our world is becoming increasingly digital and that this is profoundly affecting how we learn and live. Those that do not have access to this digital world, and those who cannot use digital tools to become independent learners and explorers of new ideas, will be at a distinct disadvantage as learners. As the authors in this section describe, and I summarize in this chapter, the educational process for much of the world is being significantly impacted on by digital technologies, and those parts of the world that are not yet there, as many envisage, soon will be. The questions that arise regarding such impact are many. For example, how will our lives change as a result of these new technologies? Who gets access to digital technologies? How are those points of access supported? And how do we as educational leaders transform ways of teaching and learning in traditional settings to accommodate new digitally enhanced learning environments? Within this chapter, readers will be introduced to a section preview of the many practical ways that educators throughout the world are using digital technology to enhance learning and the lives not only of a new generation of learners, but also of those generations who have been swept up in the digital revolution leading up to and into the new millennium.

Introduction

In January 2005, as the authors of this book were writing about enabling digital literacy among the world's populations, Nicholas Negroponte was following suit in his own way. As an MIT scholar, expert on digital technologies, and a leader in a new non-profit initiative, Negroponte was speaking at the World Economic Forum at Davos in Switzerland. His topic was 'One Laptop per Child' (OLPC).

In his speech, Negroponte remarked that he and his team envisioned a laptop that would allow children from even the poorest countries a 'window to the world', and 'a tool with which to think'. He envisaged a world where achieving literacy in such areas as reading, writing and mathematics were enabled through the digital world of computers, software applications and the internet. Ten months later, the first laptop prototype was revealed to the public in a world press conference. The $100 laptop had been born, reflecting a technology that according to Negroponte could 'revolutionize how we educate the world's children'. For many who have come to know about this initiative, OLPC has the potential to bring third world countries and poor populations into the mainstream of the digital revolution, which had its beginnings less than 15 years earlier, and an opportunity for those populations to achieve the many types of literacy needed to function in today's world.

As this book is going to press, UN leaders have signalled that they are ready to support the OLPC initiative, with the hope that these $100 laptops can help level the playing field in countries where access to educational information, tools for learning and trained teachers among the poor are lacking or in short supply. In recognition of this need, world leaders are looking for solutions, such as provided by OLPC, to help children grow, learn and be recognized as legitimate players in today's global economy. To date, initial discussions regarding the OLPC project have been held with China, India, Brazil, Argentina, Egypt, Nigeria and Thailand. Negroponte envisages up to 150 million $100 laptops being made and distributed for a new generation of children around the world. Some say that even $100 is too much for families in third world countries to spend when they make only that much or less to support a family for an entire year. But Negroponte and his supporters in this initiative have factored in educational costs for those countries and have amortized those costs over several years. It is doable and, perhaps more importantly, the ethical thing to do.

In many ways, the OLPC project illustrates a critical point that is a dominant theme in the following chapters of this book. That is, the world is becoming increasingly digital and this is profoundly affecting how we learn and live. Those who do not have access to this digital world, and those who cannot use digital tools to become independent learners and explorers of new ideas, will be at a distinct disadvantage as learners. As the authors in this section describe, the educational process for much of the world is being significantly impacted by digital technologies, and those parts of the world that are not yet there, as Negroponte and his group envisage, soon will be. As such, the authors address questions such as:

- How will our lives change as a result of these new technologies?
- Who gets access to digital technologies?
- How are those points of access supported?

- How do we as educational leaders transform ways of teaching and learning in traditional settings to accommodate new digitally enhanced learning environments?
- What qualities and skills do learners need to achieve the range of digital literacy necessary to function and thrive as a literate citizen in today's world?

The contributors to this section begin to answer these and similar questions by looking at digital literacy from a national perspective. Stephen Griffiths, in Chapter 13, 'A dense symphony of the nation,' describes and critiques a movement (Cymru Ar-lein) in Wales for ICT and information literacy support. He writes that Cymru Ar-lein is 'nothing short of an attempt to devise a national strategy for every aspect of a society's encounter with modern information and communications technology'. After a brief historical perspective about the birth of Cymru Ar-lein and a national strategy for implementation, Griffiths discusses the process and possibility for achieving universal access to information and increasing digital literacy among the citizens of Wales. He also describes how Wales is attempting to bridge the linguistic divide that currently exists on the internet by implementing a strategy with software vendors, including open-source groups, to include the native language of Welsh (20% of the country uses Welsh as their language of choice) in interfaces that citizens can use and feel comfortable with. Griffiths explains that the Welsh government is very concerned that all of its citizens have access to, and the skills to understand, critical information that is more often than not found online and through digital resources. The Cymru Ar-lein is one nation's attempt to equal the playing field for its citizens and become a viable player in today's global economy, and social and political sphere.

Whereas Griffiths focuses on one nation's attempt to promote and support a digital environment for its citizens, Jesús Lau, in Chapter 14, paints a broader picture of the impact of the digital revolution on southern hemisphere economies. He writes that a knowledge gap exists between the first world countries of North America and Europe and countries generally classified as 'developing', such as some of those found in the Southern Hemisphere. Within a broader discussion about developing economies, Lau then looks at how the economies of nations are related to their dissemination of information. That is, Lau suggests that there is a direct relationship between how much information and knowledge a country generates and makes available to its population, and how productive that country may be in terms of economic development and standard of living. Given this relationship between economic development and information/knowledge, Lau argues that information literacy skills are sorely needed for everyone, but especially for those countries that may be at an economic disadvantage. He posits that today's learners need literacy skills – such as information literacy skills – that go beyond basic reading and writing literacy, in order to compete and perhaps survive in today's global economy. In summary, Lau states that the key to bridging the knowledge gap among countries lies in education – the kind of education that is student-centred and that pays particular attention to information literacy competencies, as well as to other kinds of competencies in literacy, that are needed for today's global citizen. Further, Lau, like Negroponte, would argue that in order to support a student-centred, independent and creative environment, nations must invest in a sustainable digital technology.

As we move from the world stage to the university environment, Martin Jenkins gives readers some practical suggestions about how to support an e-learning environment that is dynamic and student-centred. In Chapter 15, he first explores the practical, theoretical and moral reasons for supporting e-learning students. For example, some students have no way to access an education at universities unless they engage in some sort of distance-learning programme. But even then, the traditional distance-learning programme, which is not necessarily digitally enhanced, may not be suitable for many students who tend to drop out at a higher rate than they would in a face-to-face experience. For those students, e-learning – that is a digitally enhanced learning environment – may be the answer. Jenkins then focuses on how universities can develop and support the skills that students require to become e-learners. Despite the praise that some have heaped on today's students for being technically savvy, the technology skills of the millennial student may not be as comprehensive as one would think, considering the time these students spend online and in a digital environment outside class. Jenkins argues that a new set of skills are needed for students to be successful at university level. Later in his chapter, he considers how learning design and delivery models can inform curriculum planning to ensure that appropriate support is in place for e-learning delivery. Finally, Jenkins describes the impact of e-learning on learning support services, and how the support they provide needs to change. This change needs to go beyond the area of ICT services as currently configured to include other services on campus, supported by such areas as the library and media.

In Chapter 16 Hester Mountifield picks up the theme of millennial students and the institutional support they need to be successful students in today's world. She begins by briefly describing today's 'digital natives', and how their learning environments need to change to reflect their knowledge, comfort zone and demand for digital environments. Mountifield then reflects on how administrators at the University of Auckland recognized that they needed to change the way University services were provided to their students. Administrators, staff and faculty realized that their support services for students were more disparate than connected. As such, the University determined that many important library support services for students should consolidate into one common space – a highly collaborative environment called an information commons, which exists to promote student learning. Thus was born the Kate Edger Information Commons, a space where once disparate areas such as the media lab, online services, reference desk and social meeting place come together. It is a bustling space for students and support staff 'where the focus is on integrating research, teaching, and learning activities within the digital and physical environments…and [it] takes as its guiding principles both the needs and characteristics of the student and changes in higher education.' As Mountifield explains, libraries, like other important academic and service units on campus, need change that reflects who we are as learners and who we wish to become.

While Mountifield examines a broad array of student services that are brought together in the information commons, Neil Anderson follows in Chapter 17 by looking more closely at one type of service, in this case defined in terms of hardware and software, that has had a profound impact on student learning in the modern university – the learning management system (LMS). In an effort to provide dynamic learning environments for their students, especially those students who do not have easy access to bricks and mortar institutions, universities are increasingly supporting a LMS through which to deliver instruction and provide training. With this in mind, Anderson explores the many facets of a typical LMS, including the types available today, the features available within the LMS, and how an online environment, in conjunction with a face-to-face environment, can support a necessary social presence for students that is sometimes lacking in more sterile and enclosed online systems. In fact, Anderson argues that a blended approach of face-to-face and online learning can provide students with an effective social network that leads to greater student participation in the class, perhaps, than the typical face-to-face model that so often provides 'time-limited opportunities' for students. Of course, not all LMSs are created equal, nor are they all capable of supporting the 'social presence' that Anderson argues is necessary for a dynamic learning environment. For excellent learning to occur online, Anderson recommends a type of LMS that can be customized for the needs of individual institutions – one that supports a variety of pedagogical methods, such as block teaching and case study, and a variety of tools that assist asynchronous and synchronous forms of communication.

In Chapter 18, Alex Reid moves seamlessly from the topic of systems support to an exploration of the various approaches universities adopt to provide and support information and communications technology (ICT) skills to faculty, staff and students. Specifically, Reid describes five areas of ICT skills programmes and strategies adopted by universities that will give readers a good idea about what kinds of programme might best support ICT training on campuses throughout the world: classroom-based courses; the European Computer Driving Licence (ECDL); self-help and peer support; online self-paced courses; and discipline-based ICT training. What Reid delivers is not just a list of key programmes that support ICT literacy, but also a detailed framework of what works and what doesn't work for those who wish to develop their own strategies, approaches and programmes. He also presents readers with a self-assessment scheme that can be used by any university when considering new or improved ICT training for their university learning community. He includes in this self-assessment a rubric that presents users with six principles or benchmarks that every university should consider when designing their own ICT support programmes.

Catherine Cardwell's focus on graduate support for ICT literacy (Chapter 19) takes us from the general support issues for ICT literacy that Reid has described to a single programme that was developed for graduate students at Bowling Green State University in Ohio. Cardwell describes an interdisciplinary graduate learning community that focuses on ICT literacy for future faculty members. She begins by reflecting on the need for future faculty members to be ICT-literate so that they can be successful in the areas of teaching, research and outreach. She also reflects on how busy graduate students need access to learning environments that are off the grid and practical for the 24/7 learner. She then describes a four-part programme developed by her university's teaching and learning centre, ITS, and the libraries that provide training in the areas of information literacy, rich media, documentation and basic IT skills. This programme is distinct in many ways, including its focus on conceptual knowledge, problem solving, cross-platform software and interdisciplinary instructors. It is also completely delivered online, in the form of modules that are media-rich, very interactive and designed to co-exist with any LMS or as standalone applications. As part of the overall flexibility of the course, students are introduced to a variety of open source applications, operating systems and computer platforms that they may encounter as future faculty members. Cardwell's co-taught online course reminds us that new technology impacts not only on what needs to be learned, but on how learning is achieved.

Moving even further beyond the walls of the university classroom, in Chapter 20 Cornel J. Reinhart writes about an outreach programme that extends the expertise of Skidmore College's faculty and staff to teachers from the Caribbean island of Antigua. Reinhart's narrative style in the beginning of the chapter does much to set the stage as the reader is deftly transported into the culture of the island's people, who struggle with many legacy issues including those of illiteracy and slavery. And once the reader becomes familiar with the island culture and its literacy issues, Reinhart unveils Skidmore's unique University Without Walls (UWW) online programme – a programme that was tailored to meet the online needs of 26 student teachers who would otherwise not have been able to attend a university, and thus not be able to advance in their profession. To get an understanding of the commitment that these 26 teachers made, Reinhart describes how they took out loans to cover the $8,000 cost of the typical annual course so that they could be better prepared as teachers and so help to curb the illiteracy rates on the island. To put this in perspective, that figure represents two-thirds of the teacher's annual income each year. Specifically, the UWW curriculum for the

Antigua teachers provided a broad-based liberal education, as opposed to the vocational education that had previously been the focus on the island. Furthermore, Reinhart tells us that the added bonus of the online environment allowed for a dynamic interaction between the island teachers and student teachers from other parts of the world. In smooth narrative fashion, Reinhart ends his chapter by bringing the reader back to some legacy issues, as he describes how within the island teachers' course projects they were able to explore their own histories in relation to the histories of the world.

To complete this section of the book with a focus on individual programmes and courses, in Chapter 21 Gill Needham and David Murphy provide readers with a case study of two courses on information literacy that were developed by the Open University of Hong Kong and the Open University of the UK. These case studies represent a historical perspective at a time when training for information literacy is still sometimes considered a controversial topic, and when professionals are still debating the kinds of information literacy courses that should be offered – or even if standalone information literacy courses should be offered at all. The authors argue that the two courses they describe are not only unique, but could also serve as models for other educational institutions, as they offer information literacy support for both faculty members and students. The authors trace the progress of both courses, developed independently, yet with similar goals and content. What stands out the most about the chapter is the authors' attention to detail, including their information on the implementation and assessment of both online courses.

The authors of Part II have much in common with all the authors in this book. That is, they all understand and would agree that any digital literacy programme, initiative, policy or support structure considered today for implementation by education-centred public and private groups should keep the following in mind. We have entered a century that promises to produce monumental changes in the way people live and learn through digital technologies. If Negroponte has it right, and I think he does, it is not just the first world countries that will have access to and contribute to the production of information, creativity and knowledge. It will truly be the citizens of the world. That is something that we all should take note of and be prepared for.

13

A 'dense symphony of the nation': Cymru Ar-lein and e-citizens and e-communities in Wales

Stephen Griffiths

Abstract

On 1 July 1999, following a referendum and elections to a new National Assembly, the UK government devolved full powers and responsibilities in the areas of health, social policy, economic development and education to Wales. Of the many new policies, strategies and initiatives pursued by the Welsh Assembly Government, one of the most innovative is Cymru Ar-lein (or Wales On-line in English). Cymru Ar-lein is an ambitious attempt to devise and implement a national strategy to empower the citizens of Wales with the e-literacy skills for a 21st century economy and society. Cymru Ar-lein is being used to address such economic matters as market failures in ICT infrastructure, and is the cornerstone of initiatives to transform public services and the 'encounters' between government, public bodies and citizens. Through major e-communities initiatives, it is seen as a means for overcoming some of the unique physical, social and linguistic barriers that exist to accessing online services and information in Wales. In the context of providing an overview of the Cymru Ar-lein strategy, and within a general analytical framework that considers questions about the relationship between technology and nation-building, this paper evaluates the nature and purpose of national initiatives of this kind.

Introduction

In 1997 the UK Government outlined proposals for devolution in Wales, the most radical change in terms of the governmental and administrative relationship between Wales and the rest of the UK since the Acts of Parliament of 1536 and 1543, that completed the process of assimilation which began with the conquest of Wales by Edward I in the 13th century (Richard Commission, 2004, 5). The proposals were subsequently endorsed in a national referendum, and the first elections for the Assembly took place in May 1999. The transfer of devolved powers and responsibilities from the UK Government to the Assembly subsequently took place on 1 July 1999.

Of the many new policies, strategies and initiatives pursued by the Welsh Assembly Government (WAG), one of the most interesting is Cymru Ar-lein: Online for Wales. Cymru Ar-lein is nothing short of an attempt to devise a national strategy for every aspect of a society's encounter with modern information and communications technology. In many ways, it is unique. Although, like many other comparable national strategies, it puts a great deal of emphasis on technical infrastructure, it is also a very human strategy. Much attention is devoted to the social dimensions of supporting and encouraging people of all ages and backgrounds to seize the opportunities offered by technology, by acquiring the 'awareness, skills, understandings, and reflective approaches necessary for an individual to operate comfortably in information-rich and IT-enabled environments' (Martin and Ashworth, 2004, 3).

Cymru Ar-lein is no doubt an attempt to drive Wales towards becoming a greater part of the 'dense symphony of nations' as Marshall McLuhan vividly described the emerging 'global village' (Maignan et al., 2003, 1). However, its role as a means, in the first instance, of strengthening and deepening the political, social and economic connections within Wales should not be underestimated.

Context

The emergence and subsequent evolution of the Cymru Ar-lein strategy has to be understood within the context of four fundamental constraints and structural dysfunctions on the development of policy in the new Assembly.

Geography and communication

Wales has a population of fewer than 3 million and has an area of 20,000 sq km. The majority of the land area is rural and the landscape is mountainous in large areas of the country, especially in the north and mid-Wales. Urban areas are concentrated in the south along the M4 corridor, and the north along the A55 corridor and around Wrexham. Average population density across Wales is 141 inhabitants per sq km, lower than the UK's average density of 242 per sq km, but large parts of Wales are even more sparsely populated. Powys has only 24 people per sq km (Digital Europe, 2003, 1). Only one major road (A470) links north and south Wales, but it exists as a dual-carriageway for only a few miles of the total distance. There are a small number of direct trains between north and south, but all travel through England, and air routes are practically non-existent.

The economy

GDP per capita is 80.5% of the UK average. In June 2002 employment in Wales stood at 68.9% of people of working age – again below the UK average of 74.6% (Digital Europe, 2003,1).Traditionally, the Welsh economy has relied on industries such as steel production, quarrying, agriculture and coal mining, although a more diverse economy has emerged since the 1980s (Digital Europe, 2003,1). Wales has only 21 companies listed on the London Stock Exchange (Leyland, 2003); the next nearest UK region (the north west) has 118. Most Welsh businesses are concentrated in the heavily industrial area along the M4 corridor; 90% have fewer than ten employees (Maignan et al., 2003, 6). In the period 2000–6, Wales is eligible for European Structural Funding, with large parts of west Wales and the south Wales valleys being eligible for Objective One funds. As of June 2005, 2435 projects had been approved, totalling £1,266,936,823 (Welsh European Funding Office, 2005).

Bilingualism

Although English predominates as the main language of communication for a large majority of the population, Cymraeg or Welsh is spoken by just under 20% of the country's population. The Welsh language has been at the heart of cultural politics in Wales since the 19th century, and remains a source of sensitivity in the making of policy. The WAG adopted a vision of turning Wales into a bilingual nation from its creation, and the language is supported by a range of legislation.

The political settlement

The political settlement that saw the creation of the Assembly involved a form of executive rather than legislative devolution, and this deprived it of primary legislative powers. As such, the powers of the Assembly are not as extensive as those granted to Scotland at the same time. However, the Assembly does have full power to develop and implement policies that reflect the particular needs of the people of Wales, and to allocate the funds made available to it from the UK Treasury. In particular, it has full power in the areas of health, social policy, economic development and education, although all initiatives have to be filtered through a statutory duty of sustainable development.

Cymru Ar-lein

Cymru Ar-lein was launched, following an electronic consultation that sought to involve 3000 organizations and individuals, by the WAG in November 2001. The vision for Cymru Ar-lein is extremely ambitious:

We want Wales to be:

- United through its use of ICT, confident in promoting our achievements on the world stage and creative in exploiting ICT for the benefits of individuals, communities and businesses.
- Committed to fostering, through the effective use of ICT, its unique and diverse identity, and the benefits of bilingualism.
- Using ICT to become more prosperous, well-educated, skilled, healthy, environmentally and culturally rich.
- Served by modern, effective, efficient and accessible public services that use ICT to enhance their services.
- Active in its use of ICT in local communities, where the voice of local people is heard.
- Fairer – a place where everyone is valued and ICT is used to give everyone an opportunity to play a full part.
- A place which values its children and where young people want to live, work and enjoy a high quality of life.

(Cymru Ar-lein, 2002)

The strategy has been divided into five themes:

1 public sector
2 private sector
3 education and skills
4 infrastructure
5 e-communities.

There are literally hundreds of initiatives associated with each of these themes, from the quietly revolutionary Informing Healthcare strategy, the investment in ICT facilities in public libraries, the Merlin Programme inside the Assembly, the rise of e-consultation (Beynon-Davies et al., 2003), the new e-procurement system, the All Wales Portal, the Meet the Mouse scheme, and the training of staff across the public and voluntary sector. All of these deserve to be analysed. However, this chapter focuses on aspects of two of the themes: ICT infrastructure and the e-communities initiative. The reason for highlighting these two is that between them they encapsulate all the intricacies and illustrate the depth, complexity and distinctiveness of the overall approach taken by the WAG.

ICT infrastructure
Market failure and broadband

For the WAG, 'higher bandwidth telecommunications is an ever more crucial aspect of ICT infrastructure as usage of connectivity increases and as a convergence of content and of delivery technologies blurs the boundaries between broadcasting, publishing, and the Internet' (Cymru Ar-lein, 2002).

Broadband has been identified as the technical catalyst for the whole range of desirable transformations associated with Cymru Ar-lein and other strategies developed by the WAG. However, as a result of the geography and population distribution of Wales, the supply of commercial higher bandwidth services has tended to concentrate in the urban areas of south Wales, leaving the rest of the country mostly underserved.

As a consequence of this, the WAG unveiled a £115 million programme to address these market failures and facilitate the take-up of broadband throughout Wales. In July 2002 a target was set to increase the availability of affordable terrestrial broadband services in Wales by approximately 30%, with 310,000 extra homes and 67,000 extra business lines potentially able to access broadband. This target was met in September 2004 (Broadband Wales, 2005, 15). By Summer 2005 it was estimated that standard 512 kbps ADSL broadband coverage would peak at between 95.5% and 98% of Wales. To gauge the significance of this, it was estimated in 2002 that only 67% of Wales (compared with a UK average of 80%) would ever be able to access a commercial broadband offering (Broadband Wales, 2005, 16).

As to the qualitative use that is being made of broadband, it is unclear and probably too early to determine whether it is having the anticipated impact. In a recent survey of large SMEs (small and medium-sized enterprises) in Wales, 75% were now using broadband. However, less than half of those surveyed were using it to improve customer services and business processes, only one-quarter used the internet to sell their goods or services online and only 2% were taking advantage of broadband grant funding (National Assembly for Wales, 2004).

Bridging the linguistic digital divide:

In a speech to students at UCLA in January 1994, Vice-President Al Gore told the following story:

Last month, when I was in Central Asia, the President of Kyrgyzstan told me his eight-year-old son came to him and said, 'Father, I have to learn English.'
'But why?' President Akayev asked.
'Because, father, the computer speaks English.'

(Gore, 1994)

A major contemporary anxiety for the guardians of minority languages has been the domination of cyberspace by the English language. Although this has begun to diminish in recent years, and it is now possible to use the internet as a multi-lingual forum, it remains problematic to create common computer applications in minority languages or to create bilingual software. This is particularly impor-tant in a country like Wales, where the equal status of English and Welsh in conducting public business is enshrined in the Welsh Language Act 1993, and the WAG has declared its ambition to create a 'truly bilingual Wales'.

Three developments illustrate the progress that has been made in this area in Wales since the launch of the Cymru Ar-lein strategy:

- The Welsh Language Board has created a pioneering document that seeks to outline guidelines and draft standards for bilingual software (Welsh Language Board, 2004).
- Again, the Welsh Language Board has co-operated with Microsoft to create Office 2003 and Windows XP in Welsh.
- A software community has evolved to create open source applications in Welsh. The first of these, Cymrux, is the first Linuxlive CD in Welsh (Cymrux, 2005).

E-communities

The e-communities initiative is aimed at helping individuals, families, busi-nesses, voluntary organizations and schools in communities across Wales to make effective use of the internet and ICT. While concentrating mostly on giv-ing community leaders and voluntary groups access to ICT resources and expertise, skills training and careers guidance, it has also thrown up a series of distinctive initiatives, two of which are described below.

Funky Dragon

Funky Dragon is the website of the Children and Young People's Assembly for Wales. It is a platform for young people in Wales to gain access to online forums where current issues and interests can be discussed. They can vote and let their views be heard by the Assembly. Funky Dragon enables young people to gain a presence on the web. The Funky Dragon site also has a magazine section, which allows groups to publish less formal, more entertaining material (Funky Dragon, 2005).

Penrhyndeudraeth

Penrhyndeudraeth is a village in north Wales, close to Portmeirion, the set for the television series, *The Prisoner*. It has a population of less than 1900 people, and has been the site of an experiment to create the first networked village in the UK. The creation of the first networked village has been overseen by a regeneration company, whose aim was 'to accelerate the take-up of ICT, and participation in the Information Society by pro-actively encouraging a community to get online' (Deudraeth, 2005). The aim of the scheme was to bring the most up-to-date technology to a rural village, and measure its influence on the community. By developing strong partnerships with the public sector and the local community, computers have been distributed to some villagers, and the library offers a laptop loan scheme. CySill and Cysgair, the Welsh-language spellchecker and English/Welsh dictionary for Windows, are now available free of charge to businesses and residents of the networked village.

Although the e-communities theme of Cymru Ar-lein has been the most controversial, originally failing to win matching funding from the government, it has also been the most dynamic and creative, in terms of the range of initiatives that has been launched across Wales (Colvile, 2004).

Conclusion: the e-literate nation

On one level, Cymru Ar-lein is a straightforward strategy to use the newly acquired devolved powers of the Assembly to address what are perceived to be 'market failures' in the provision of ICT infrastructure in Wales. On another level, the strategy is a rather more complex effort to introduce Wales to the 21st century, and to overcome rapidly many of the major geographical, communication, economic, health and social problems faced by the nation.

Cymru Ar-lein has much in common with other strategies and initiatives of this kind around the world: for example, the SUPERNET broadband network has been built to link rural communities across Alberta, Canada; subsidies have been offered in Italy to allow schoolchildren to buy PCs; the Networking the Nation programme in Australia includes the development of ICT skills; and, in the USA, the Departments of Commerce and Agriculture have offered grants and loans for the development of rural broadband (Analysys, 2001).

In other ways, it is very different. The strategy is extremely ambitious in its scale, but also accessible and non-technical. It attempts to weave together hundreds of initiatives, many of which are dependent on the development of related initiatives in other strategy documents. In this sense, Cymru Ar-lein is very much a product of the 'strategy factory' mentality, which understandably overcame the Assembly in the first few years after its creation (Welsh Local Government Association, 2003). However, its creation has allowed Wales to think about itself on its own terms, and it has surprised itself with its ability to come to distinctive conclusions. The strategy also recognizes that technology itself is not the goal of policy, but instead a means of delivering change.

Questions arise about the long-term value of public intervention to correct what are characterized as market failures in the provision of ICT infrastructure, and focusing wider investment on providing public facilities rather than improving private access. ICT markets are extremely dynamic and many of the opportunities associated with new technologies are most efficiently utilized in the private realm. As such, it is debatable whether public interventions can respond to ICT developments in a way that is sustainable and flexible in the long term, and the focus on the public rather than the private realm might be misguided.

Beyond the debate about Cymru Ar-lein as a government strategy and the questions about its focus, it is its ambition to use new technologies and the e-literacy skills required to utilize them, to create a new, stronger and more self-consciously united nation that marks it out from other comparator strategies. Nation building has always been facilitated by new communication technology, and ICT is an obvious means of seeking to strengthen a nation with structural dysfunctions. This raises an interesting question about the relationship between Cymru Ar-lein and contemporary debates about technology and geography. On one level, new information and communication technologies promise to free us from the limitations of geography, and there is no doubt that the strategy is designed to help people in rural communities in particular to join the global community. However, the flip side of this debate is that geography is vital to shaping technology in ways that suit a people. In this regard, while technologies might free us to work anywhere and at any time, this actually occurs in specific political, economic, geographical and social contexts and these can be shaped and honed by nations and governments.

In that sense, although Cymru Ar-lein is a strategy designed to empower citizens and communities for the 21st century, most importantly it is a strategy designed to empower the citizens and communities of Wales. In some ways, it is in its role as a contribution to nation building that the strategy is promising to make its greatest contribution. In this respect, Cymru Ar-lein is about the creation of a 'dense symphony of the nation', rather more than it is a contribution to the creation of a 'dense symphony of nations'.

References

Analysys (2001) *Ubiquitous Broadband Infrastructure for Wales*, report prepared for the Welsh Development Agency, Annex E, www.wis.org.uk/english/whats%20new/docs/PDF/.

Beynon-Davies, P., Owens, I., Williams, M. D. and Hill, R. (2003) *Re-energizing Democracy?*, Electronic Consultation at the National Assembly for Wales, EBMS Working Paper, Swansea University.

Broadband Wales (2005) *Programme Strategy 2005–2007*, www.bbwo.org.uk/broadband-2238.

Colvile, R. (2004) *New Statesman/ BT Round Table: Cardiff – from farce to treasure trove*, www.newstatesman.co.uk/considerthis/ctwalessummary.htm (accessed 1 June 2005).

Cymru Ar-lein (2002), www.cymruarlein.wales.gov.uk/ (accessed 4 March 2005).

Cymrux (2005), www.cymrux.org.uk/index.php (accessed 13 May 2005).

Deudraeth (2005), www.deudraeth.net/opencms/opencms/english/index.html (accessed 13 May 2005).

Digital Europe (2003) Cymru Ar-lein and Sustainable Development: case study in *Digital Europe: business and sustainable development* (DEESD IST – 2000-28606).

Funky Dragon (2005), www.funkydragon.org/fe/master.asp?n1=399 (accessed 13 May 2005).

Gore, A. (1994) Remarks by Vice-President Al Gore, Royce Hall, UCLA, 11 January, www.ibiblio.org/icky/speech2.html (accessed 12 May 2005).

Leyland, A. (2003) Could This Really Happen in Swansea? *Real Business*, (December) www.realbusiness.co.uk/showdetail.asp?ArticleID=2606 (accessed 4 March 2005).

Maignan, C., Ottaviano, G., Pinelli, D. and Rullani, F. (2003) Comparative Regional Case Study Piedmont, Wales and the Ruhr, *Digital Europe: e-business and sustainable development* (DEESD IST– 2000-28606).

Martin, A. and Ashworth, S. (2004) Welcome to the Journal of eLiteracy!, *Journal of eLiteracy*, **1** (1).

National Assembly for Wales (2004) *David Slays Goliath: broadband helps Welsh SMEs prove they are small but mighty*, www.cymruarlein.wales.gov.uk/fe_irc/details.asp?ircid=92 (accessed 4 March 2005).

Richard Commission (2004) *Commission on the Powers and Electoral Arrangements of the National Assembly of Wales*, report, www.richardcommission.gov.uk/content/template.asp?ID=/index.asp.

Welsh European Funding Office (2005), www.wefo.wales.gov.uk/ (accessed 29 May 2005).

Welsh Language Board (2004), www.bwrdd-yr-iaith.org.uk/en/index.php, (accessed 16 February 2005).

Welsh Local Government Association (2003) *Response, Consultation on the Review of the Sustainable Development Scheme*, www.cymru.gov.uk/themessustainabledev/content/review/responses/wlga-w.htm (accessed 12 May 2005).

14

The impact of information competencies on socio-economic development in Southern Hemisphere economies

Jesús Lau

Abstract

This paper discusses the North–South knowledge gap and its relationship to socio-economic development, information development, education and information literacy. Information development – the information progress of a country – is analysed using indicators of production, storage and demand of recorded information/knowledge. Most concepts are discussed from the point of view of developing countries – nations that basically fall within the Southern Hemisphere. The term 'developing economies' is used to group middle-, low- and lowest-income nations that share general characteristics but also have several differences even within their own regions/states. The analysis is simplistic and does not attempt to give a full conceptual scientific explanation of North–South knowledge gaps. The term 'literacy' is used to denote the various competencies that citizens are required to master at a basic level. The most familiar meaning of literacy is the one related to basic reading and writing. However, literacy has become a common word to denote elementary skills that are needed by most, if not all, members of society, such as information literacy.

Text originally presented as the Mortenson Distinguished Lecture, at the Mortenson Center for International Library Programs, University of Illinois at Urbana-Champaign.

Information development

The development of a nation can be measured according to the dissemination of information because it shows how a country generates and uses knowledge, especially the printed type. Recorded knowledge has a production cycle: authors, inventors and researchers generate information and knowledge in the form of arti-

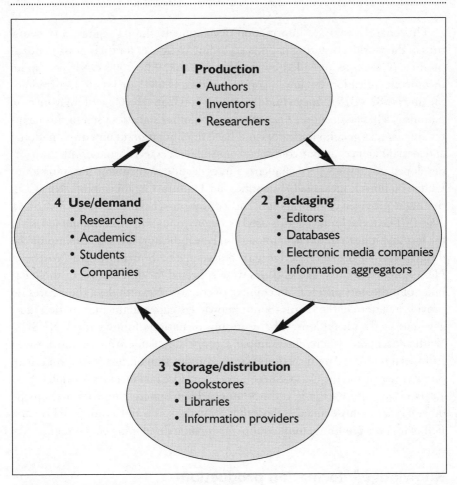

Figure 14.1 *Knowledge/information cycle*

cles, books, texts and patents that are then processed by publishers, database builders, webmasters and electronic media companies. Processed information is, in turn, stored and distributed by bookstores, libraries and other information providers to meet the demand (if the proper competencies to use information are present) of researchers, faculty, students, companies and society in general (see Figure 14.1). It is assumed that citizens need a working knowledge of the social, economic and political activities of their own country to improve their personal, family and business life. If this is true, it is also assumed that information literacy is a crucial set of skills that enables individuals to benefit from the wealth of knowledge available in paper or electronic format, and that these competencies are basically fostered by the country's educational system.

This chapter analyses information development among regions and countries of the world, clustering nations according to figures for their gross national product (GNP), as provided by the World Bank. The 2004 GNP per capita income classification for low-income countries is $825 or less; lower-middle-income is $826–3255; upper-middle-income is $3256–10,065; and high-income nations is $10,066 or more. These figures and other statistics used in this chapter are taken as general indicators and have the limitation of obscuring national and local differences among countries. Some nations, especially those with the least-developed economies, face challenges in collecting and submitting statistics to United Nations Educational, Scientific, and Cultural Organization (UNESCO), the main provider of information and education-related data (see UNESCO, 2006a). The term 'knowledge' is used as synonymous with 'information', despite the fact that it has a different connotation. Few indicators are used to simplify the description of the knowledge gap between the Southern and Northern Hemispheres. Because the statistics were collected for different years, the reliability of indicators differs from country to country. Nevertheless, the figures do provide a pattern of the North–South knowledge gap, and the information literacy status of both regions. The grouping of nations follows the UNESCO Yearbook scheme, where, for example, Europe stands for Western and Eastern European nations; America covers North America (including Central America), South America and the Caribbean countries; and Oceania includes Australia, New Zealand and the Pacific islands. Southern Hemisphere countries are, on the other hand, roughly defined as those that are in the south and around the Equator. Following this grouping, most continents include developing economies.

Knowledge/information production

Knowledge is generated by authors and researchers, among other key players. The recording of scientific discoveries, technological developments and human experience in general is normally measured by the number of patents and publications, such as reports, articles and books. Statistics for individuals engaged in research are a good indicator of knowledge creation and information demand in a nation. The knowledge-generation differences between continents and countries are dramatic when this indicator is taken into account. For example, Africa has fewer researchers (71,000) than the developed country of Canada (80,000). The American continent without the two major economies of Canada and the USA also has an abysmal difference: there are 125,000 researchers – compared with more than 1 million when the numbers for Canada and the USA are included. European countries and Japan and Asia generally rank high in the number of researchers. However, the Asian group includes China and India, two highly populated nations that fare better in this indicator. If researchers are distributed per capita, China and India would rank low (see Table 14.1).

Table 14.1 *International distribution of researchers (UNESCO, 2006c)*

Continent/country	Researchers
Africa	71,308
America*	124,899
Asia	4,483,881
Europe	1,892,307
Oceania	60,066
Canada	80,510
Japan	651,099
USA	962 700

*Excludes USA and Canada

Research is an important activity in fostering socio-economic progress because it contributes to the generation of discoveries that industry can develop into new products and services to solve local problems. The lead of the developed world in the number of researchers gives it an advantage in the production of science and technology. Research activities are highly dependent on information competencies. Researchers must possess strong information skills to successfully benefit from the research work of others and to avoid inquiry overlap.

A second strong indicator of knowledge production is the number of registered patents of countries. Statistics for 2003 show that developing countries generated 14% of patents compared with the striking figure of 86% for the highly developed nations (see Table 14.2).

Table 14.2 *Patents (WIPO, 2003)*

Country/region	Patents	Percentage
USA	44,609	40
Germany	15,269	13
Japan	13,531	12
Subtotal	*73,409*	*65*
UK	6,274	5
Other developed economies	19,115	16
Subtotal	*25,389*	*86*
Rest of the world	16,202	14
Total	*115,000*	*100*

Information packaging

The recording of information takes different forms, among them books, serials, databases and websites. The recorded output of a country, i.e. publishing, reflects the national capability for knowledge packaging, an activity that is also heavily concentrated in the developed world. Traditionally, scientific serials have been published in the developed world. Table 14.3 shows that Africa had slightly more than 7000 International Standard Serial Numbers (ISSNs). Latin American countries had fewer than 30,000 ISSNs, while the USA held the rather high figure of more than 160,000 and Canada more than 110,000 records (ISSN, 2002). Because journals represent a key form of knowledge encapsulation, the rather minimal number of serial titles produced by the developing world, as cited for Africa and Latin America, is a strong indication of the state of information in these countries (see Table 14.3).

Table 14.3 *Serial titles (ISSN, 2002)*

Continent/country	ISSN records
Africa	7,094
Asia	37,369
Europe	584,632
South America/Caribbean	27,842
Oceania	51,691
Canada	111,618
Japan	30,947
USA	161,031

Another information medium is the newspaper. They document the current, daily in most cases, information of a society and, because dailies are cheaper than books and other serials, they are accessible to the general citizen. However, even with this indicator, the difference between developed and developing economies is significant. Statistics for 1996–1997 show that circulation was 226 copies per 1000 inhabitants in the developed countries – a large three-digit figure compared with the 60 copies that circulated in developing nations and the eight copies in the least-developed countries. The newspaper-reading gap between North and South is similar to that of serial publications. Table 14.4 shows in greater detail the geographical differences between continents, where some of the largest economies represent the greatest newspaper demand.

Newspaper publication in paper is decreasing because leading newspapers have summaries or are published in full text on the internet. However, newspapers are still a good measure of information packaging in developing countries because they are printed on traditional presses and the internet is not yet readily available to all members of society.

Table 14.4 *Newspaper circulation (UNESCO, 2006b)*

Continent/region	Number of dailies (000)	Circulation total (millions)	Per 1000 inhabitants
World total	8391	548	96
Africa	224	12	16
America	2939	111	141
Asia	3010	229	66
Europe	2115	190	261
Oceania	103	6.4	227
Developed countries	3972	276	226
Developing countries	4419	272	60
Least developed	172	3.9	8

Storage and distribution

Information stocks are held and distributed in different types of places, for example, bookstores, information centres and libraries. Libraries, library holdings and computer networks are useful indicators because statistics are available for most countries. The most comprehensive library statistics are from national and public libraries. The holdings of national libraries are excellent indicators of national information wealth, because national library collections represent the local information production in different media, not only printed material. In other words, the stocks of national libraries are the indicators of nationally produced information. These holdings vary dramatically from North to South. Statistics for 1995 show that Europe had nearly 300 million volumes, a figure that looks astronomically large compared with Africa's holdings of fewer than 3 million. Asia, a highly populated continent, held 46 million volumes, but a significant share was held by a single nation, Japan, the leading information economy on the continent (see Table 14.5). US statistics were not available because the USA had not made its payement to UNESCO.

Table 14.5 *National library collections (UNESCO, 2006b)*

Continent/country	Libraries	Volumes (000)
Africa	13	2920
America	10	20,560
Asia	26	45,992
Europe	63	278,194
Oceanía	1	2441
Canada	1	6387
Japan	1	5528

Public libraries, on the other hand, represent an indicator of information availability to the general citizen. Here, again, there are large disparities among
regions. Statistics for 1995 show that Africa accounted for 6 million volumes, and
the Latin American continent held 18 million volumes, compared with Europe
with the outstanding figure of 2500 million volumes. Canada and Japan had 70
million and nearly 200 million volumes respectively. Asia ranked higher but its
population is also high, so per capita indicators would be lower than those from
Latin America. The difference in number of libraries or library service points, the
prime centres to keep the public recorded knowledge, is also dramatic. The gap
in public library service points follows the trend of holdings (see Table 14.6). Library
figures reflect information gaps between the hemispheres and regions, because the
statistics are valid in both the developed and developing world, unlike websites
or other high-technology information media that are mainly concentrated in the
Northern Hemisphere.

Table 14.6 *Public library collections (UNESCO, 2006b)*

Continent/country	Libraries	Volumes (000)
Africa	358	6271
Asia	22,741	597,394
Europe	127,271	2,568,421
Latin America	2060	18,231
Canada	1045	70,077
Japan	2172	195,390

The creation of home pages, portals and websites is the latest indicator used to
identify the current information gaps throughout the world. The internet, the electronic information highway, has become the most powerful world information
repository. It amalgamates the production, packaging, storage and distribution of
the information cycle. However, the internet is predominantly an asset of the North.
Nearly all, i.e. 90%, of internet demand comes from developed countries, and 70%
of computer servers are located in those countries. In addition, English is the lin-
gua franca for internet material: between 60 and 80% of internet records are in
this language, a major information barrier for non-Anglo-Saxon societies. The enormous internet gap between North and South is dramatic because the internet is
such an important tool for socio-economic and information development. The
macro-network comprises all the advantages that a nation requires to foster social
progress. The differences between the internet-haves and the internet-have-nots
are higher than in the printed information indicators (see Figure 14.2).

USA, Canada, Japan and Western Europe
90% internet demand
70% computer servers

English language
60–80% internet content
60% English-speaking users
8% English speakers in total world population

Figure 14.2 *Use of the internet (UAB, 2004)*

Information use/demand

The number of researchers can be used as a proxy for information demand, an indicator explained earlier in the chapter. As stated above, there are striking differences in the number of researchers between the North and the South. Figures for the North seem astronomically large when compared with the small number of people engaged in research in the developing nations of the South. The number of graduates could also be another good indicator of information demand (see RICYT statistics, 2002). Internet use is another excellent indicator of how a country can access international information repositories. English speakers, mainly citizens of the wealthy regions of the world, account for 8.3% of the total world population, but they represent nearly 60% of internet demand (see Figure 14.2). Although the number of indicators used to describe international information demand is small, they do depict information use gaps among countries.

The international trends in the cycle of production, packaging, storage/distribution, and use/demand of information/knowledge illustrate, in general, the information and knowledge gaps between the two hemispheres. The ranking of countries in this cycle is closely related to the information competencies of a society. People who identify and succeed in achieving their information needs perform better in the different stages of the information/knowledge cycle. Countries with greater information demand and a greater supply of printed materials are nations with greater information development. These nations are basically located in the northern part of the world, and they are, by analogy, the knowledge nations who lead in information competencies.

The knowledge bridge

Knowledge is the product of a cognitive process, where information becomes the key ingredient to enhance human perception, understanding, awareness, thinking, intelligence and memory. Each of these cognitive stages relies or spins around information. Therefore, the competencies of searching, retrieving and using recorded knowledge, i.e. information, is vital for individual and collective socio-economic development. These information competencies are mainly fostered by education, although parents and the work environment also play key roles. All citizens must develop information literacy skills to benefit from and participate in the knowledge cycle. For example, an information-literate worker who can learn constantly is able to adapt to short-term jobs that predominate in the current economy, including those from the more industrialized and service-oriented strata of less-developed countries, sectors that share similar characteristics with more advanced economies. The workplace is moving from routine to rich-thinking activities; information literacy enables workers to respond to the lifelong learning environment currently present in manufacturing and service industries. If education is an important process in an individual's personal and professional growth, including the development of information competencies, then developing economies may need to improve this crucial process in order to bridge the information competencies gap (Figure 14.3).

- Education enables people to be better citizens.
- Education helps economic mobility of individuals.
- Education determines national progress.
- Education access is a challenge.
- Education quality is an even greater challenge.
- Information development is related to education.
- Education fosters information competencies.

Figure 14.3 *Education and development*

Conclusion

According to the printed information indicators, less developed countries, mostly located in the Southern Hemisphere, have made limited information progress with a general correlation to their socio-economic development. The production and use of recorded knowledge, especially of the printed type, is low. The recorded knowledge production cycle of authors, inventors and researchers indicates a low generation of information/knowledge, as indicated by the production of articles, books, texts and patents. Based on the statistics used in this chapter, the information-processing infrastructure, e.g publishers, database builders, webmasters and electronic media companies, is also limited. The process of storing and distributing information (by bookstores, libraries and other information providers) is, again, limited. On the other hand, the demand for information/knowledge follows the same trend when the number of researchers was analysed. The most easily identifiable cause for such information development gaps, although there could be many socio-economic reasons, is the limited information skills of citizens that prevent them from playing a full role in the knowledge creation/use cycle. Limited information competencies may, in turn, be due to the quantity and quality of national educational systems, factors not analysed in this chapter.

Countries from the Southern Hemisphere could narrow the knowledge gap and achieve better information development if they improve their educational systems. It could be argued that reduced budgets are a barrier. However, this limitation heightens the need for better education. Students can be better educated, with higher learning outcomes, if those learning outcomes are based on the development of competencies that, in turn, include the core information skills needed to access knowledge.

References

ISSN (2002), www.issn.org/en/node/330.

RICYT (2002), www.ricyt.org/Indicadores/Comparativos/18.xls.

UNESCO (2006a),
www.uis.unesco.org/ev_en.php?ID=2867_201&ID2=DO_TOPIC.

UNESCO (2006b), www.uis.unesco.org/ev.php?ID=5066_201&ID2=DO_TOPIC.

UNESCO (2006c), www.uis.unesco.org/ev.php?ID=5753_201&ID2=DO_TOPIC.

Universitat Autónoma de Barcelona (UAB) (2004) Importancia (y Desigualdades) de los Niveles de Acceso a Internet, *Hacia 2004: estudios interculturales, textos básicos para el forum 2004 (October, 1997 – August, 1998)*,
www.blues.uab.es/incom/2004/portada.html.

World Intellectual Property Organization (WIPO) (2003),
www.wipo.int/edocs/prdocs/es/2003/wipo_pr_2003_338.html.

15

Supporting students in e-learning

Martin Jenkins

Abstract

The majority of e-learning developments are supplementary to face-to-face teaching. This means that support issues, which are best planned as part of the curriculum design, are not fully developed. In addition it means the opportunities presented by e-learning are not fully exploited. This chapter considers the reasons why support should be integral to e-learning provision, how this impacts on support provision and how the use of learning-design models can help to inform student support and skills development.

Introduction

The use of e-learning encompasses a wide continuum of potential uses of learning technology. Phillips (2004) identifies four e-learning design dimensions: student–student interaction, student–teacher interaction, student–resource interaction and student–computer interaction. However e-learning is employed, it is critical that students are supported in the development of the e-learning skills required and provided with the appropriate support structures and opportunities.

The majority of e-learning developments have been supplementary to face-to-face delivery. This has meant that the full implications for supporting students in e-learning are not always fully considered. The reason for this is that supplementary applications are often 'bolted-on' to traditional forms of delivery. As a consequence e-learning is not considered in the design and delivery of the learning event.

This chapter is divided into four main sections. The first considers the reasons for supporting e-learning students. The second focuses on developing and supporting the skills that students require to become 'e-learners'. The third considers how learning design and delivery models can inform planning to ensure appropriate support is in place and how this can be delivered through the curriculum. The fourth section considers the impact of e-learning on learning support services and how the support they provide needs to change.

Supporting students in e-learning

Simpson (2002) suggests student support is required for practical, theoretical and moral reasons. Building on Simpson's list for students studying via open and distance learning, the reasons it is important to make student support integral for e-learning are:

- Retention: flexible and distance learning provision has been particularly associated with high drop-out rates; based on experiences with traditional correspondence forms of distance learning. E-learning presents opportunities to improve retention through monitoring, tackling isolation and helping provide structure.
- Access and widening participation: the demand for life-long learning has created a more diverse student population. It can no longer be assumed that the full-time student is wholly on-campus; and they may now face constraints typically associated with part-time and distance students (Kirkwood and Price, 2005, 258).
- Competition: a more 'customer focused' view of education means that a student's choice of institution will be influenced by the services and support provided.
- Student isolation: this has always been a potential problem with distance courses; however, with effective planning and support e-learning provides opportunities for communication and collaboration.
- Quality assurance processes: for example, in the UK the Quality Assurance Agency for Higher Education (QAA) *Code of Practice for the Assurance of Academic Quality and Standards in Higher Education: section 2, collaborative provision and flexible and distributed learning (including e-learning)* (2004) contains clear guidance for student support. This includes information provision, reliability of systems, learner support and assessment.
- Skills development: having the experience of using the internet, which most students now have, does not equate to students having the skills to be e-learners. E-learning requires specific and often different skills.
- Emotional and affective support: online collaborative learning is still a new experience for most students, support is required to ensure they feel comfortable, welcome and valued and not at risk.

- Engagement and structure: the majority of student learning time, even for campus-based students, occurs away from staff–student contact time (McAlpine, 2004). Through e-learning contact time can be extended and structure provided to 'non-contact' time.

Skills development and support

Any learning event is a unique experience for a student. Prosser's and Trigwell's (1999) model of learning and teaching identifies five factors that influence any learning event. They are the student's:

- prior experience
- approaches to learning
- perceptions of their situation
- situation
- learning outcomes.

In the case of e-learning this includes familiarity with the technologies involved. Working in an online environment requires new skills and expectations of the student. Even with an increase in e-literacy skills within the general population and particularly the younger generations (Oblinger, 2003; Kirkwood and Price, 2005), it cannot be assumed that students will have the skills or knowledge to operate in an online learning environment, to be online learners. Jochems, van Merrienboer and Koper (2004, 201) believe that integrated e-learning, a holistic approach to e-learning design and delivery, is not the best approach for the 'low-ability' learners, those suffering from motivational problems or from cultures where the traditional school system does not allow for any form of self-directed learning or its development. Using e-learning, students have to be more self-directed in terms of choosing task, media and collaborating, requiring higher order skills (Jochems, van Merrienboer and Koper, 2004, 200). However, through good design and support, an appropriate environment for even low-ability learners can be created, but they must be actively supported: 'Merely putting students into an online laboratory or a forum for discussion does not necessarily lead to learning taking place' (Bates and Poole, 2003, 230).

Within the broad spectrum of e-learning students will require a suite of e-literacy skills. Core, Rothery and Walton (2003, 22) identify these skills as:

- Local basic skills: how to access and use local networks and facilities.
- IT skills: basic word-processing and spreadsheet skills.
- Specialist ICT skills: the use of specialist ICT software for data analysis, including packages such as SPSS and QSR Nvivo.

- Information management and communication: information literacy skills, presentation techniques and software; use of communication tools including e-mail, bulletin boards, chat and video conferencing and the use of learning support software such as virtual learning environments (VLEs).
- Assessment: using and coping with online assessment, including the use of collaborative learning, uploading assignments, use of computer-aided assessment (CAA) and a full awareness of plagiarism, copyright and appropriate referencing skills.

Students are often 'expected' to be able to use e-learning without any formal induction (Browne and Jenkins, 2003). The opportunity for skill development is limited especially within modular schemes with very short modules. In such circumstances induction programmes or learning skills modules provide opportunities to prepare students for e-learning. The University of Gloucestershire operates a modular system and has a compulsory study skills module for all first-year students. Some disciplines, such as media communications, use the University VLE to deliver this module. They have created a series of structured online activities, in place of lectures, and supported by online discussions. This has proven successful in meeting the learning outcomes of the module but has also served as a means of inducting the students into the use of the VLE, which is used extensively in other modules in this discipline.

Learning design and delivery

E-learning developments should be pedagogically led, with appropriate consideration of organizational and technical issues. This ideal situation is often not achieved when e-learning developments are introduced supplementary to courses that are already being delivered. In such situations the focus of attention tends to focus on technical considerations rather than the pedagogy and improving the student learning experience.

The provision of both coaching (guidance and help in the learning setting) and scaffolding (support for skills, learning strategies and provision of appropriate resources) must be part of the learning design process. Providing for coaching and scaffolding requires an active and engaged teacher/facilitator with support structures. Oliver's (2001a) framework for learning design describes three key elements: learning tasks, learning resources and learning supports. This model demonstrates how taking a different emphasis at the learning design stage can lead to the creation of very different learning environments. Adopting a student-centred, constructivist approach places the emphasis on tasks at the learning design stage. Alternatively, emphasizing content will create a resource-focused programme with the teacher as expert. While the latter can be said to not fully exploit the benefits of learning technology this design model can be used to help consider and plan the balance between tasks, resources and support. McAlpine (2004) emphasizes that strong support (scaffolding) is required early on but should be phased out to encourage more active engagement.

Salmon's (2000) five-step model of e-learning delivery is based on the recognition that to achieve participation and success e-learning participants need to master technical and online communication skills. This model emphasizes the role of the tutor and course team, who need to ensure these skills are developed and support is in place. The five stages of the model are, with e-moderator tasks:

- access and motivation – welcoming and encouraging
- online socialization – familiarization, socialization
- information exchange – task facilitation and use of learning materials
- knowledge construction – facilitating process
- development – supporting and responding.

However, the outcomes of any planned learning event cannot be fully predicted, particularly so with online collaborative learning. As Oliver (2001b, 85) states, 'With online learning, there is a real need for the teacher to monitor learners' activities … there are so many things to go wrong and so many things that can impede.' The tutor must therefore be continually monitoring and responding to developments. Tutors need to be skilled in the management and support of online courses and learners.

The use of these models highlights the importance of focusing on tasks and activities for successful e-learning. McAlpine (2004) has developed a model of learning design which emphasizes that most learning takes place in non-contact time, when tasks are worked on independently. Her model can be used as a tool to illustrate the provision of structure to this non-contact time. Table 15.1 summarizes the key elements of the student support required at the different stages.

Institutional support

Educational institutions need to provide support for the affective, practical, pastoral, financial and social aspects of the student experience. This covers a broad spectrum of support and support providers. The use of e-learning impacts on all aspects of learning support, notably on library and ICT services (Bricheno, Higgison and Weedon, 2004, 110), but also enrolment processes.

Table 15.1 *Examples of student support for different phases of the McAlpine learning design model (based on McAlpine, 2004, 126)*

Phases of McAlpine learning design model	Examples of student support related to e-learning
Engagement: gain full attention of students	• motivation • students to be clear about why they are using e-learning • information produced in advance so that students can make informed choices • designing and creating an accessible system.
Informing: advise students about the subject matter or task	• provision of well structured information and resources, including FAQs • produce clear guidelines and establish ground rules • expectations of students to be clear, including skills required • expectations of tutor, including availability, and institution to be clear • ensure relevant support is available within institution.
Practice: provide activities for students to rehearse, perform, apply	• ensure opportunities to develop e-learning skills are available, either through the curriculum or induction/support services • provide regular opportunities for regular engagement and feedback • phase the scaffolding provided as students develop the skills and knowledge. • ensure learning environment is structured appropriately to support tasks, e.g. size of discussion groups • be prepared to offer students a choice in how they engage with activities.
Summative assessment: judge student outcomes	• assessment to take advantage of the opportunities provided by e-learning • provide opportunities for students to familiarize themselves with any testing software • provide guidelines for computer-based assessment.

ICT services

This chapter has already discussed the importance of e-literacy skills development. Complementary to this is the need for ICT support. Issues for which support will be required include:

- students who have forgotten login details
- requests for access to VLE sites
- technical queries on student's own ICT equipment and browser problems
- and a myriad of specific requests which emphasize the personal nature of this support.

Such queries can be particularly challenging from e-learning students who are studying off-campus where their computer set-up is unknown. ICT staff should play a proactive role, not just in providing support to queries, but in making advice available on the set-up of computers to minimize access problems. With the increasing flexibility of study patterns, the demand for 24-hour access to support increases. For most institutions this is a significant resource issue. Some have sought to provide solutions through collaborative arrangements with institutions around the globe.

E-learning also impacts on physical learning spaces. The increased use of e-learning creates demands for internet access, projection facilities and interactive whiteboards in classrooms. The learning spaces themselves are also extending through the provision of network access to residences and wireless provision across and even beyond campuses.

Library

Distance learning courses have often led to the development of special services, such as postal library services. Such services may still be required but should be combined with access services such as UK Libraries Plus (http://uklibraries-plus.ac.uk/). In common with ICT services, a particular demand is the provision of an enquiry service to students who are no longer in the library or with very different study patterns. Web-based services including FAQs and online enquiry services are now commonplace in response to such demands.

On campus the use of e-learning is leading to changes in physical learning spaces, including both classroom and study spaces. Many institutions, often through libraries, are developing new learning spaces, such as information commons (see Chapter 16). These spaces based on a model of social learning create an integrated environment with appropriate student support.

Enrolment

Trouble-free access to systems and resources is of particular importance to e-learning. Enrolment, in programmes and individual modules is a key process to accessing online courses and resources; as a consequence many educational institutions are now integrating systems.

Informing – enquiring – counselling

Whatever support is being provided there is a continuum from the provision of information through personal interaction with the student; these could be identified as informing, enquiries and counselling.

How services provide this support needs careful consideration and skill development for the staff providing the service, especially when dealing with enquiries and counselling. It is now an expectation that information will be provided via the internet, often as well as in print, and increasingly technologies such as SMS messaging and web portals are being used to provide more personalized access to information.

Dealing with enquiries and counselling support requires more specialist support and staff with appropriate skills. Many institutions are now developing a one-stop-shop approach, providing one clearly identifiable point of contact to overcome the complexity of educational systems which can deal with basic enquiries but pass on enquiries to the appropriate expert.

Media

The QAA *Code of Practice* (2004) clearly indicates that in addition to what support is provided, the means of delivering that support and how it is accessed must also be considered. E-learning provides opportunities to increase access but is not suitable for all, and alternatives must be provided to support students with particular needs and cover situations where problems might occur with online sources. Simpson (2002, 116) notes 'in order for a particular medium of support to be useful to a student it must be accessible, in terms of reasonable cost and time taken, and add "study value".' What is important is that students are provided with opportunities for support that are worthwhile and valued. High-quality support can be provided by face-to-face, telephone and online means, such as e-mail communication or via conferencing support. The important point is the provision of opportunities. The use of residential events is one way that opportunities for face-to-face contact are provided, though it should be recognized that making these compulsory can exclude students and so even in these circumstances alternatives are required.

The requirements of disability legislation (Disability Discrimination Act 2005 in the UK) must be considered in the design of learning events and of the support provision. The use of e-learning presents opportunities for improvement, including accessibility and personalization of interfaces. However, if a particular e-learning application is inaccessible to students with a specific disability then reasonable adjustments in provision will be required to provide those students with a comparable learning experience.

Conclusions

The use of e-learning presents education institutions with both challenges and opportunities to the support of students. To meet these challenges and reap the potential benefits, it is important that a holistic approach is taken to developments. There will be no one-size-fits-all approach; however, there are key principles that institutions can consider. First, we must recognize that support for e-learning must be considered at the learning design stage. The use of e-learning must be clearly and carefully considered and the implications for skills development and support considered to ensure the support is embedded. Reference to appropriate learning design and delivery models can help this process. Second, skills development is particularly important to ensure students are equipped to best take advantage of e-learning. This and the provision of 'non-academic' support require a holistic approach by the institution. Bricheno, Higgison and Weedon (2004) found that successful implementation of networked learning in UK further and higher education was found where enthusiast-led e-learning developments occurred within a top-down strategy. The increased use of e-learning changes the education landscape and the way students need to be supported. Bolting on changes to existing means of course delivery and support will not make the necessary changes; an integrated and holistic view is required.

References

Bates, A. W. and Poole, G. (2003) *Effective Teaching with Technology in Higher Education: foundations for success*, San Francisco CA, Jossey-Bass.

Bricheno, P., Higgison, C. and Weedon, E. (2004) *The Impact of Networked Learning on Education Institutions*, Final Report of the JISC INLEI Project, October 2004, UHI Millennium Institute, University of Bradford and Scottish Further Education Unit, www.sfeuprojects.org.uk/inlei/Final_Report.pdf.

Browne, T. and Jenkins, M. (2003) *VLE Surveys: a longitudinal perspective between March 2001 and March 2003 for higher education in the United Kingdom*, www.ucisa.ac.uk/groups/tlig/vle/index_html.

Core, J., Rothery, A. and Walton, G. (2003) *E-learning Series No 5: a guide for support staff*, York, LTSN Generic Centre.

Jochems, W., van Merrienboer, J. and Koper, R. (eds) (2004) *Integrated e-Learning: implications for pedagogy, technology and organization*, London, RoutledgeFalmer.

Kirkwood, A. and Price, L. (2005) Learners and Learning in the Twenty-first Century: what do we know about students' attitudes towards and experiences of information and communication technologies that will help us design courses?, *Studies in Higher Education*, **30** (3), 257–74.

McAlpine, L. (2004) Designing Learning as well as Teaching: a research-based model for instruction that emphasizes learner practice, *Active Learning in Higher Education*, **5** (2), 119–34.

Oblinger, D. (2003) Boomers, Gen-Xers and Millennials: understanding the new students, *Educause Review*, (July/August), 37–47.

Oliver, R. (2001a) Developing e-Learning Environments that Support Knowledge Construction in Higher Education. In Stoney, S. and Burns, J. (eds), *Working for Excellence in the e-Economy*, Churchlands, Australia, We-B Centre, 407–16.

Oliver, R. (2001b) It Seemed Like a Good Idea at the Time. In Murphy, D., Walker, R. and Webb, G. (eds), *Online Learning and Teaching with Technology: case studies, experience and practice*, London, Kogan Page, 81–7.

Phillips, R. (2004) The Design Dimensions of e-Learning. In Atkinson, R., McBeath, C., Jonas-Dwyer, D. and Phillips, R. (eds), *Beyond the Comfort Zone: proceedings of the 21st ASCILITE conference*, Perth, 5–8 December, 781–90, www.ascilite.org.au/conferences/perth04/procs/phillips.html.

Prosser, M. and Trigwell, K. (1999) *Understanding Learning and Teaching: the experience in higher education*, Buckingham, SRHE and Open University Press.

Quality Assurance Agency for Higher Education (2004) *Code of Practice for the Assurance of Academic Quality and Standards in Higher Education: section 2, collaborative provision and flexible and distributed learning (including e-learning)*, 2nd edn, Gloucester, QAA.

Salmon, G. (2000) *E-moderating: the key to teaching and learning online*, London, Kogan Page.

Simpson, O. (2002) *Supporting Students in Online, Open and Distance Learning*, 2nd edn, London, RoutledgeFalmer.

16

The information commons: a student-centred environment for IT and information literacy development

Hester Mountifield

Abstract

This chapter discusses the concept of an integrated information commons, its success and the benefits it delivers to student learning. The Kate Edger Information Commons at the University of Auckland, New Zealand, is placed in the critical context of current information commons models. This large student-centred learning facility provides proactive integrated learning support in a collaborative, interdisciplinary physical and virtual learning environment. It is the hub of the City Campus, providing an optimum learning experience by facilitating access to the learning resources and support that students need in one location. This chapter examines how opportunities for IT and information literacy (e-literacy) development are integrated into service delivery. Some of the e-literacy challenges still facing the University are also considered.

Introduction

Developments in information technology and the changing student profile have prompted universities and, in particular, university libraries to reconsider the learning and teaching support they provide. The past decade has brought an increasing rate of computer use for learning, teaching, research and communication and has led to significant changes in student characteristics, needs and expectations. The Net Generation or Net Gen, as the group born after 1987 is sometimes called, are 'digital natives', implying that they have grown up with technology (Prensky, 2001). Several authors (Abram and Luther, 2004; Kvavik, 2005; Oblinger and Oblinger, 2005) regard the Net Gen as digitally literate, always connected, highly mobile, able to multitask, format agnostic, comfortable in a visual-rich environment, favouring teamwork and experimental learning, achievement oriented, able to move seamlessly between the physical and virtual environments, and expecting service excellence and immediate responses.

Students arrive at higher education institutions with a variety of digital technologies they use for entertainment, communication and learning. They expect universities to be a continuation of the wired world they are familiar with and allowing them connectivity, control and convenience in their educational experience.

Higher education continues to invest heavily in information technology infrastructure and systems to keep up with progress and to meet the expectations of students and faculty. Conventional and wireless networks, portals and online student services facilitate communication and connection, while course management systems, online library resources and systems, student computers, networked file storage and e-portfolios allow students to plan and manage their learning. This IT-rich learning environment offers ways for the more effective implementation of student-centred learning models such as problem-based learning, evidence-based learning, reflective study and collaborative learning, in turn requiring flexible learning spaces. The impact of the digital revolution on the university library sector is evident in the proliferation of electronic content delivered and supported anywhere and anytime via web-based services, the creation of institutional repositories and the transformation or emergence of physical facilities to address the pervasive impact of technology on resources, services, facilities and customers. An example of such a facility is the information commons. The information commons, not long ago considered an innovation, is fast becoming a mainstream approach to providing a student-centred virtual and physical environment suitable for all styles of learning and research.

It is tempting to conclude that students, particularly the Net Generation, have the appropriate IT and information literacy skills required to succeed in higher education. However, the growth in online and blended learning activities, multitude of database interfaces and the specialist software applications used in education call for a certain level of IT and information literacy among students. The information commons has the potential to play an important role in developing higher-level IT and information literacy attributes among students through its resources and services.

The information commons as a learning environment

Beagle (1999) defines the information commons as 'a new type of physical facility specifically designed to organize workspace and service delivery around the integrated digital environment'. The information commons first appeared in the early 1990s in North America with the Leavey Library at the University of Southern California, the Information Arcade at the University of Iowa and the Information Commons at the University of Toronto as early innovators. Information commons facilities are predominantly located in renovated spaces within university libraries, but purpose-built facilities have started to emerge recently.

Different models and configurations are available, all of which have remarkably similar goals or objectives (Mountifield, 2004; Seal, 2005) that encompass:

- convenience: a centralized and one-stop shop for IT, information and learning needs
- expert support at hand: collaboration between librarians, IT professionals, writing consultants, media specialists, language and learning advisers
- access to a seamless technology-enabled learning environment: latest hardware, software, multimedia, networks and file storage
- accommodating different learning styles: collaborative and individual learning
- promoting IT and information literacy development
- service excellence: self-service, satisfaction and seamlessness
- comfort and collaboration.

Regardless of the variation, three common models can be identified, each more sophisticated than the former. The information commons as a virtual space is described by Beagle (1999) as 'an exclusively online environment in which the widest possible variety of digital services can be accessed via a single graphical user interface'. This model may suit some student needs and preferences but it does not consider the physical and social requirements of learning. The computer laboratory model (White, Beatty and Warren, et al., 2004) focuses on technology, providing a variety of hardware, software and network resources. Collaboration with other campus units is rare and the service model is limited to technical assistance. The third model, on the other hand, advocates integration and collaboration and seems to hold the greatest potential for sustainability and learning.

The integrated model, identified by Bailey and Tierney (2002), focuses on integrating research, teaching and learning activities within the digital and physical environments. This is emerging as the most successful model because the design takes as its guiding principles both the needs and characteristics of the student and changes in higher education. This collaborative environment provides a holistic approach to student learning by integrating the facilities, tools, resources and expertise of learning support providers such as IT professionals, librarians, learning advisers, instructional technologists, multimedia producers, language advisers, writing advisers and others (Mountifield, 2004).

Mountifield (2004), Seal (2005) and White, Beatty and Warren (2004) summarize the benefits and subsequent success of the integrated information commons:

- Students have a common and inclusive experience through consistent and holistic learning support and access to computers with a common software environment, rich in e-content, high-speed networks, multimedia and personal file storage.

- The learning and social needs of all students are met effectively and conveniently.
- It provides a continuum of service that supports the access, use, evaluation, management, integration and creation of information.
- There is flexibility to adapt the physical, virtual and service elements to accommodate changes in technology and in the expectations and needs of students.
- It encourages social and learning communities by providing a convenient, central and comfortable space for learning and socializing, ideal for activities such as collaboration, groupwork, discussions and peer coaching.
- It develops the IT and information literacy skills required to prosper in a complex and multidimensional environment.

The Kate Edger Information Commons

The Kate Edger Information Commons (www.information-commons.auckland.ac.nz), at the University of Auckland in New Zealand, is an example of the integrated collaborative model located in a purpose-built facility. The five-storey facility opened in late April 2003 and provides in different configurations over 1200 seats, including more than 500 full-productivity computers. The Information Commons, a University Library service, presents a collaborative student-centred infrastructure for IT, information services and learning support that facilitates the delivery of customized, comprehensive and convenient services. The facility reflects the transformation of higher education and trends in IT and associated electronic information resources, and was designed to be a welcoming space for the Net Generation student. It includes facilities and spaces that accommodate solitary and collaborative learning; integrates new technologies with services; and establishes dynamic and innovative partnerships between information and learning support providers on campus. The groupwork areas, open consultation and adaptable service points allow a greater tolerance of noise and activity.

Opportunities, strategies and collaboration

The substantial size of the facility created the opportunity to co-locate and consolidate previously geographically dispersed but related learning support services such as:

- The University Library's high-demand print and video collection for arts, science, business and economics students. The collection consists of over 8000 prescribed and recommended texts.
- The University Library's Information Skills team, which works closely with subject librarians across the Library system to design, develop and deliver the Library's multifaceted information literacy programme, initiatives and resources.
- The Student Learning Centre, which assists undergraduate and postgraduate students with the development of learning and performance skills through workshops and individual consultations. The Centre also offers a range of courses covering introductory computing, Microsoft Windows, Microsoft Office, EndNote, SPSS, N4 Classic, Nvivo, SAS and Latex.
- The English Language Self-access Centre (Elsac), which assists all students from non-English speaking backgrounds. It supports the growing number of 'English as another language' students at the University in improving their English language skills through guided self-study in an electronic learning environment available in the Elsac. The electronic learning environment is a programme that gives students access to learning resources, monitors their learning and aids the development of successful self-study skills. The Elsac was transferred to the University Library's Learning Services department as a strategic move to create an integrated and collaborative learning environment.
- The IC Help Service, which was created by merging the IT directorate's Electronic Campus Help Desk with the University Library's Learning Services. The service, consisting of two components, operates in a cross-functional multi-skilled team environment. The IC Help Desk provides walk-in support to students, while the IC Consultants, who are senior students, provide first-tier roaming support on the different levels. They support students using the computers in the Information Commons, work shifts on the IC Help Desk and assist with special projects. IC Consultants have a general knowledge of electronic resources, software and databases in the Information Commons, on the internet, and on the campus network. They are well trained in MS Office software, and are able to provide qualified assistance to users in creating documents and spreadsheets and in other production-related issues. They provide general PC skills support (e.g. accessing files from drives), assist students in the use of the NetAccount authentication system, the Cecil learning management system and the nDeva student administration and online enrolment system, as well as supporting the print, scanning and photocopying systems. The IC Help Desk team offers IT courses which teach students how to use the University's electronic enterprise systems, the extensive IT facilities available to students at the Information Commons and the Library, as well as the basics of the available software, saving, printing, photocopying and scanning.

Strategic partnerships and collaboration between student learning support providers resulted in an enhanced and attractive learning environment. The Kate Edger Information Commons student support service, a new model based on the re-engineering of existing services, is founded on a commitment to service innovation and excellence. The development of IT and information literacy skills in the University community, especially undergraduate students, is a key focus area of the Information Commons. The University Library's Learning Services department collaborates with faculty, the Student Learning Centre and other University units to develop the information literacy of students.

'Vibrant new heart' was how the cover of the *University of Auckland News* (Wilford, 2003) described the Kate Edger Information Commons one month after opening. The Information Commons provides a general learning environment that is considerably different from others on campus. There is a greater tolerance of noise and group collaboration, social activities and food and drink. It is likely to be closer to the working environments that students will experience in their ensuing careers than anywhere else on campus. It accommodates different styles of learning, and the open and flexible nature provides students with greater choice of where, when and how they learn. In keeping with the preferences of the Net Generation, the Information Commons supports collaboration by facilitating the development of learning and social communities.

Staff and students are operating in a complex and multidimensional environment that mandates collaboration. It has become vital to develop partnerships and strategic alliances in order to provide and maintain a student-centred learning environment that improves student learning. The learning support providers in the Kate Edger Information Commons have found that working collaboratively within the learning support environment has significant benefits such as:

- the opportunity to provide a student-centred, integrated seamless support service
- interworking across departments or domains resulting in a cross-functional multi-skilled team environment
- sharing of resources and expertise
- developing new standards and best-practice models
- innovation.

Enabling e-literacy development

The Information Commons at the University of Auckland has responded in a creative and innovative way to contemporary student-learning needs. The learning environment and services are strategically aligned with the University's strategy, direction and commitments to student learning.

For example, several institutional strategic documents and plans, published prior and subsequent to the development of the Information Commons, endorse an institutional approach to lifelong learning and IT and information literacy development. The University of Auckland Academic Plan (2004) articulates the University's commitment to providing 'its graduates with key, high-level generic skills such as the capacity for lifelong critical, conceptual and reflective thinking, and attributes such as creativity and originality'.

The University of Auckland Graduate Profiles (2003) assert that graduates should:

- be able to recognize when information is needed and have the capacity to locate, evaluate and use this information effectively
- have appropriate computer literacy skills
- have a lifelong love and enjoyment of ideas, discovery and learning.

The stated vision for the Kate Edger Information Commons is to provide a highly visible, modern and unique facility which will inspire students to acquire new skills so they can participate more actively in the learning process. The vision is supported by four desired outcomes: e-literacy development, effective information access, access to good-quality facilities and improved support. Developing the information literacy and IT skills of students is the pedagogical intent common to these outcomes and they underpin the service design and delivery as well as ongoing evaluation and enhancement. For example, students are assisted in acquiring skills to locate, retrieve, evaluate and use information effectively through:

- courses in computer, information and learning skills presented in flexible teaching spaces with state-of-the-art audiovisual and presentation technology
- individualized instruction provided through roaming support and in consultation spaces throughout the building
- several layers of instruction, catering for different needs and preferences, in a wide-ranging collection of guides and self-paced tutorials in both print and electronic format.

The University Library offers a multifaceted information literacy programme that has both specialized subject-based and generic components to students and staff. The Information Skills team, based in the Information Commons, provides leadership in developing the programme and co-ordinates the library teaching activities. There has been a significant increase in student and faculty participation in the information literacy programme since the opening in 2003 of the Information Commons. That year there was a 36% increase in student attendance at all library courses, followed by another 21% increase in 2004. Attendance of optional generic courses grew by 109% in 2003 and by 22% in 2004, indicating that students value opportunities to develop their information literacy and are increasingly aware that it enhances their learning. The high visibility of the programme, targeted marketing, increased tailoring of content and the excellent teaching facilities in the Information Commons are major contributors to its ongoing success.

IT literacy, another key-focus of the Information Commons, is developed through the point-of-need roaming support provided by the IC Consultants and through hands-on courses offered by the Student Learning Centre and the IT Help Service. IT literacy is a key attribute required to support learning, teaching and research. Most students in higher education require a diverse range of skills in the use of computer applications and technologies relevant to their discipline (Mountifield, 2004). The approach to IT literacy at the University of Auckland is for the most part low-key and not as well developed as the information literacy programme.

E-literacy challenges

Martin (2003) identifies several challenges in advancing e-literacy at an institutional level. The system-wide implementation of institutional policies and plans is a strategic challenge facing university and faculty management structures. Although these documents and policies demonstrate a clear commitment to IT and information literacy development, the coherent and systematic implementation varies greatly among disciplines. However, implementing policies and plans often requires additional financial, operational and staffing resources, as well as conceptual buy-in.

Martin (2003) states that collaboration within the institution or between institutions has the potential to improve the delivery of e-literacy initiatives. Collaboration, however, is often encumbered by the cultural, administrative and political barriers between partners. A collaborative approach to e-literacy development requires careful planning, a shared understanding of the desired outcomes, clearly defined and interconnected roles, as well as recognition of expertise and differences. The successful collaboration between learning support providers in the Kate Edger Information Commons has resulted in redefining the approach to e-literacy and the new initiatives are supported by University management. Integrating e-literacy development as a core focus area of an integrated and collaborative learning environment such as the information commons is a direction to consider when addressing e-literacy issues.

Conclusion

The integrated information commons model at the University of Auckland was extended through the opening of satellite facilities at the Medical and Education campuses. In student surveys of both undergraduates and postgraduates, the information commons facilities are consistently given the highest satisfaction rating of any University of Auckland service or facility evaluated.

The integrated collaborative information commons model is an innovative, holistic and learner-centred approach to supporting and improving student learning. It facilitates autonomous, resource-based learning in an open and flexible environment and fosters lifelong learning by promoting, developing and supporting the acquisition of transferable skills such as IT and information literacy. Critical to this model's ongoing development and success are:

- ongoing research into current and emerging trends in higher education, information and communication technology and e-learning
- reflection and reappraisal of services, activities and feedback
- a flexible design that can adapt in response to the results from research and reflection
- the ability of collaborators to integrate their services, capabilities and potential into the learning process and campus-wide learning initiatives.

This particular model has proved to be very successful at the University of Auckland. The rewards in terms of student usage and improved learning support provide an ongoing return on the strategic, operational and financial investment made by the University.

References

Abram, S. and Luther, J. (2004) Born with the Chip, *Library Journal*, (May), 34–7.

Bailey, R. and Tierney, B. (2002) Information Commons Redux: concept, evolution, and transcending the tragedy of the Commons, *Journal of Academic Librarianship*, **28** (5), 277–86.

Beagle, D. (1999) Conceptualizing the Information Commons, *Journal of Academic Librarianship*, **25** (2), 82–9.

Kvavik, R. B. (2005) Convenience, Communication, and Control: how students use technology. In Oblinger, D. and Oblinger J. (eds), *Educating the Net Generation*, EDUCAUSE, www.educause.edu/educatingthenetgen (accessed 31 May 2005).

Martin, A. (2003) Towards E-literacy. In Martin, A. and Rader, H. (eds), *Information and IT Literacy: enabling learning in the 21st century*, London, Facet Publishing.

Mountifield, H. (2004) The Kate Edger Information Commons – a student-centred learning environment and catalyst for integrated learning support and e-literacy development, *Jelit: Journal of eLiteracy*, **1** (2), www.jelit.org/archive/00000035/ (accessed 31 May 2005).

Oblinger, D. and Oblinger, J. (2005) Is It Age or IT: first steps toward understanding the Net Generation. In Oblinger, D. and Oblinger J. (eds), *Educating the Net Generation*, EDUCAUSE, www.educause.edu/educatingthenetgen (accessed 31 May 2005).

Prensky, M. (2001) Digital Natives, Digital Immigrants, *On the Horizon*, **9** (5), 1–6.

Seal, R. A. (2005) The Information Commons: new pathways to digital resources and knowledge management. In *The 3rd China–United States Library Conference: proceedings of an international conference held on 22–25 March 2005, organized by the National Library of China*, www.nlc.cn/culc/en/call.htm (accessed 9 March 2005).

University of Auckland Academic Plan 2005–2007: Draft (2004), www.auckland.ac.nz/docs/teaching/pdfs/Academic_plan_2005-2007.pdf (accessed 31 May 2005).

University of Auckland Graduate Profiles (2003), www.auckland.ac.nz/cir_teaching/index.cfm?action= display_page&page_title=graduate_profiles (accessed 31 May 2005).

White, P., Beatty, S. and Warren, D. (2004) Information Commons. In *Encyclopedia of Library and Information Science*, Marcel Dekker Inc., www.dekker.com/servlet/product/DOI/101081EELIS120020359.

Wilford, J. (2003) Information Commons Packed from the Start, *University of Auckland News*, **33** (5), 3–4.

17

Socio-cultural approaches to literacy and subject knowledge development in learning management systems

Neil Anderson

Abstract

Literacy development is increasingly mediated in digital, online environments such as learning management systems (LMS). These systems have been criticized for their lack of social presence, thereby reducing their impact for literacy and subject content learning. This chapter examines the definitions and descriptions of LMS and their characteristics. It then describes a blended model of on-campus and online delivery of courses in Australia and Singapore and examines some issues concerning advantages and disadvantages of LMS, with particular reference to enhancing the social elements or 'social presence' embedded in the system. Student feedback, survey data and a literature review inform an examination of issues such as ease of access, equity and the critical notion of 'social presence' in online spaces. Feedback was collected from public postings on a discussion board, online surveys, e-mail communications and paper-based surveys. This involved 495 students across three subjects in an Australian teacher pre-service preparation undergraduate course and one subject from a Singapore-based Master of Education subject.

Introduction

In the past, online learning environments have been characterized by a wide variety of features depending on the operating system, software tools and experience of the creator. Often, in educational contexts the knowledge of effective pedagogy has not been matched by equivalent knowledge of programming, web design or competency in using appropriate online tools. This sometimes created a tension between educators on one hand and technicians on the other, when the technical construction of online environments was outsourced or created in teams.

Learning management systems have developed as a means to cater for the needs of educators who may not have a high level of knowledge, or the time to construct their own custom-made e-learning environment. These systems provide a standardized 'shell' that includes a set of tools commonly used in online courses. Terms and definitions attributed to these systems are still in a state of evolution and are sometimes confusing or contradictory.

Merely paying attention to technical competencies and efficiencies in some cases has led to barren and impersonal environments with few opportunities for students to develop literacy and subject knowledge in ways that take advantage of social and cultural shared understandings and engagement. Lankshear (2003, 183) emphasizes the 'socio-cultural approach to literacy' within 'new literacies' that he describes as 'literacies associated with new communication and information technologies, or in more general terms, the digital apparatus'. Gee, when discussing socio-cultural approaches to literacy, alludes to the importance of 'social presence' and the intersection and interplay of elements in any learning environment. He argues that 'each element in a coordination, whether human or not, simultaneously plays two roles: it actively coordinates the other elements and it passively gets coordinated by the other elements in the coordination … within such coordinations we humans become recognizable to ourselves and to others and recognize ourselves, other people, and things as meaningful in distinctive ways,' (see Lankshear, 1997, xiv). This is a powerful way of thinking about the use of learning management systems because they are clearly sets of non-human elements associated with the ICT system and human elements that need to be co-ordinated in ways that lead to dynamic, interesting and socially and culturally rich environments where learning can flourish. In the following sections of this chapter, the technical elements and definitions of LMS will be discussed along with the important notion of increasing 'social presence' through the use of blended (face-to-face and online) delivery and through additions to the elements included in the learning management system.

Definitions of learning management systems

In Australia, Hong Kong, Singapore and the USA, the term 'learning management system' (LMS) is commonly (but not exclusively) used, whereas in the UK, the commonly used term is 'virtual learning environment' (VLE), and this fits within the broader 'managed learning environment' (MLE). In various research papers concerning these systems, the terms can be synonymous and therefore confusing. Wilson, cited in Anderson and Baskin (2002), defines common LMS functionalities as 'integrating all of the well established advantages of the world wide web … [and] as a place where learners may work together and support each other as they use a variety of tools and information resources in their pursuit of learning goals and problem solving activities'. On the other hand, Everett (2002) argues that 'the term Virtual Learning Environment (VLE) is used to refer to the "online" interactions of various kinds, including online learning … Managed Learning Environment (MLE) is used to include the whole range of information systems and processes of a college (including its VLE if it has one) that contribute directly, or indirectly, to learning and management of that learning.'

In contrast, Hicks and Ingram (2001) define the MLE as synonymous with the LMS (VLE): 'a managed learning environment (MLE) is a web based system that provides academic staff with a coursework shell to manage an online learning environment.' While Hicks refers to these systems as tools for academic staff, others describe these systems as commercial programmes that provide a set of standardized, web-based tools. These definitions are defective in that learning management systems are not only for academics and tertiary systems because they are now commonly used in schools, clubs and organizations or for community-based training. Nor are they strictly commercial products – a free open-source program, Moodle, is becoming increasingly popular. Defining the MLEs as an overarching system that includes all of the information managements systems of the organization is a useful one. The term 'virtual learning environment' conjures up a very general and open image of an online environment, whereas 'learning management systems' more appropriately describes the limited and standardized model that these software systems embody. The description of an LMS as a 'shell' is appropriate because the standardized tools can be used to wrap around a standard website. This is a model often used in tertiary settings as the standard website within the shell offers a greater degree of flexibility. For the purposes of this chapter, an LMS refers to a set of standardized, user-friendly tools that operate within a 'shell' that allows experienced and non-experienced users to set up an online learning environment.

Anderson and Baskin (2002) point out that there are numerous authoring tools available that allow non-programmers to create their own instructional environment within the confines of the particular LMS. Each LMS varies slightly according to the preferences of the developer and these parameters confine the user in various ways. However, the basic components of an LMS are common. The JISC (2003, 19) lists the principle functions of an LMS to include 'controlled access to a curriculum – mapped into chunks, tracking of student activity and achievement; support of online learning such as access to learning resources, assessment and guidance; communication between the staff–students, student–student, other specialists and to build a sense of group identity and community of interest; links to the administrative system'. These systems typically link to the administrative system in rudimentary ways such as using the student enrolment database so that student names for each subject do not have to be entered manually. It is anticipated that the LMS will link to administrative databases in more powerful ways in future developments and that there will be easier ways to export and import data across different types of LMS.

Open-source and low-cost learning management systems

Many universities support the concept of using and developing open-source software, such as the increasingly popular Moodle. Perceived benefits include flexibility and cost saving along with participation in an open development community. Brandl (2005, 11) reports that Moodle stands for 'Modular Object-Oriented Dynamic Learning Environment' and points out that its development 'is based on social-constructivist pedagogy', since it supports an inquiry-based and discovery-based approach to learning. Moodle includes many of the features described in the preceding section, as well as some features unique to this open-source offering. Pfaffman (2005) outlines a useful feature concerning the generation of an automatic calendar where students can quickly and easily see when assignments are due and praises another feature that allows teachers to switch quickly from the view students see to the 'edit' mode used by instructors. Hinton (2005) describes Moodle as 'a viable, high-performing product'. Hall (2005) also outlines six 'low-cost' products that are alternatives to either open-source or higher-end commercial learning management systems. Obviously, educators and administrators have several choices when deciding on the best LMS solution to their particular needs.

Blended models of learning management systems

This chapter examines a 'blended' model where the LMS is not used to deliver a course or subject totally externally. It examines feedback from students enrolled in courses where there was a mixture of face-to-face and external delivery. In all cases the number of face-to-face lectures had been reduced from a more traditional model to an alternative where students had reduced contact hours in terms of lectures and onsite tutorials. Moore and Barab (2002) used a blended approach in teacher preparation and concluded that the face-to-face sessions had great value in establishing long-term relationships. In a similar vein, Brosnan and Burgess (2003) found that the initial face-to-face component resulted in the establishment of more effective social networks and therefore greater student participation. Wiesenburg and Willment (2001) argue that a particular strength of a blended approach is that it can 'extend beyond typically time-limited opportunities' of face-to-face models. Taylor (2002) claims that courses offering a blended model of on- and off-campus delivery are becoming more popular with working students and busy parents because they often have less time required at the university but still offer face-to-face support. This claim is supported by the data from both Australian and Singaporean students. In the Australian context, many of the students were studying full time but also supporting themselves by part-time employment that sometimes approaches full-time employment. Many of the mature students reported time constraints associated with family commitments. In Singapore the students undertaking masters degrees worked full time in teaching and appreciated the opportunity to undertake courses in block mode that entailed two weeks of intensive face-to-face and online contact followed by external studies online. In this case the blended approach was perhaps the *only* way that students could undertake study.

Considering that blended courses are a convenient model for students and that learning management systems offer academics a relatively easy way to construct online environments, it is an important area for investigation in terms of the advantages and disadvantages of such systems and how the online component can more effectively support the face-to-face component. Simply providing lecture notes and text online does not constitute an effective online learning environment. Baskin and Anderson (2003) and Baskin, Barker and Woods (2003) point out that although using learning management systems in education is seen as a desirable innovation, the claims of great success attributed to the LMS is largely unsubstantiated and further research needs to be undertaken in this area.

Characteristics of learning management systems

'Ease of use' is often cited as the main advantage of the LMS and, in support of this claim, Morgan (2003) found that this was the main criterion for initial selection. Ease of use is also linked to advantages in terms of economics. If academics can easily produce their own learning environment, extra money once paid to multimedia and programming experts could be saved. Professional web-based courses were initially very expensive to produce. Potential savings, particularly in the current, cost-cutting environment, were recognized by the JISC (2003, 119) when it pointed out that 'colleges need to juggle the realities of increased competition and heightened quality expectations at a time of reduced real-time funding. Only through change can they succeed. Technology may provide a solution – through Managed Learning Environments.' Critics would argue that constructing effective online environments is still expensive in terms of time and cost, despite using an LMS.

Some critics such as Huang et al. (2004) argue that learning management systems do not adequately cater for different learning styles and teaching methods. Counter-claims are that course materials can be presented in many different ways, e.g. text, graphics, audio, animations or video; and many different learning styles can be catered for, providing the instructor deliberately uses a variety of presentation techniques. Another argument is that an LMS can also display an external web page within the standard shell. This way the students or participants see the standard buttons and layout of LMS shell (usually on the left) and the external website on the right, thus providing consistency with other offerings, and an integrated look. This is an obvious way of supporting items such as complex learning objects or interactions that are not supported by the LMS shell alone. As far as the student is concerned, it appears as an integrated page as the LMS shell wraps around the web page. Although this negates the restriction of the system it also means that academics need to construct a web page or learning objects, interactions, etc., or pay someone else to do it.

Some systems may prove to be constraining, although they may be economical in terms of purchase and training costs. Hicks and Ingram (2001) suggest that 'because of its generic nature it is unlikely to be suitable for all the needs of each academic or for all of the particular needs of teaching within specific disciplines'. They claim that a single LMS is controlling, vulnerable to changes in the market and limited in its ability to suit all comers and advocates the use of more than one LMS within an institution. Having a suite of learning management systems within one institution would be costly and also difficult to manage.

In terms of supporting effective pedagogy, the LMS has critics and supporters. Hong, Lai and Holton (2001) report that the LMS environment can support constructivist pedagogy and need not be a content-driven transmission model. They recommend activities that are connected to 'realistic' professional activities and involve problem solving. In this model the LMS tools are used by students to create and post-graphic organizers so that their thinking processes are made explicit, and they are often given a choice of problems to solve that are connected to the topic of study. Likewise, Johnston and Cooley (2001) argue that virtual learning environments 'are forcing pedagogical shifts – shifts from the teachers controlling the teaching to the students controlling the learning'. However, this is not necessarily the case because an LMS can more easily support a content-driven delivery that is very much in the control of the teacher, although creative teachers can often use a set of tools that appears to support a content-driven model in a subversive way that opens up all sorts of possibilities.

Another challenge reported in the literature by Burford and Cooper (2000) is that some excellent face-to-face teachers have difficulty transposing their skills to the LMS environment and that there isn't an automatic transfer of skills and success from one environment to another. This highlights the need for professional development that includes not only the skills in using the tools inherent in the LMS but also ways of using effective pedagogy in online environments. An emerging area of research concerning pedagogy is the notion of 'social presence' in online environments.

Social presence in learning management systems

Garrison (cited in Stacey 2002, 288) defines social presence as 'the degree to which participants are able to project themselves within the medium'. In addition, Rice (cited in Stacey, 2002, 288) argues that 'social presence can be projected best when verbal and non-verbal cues and the context can also be communicated'. Stacey's (2002) research confirms the importance of the teacher's role in establishing social presence of all participants in the online environment. Some institutions require that all online students attend some activities on campus so that students can get to know their professors and their peers. These activities, which may be orientation or social activities rather than academic tasks, highlight the importance that these institutions place on social aspects of learning (Taylor, 2002). It is also important that the online learning environment supports the continuation of these critical social elements. Despite the addition of many features to enhance social presence in one of the author's Australian undergraduate causes several students posted comments such as:

> Given that most of this subject occurred online, it lacked the student/teacher feel. Also the fact that computers can sometimes be very unreliable created some difficulties amongst students i.e. freezing during quiz's and whilst entering topics.
>
> (Student posting, 2004)

Some students, however, object to online discussions being used for social and academic communication. One Singapore-based student posted the following thoughts:

> The bad thing is that the blackboard can be 'messy' because students can write whatever they wish, whether relevant or not. So, there has to be a mediator. I know, this allows for 'creativity', but yet on the other hand, it can be confusing.
>
> (Student posting, 2004)

Smith, Ferguson and Caris (2001) report on research that demonstrates that many teachers feel that 'social presence' is a diminished factor in online delivery in that they 'cannot use their presence and their classroom skills to get their point across. Nor can they use their oral skills to improvise on the spot.' Educators need to closely examine various means of increasing social presence in online environments. Key areas for examination include the way synchronous and asynchronous communications are used, the way that group identity is established and maintained, and the advantages of using video and audio.

Although synchronous and asynchronous discussions are supported in learning and management systems, Wang and Newlin (2001) lament that there is often an absence of synchronous discussions in online courses and argue the case for the inclusion of synchronous models where 'instructors can lecture to students and questions can be answered immediately. Follow-up questions can also be addressed immediately at an appropriate level of detail. Moreover, the instructor can inquire as to whether the students are clear on aspects of course materials.' They rate synchronous communication highly in regard to increasing social presence and point out that

> research has shown that increasing the social presence of others serves to increase student satisfaction and performance in a computer mediated environment. We have found that chat rooms enhance the social presence of instructors and their students in a way that cannot be done by asynchronous communication.

They feel that using this type of communication helps reduce the loneliness and isolation experienced by students involved in online learning. Although these factors can be somewhat mitigated by the use of blended models, the sense of belonging engendered in the initial face-to-face sessions needs to be extended in the online environment.

Group identity may be strengthened by the use of synchronous discussion. Coghlan (2004) supports this notion and argues that group identity is enhanced through synchronous communications: 'group identity is better, more quickly and more powerfully formed through synchronous interactions, and even more so if the interactions are voice based'. These interactions need to be between the instructor and the students and between the students themselves. Although asynchronous discussions do not have the immediacy of synchronous communication, they can enhance social presence in different ways, for different kinds of students. Taylor (2002) asserts that asynchronous discussion boards are particularly beneficial because students have extra time to respond and personality traits such as shyness, cultural differences or disability are not as constraining as in face-to face models of delivery. Many student postings support this point of view:

> I like working on the discussion board because of its ease of use. It is also the only place where I feel comfortable as discussions take a relaxed stand. I can look at a question, ponder over it and take my time to answer it. At the same time I can read what my fellow comrades have got to say. I do not mind looking at comments on other related areas as long as they stay relevant to the topic.
>
> (Student posting, 2004)

Another student responded:

> The subject site is great. So is the blackboard. I think the subject site is very organised and it's easy to use. The fact that you can take your own sweet time to go through the material and answer the questions, allows us time to reflect and engage in critical thinking.
>
> (Student posting, 2004)

Lavooy and Newlin (2003) report that asynchronous discussions allowed them to address the concerns of students throughout the course; this resulted in less confusion and in an environment more conducive to learning. In blended approaches, students who are reticent to speak up in on-campus classes may feel more comfortable about voicing their concerns online, particularly if they have time to consider their response and alter it before posting.

Hong, Lai and Holton (2001, 235) argue that, in either synchronous or asynchronous models, it is essential to have students working in groups for some of the tasks. They emphasize the importance of mandated groupwork in which 'students can be given questions and activities that must be completed in groups rather than individually. The web is an improvement over normal group-based activities because what each student does is published in some way.' This type of group work could add substantially to establishing group identity.

Use of video in online environments can enhance the quality of social presence, although difficulties in viewing video over low-bandwidth modem connections remain a challenge. Some researchers claim that these techniques can be expensive if supported by professionals. For example, Walstad et al. (2003, 4) argue that investments of US$100,000 plus are necessary for developing courses with video because 'specialists in media production and web page development are crucial to success. This allows faculty to focus on scope, content, organization, and delivery while the media experts handle the technology and facilitate effective presentation of the material.' After a trial they conclude that 'video and web-based distance education courses are convenient and effective ways to reach motivated but place-bound students and professionals ... they also provide a convenient alternative for campus-based students with scheduling difficulties'.

In contrast, the author and colleague Ruth Hickey (Hickey and Anderson, 2003) used low-cost digital cameras and computer hardware with pre-service teachers as actors to produce a video-based website to highlight practical science experiments and how to assess the results. This economically produced website was partly develoed to add an additional 'practical' experience of science in a classroom setting to overcome the minimum time that students spend in practical school-based settings. Though the production costs were minimal, the result was very effective according to a student survey and follow-up interviews. Students responded to questions after making use of the site in their elementary school science curriculum subject. See Figure 17.1.

In this case, preparation prior to production with an emphasis on using video to provide powerful, thought-provoking examples, coupled with activities leading to intellectual engagement, were more important than slick production. Responses to important questions about conceptual development, relevancy and making decisions about assessment were rated by almost all students as OK ranging to very good, with the majority in the higher rating levels.

Question	1	2	3	4	5	n/a
1. How well did the video download on your computer?	1		3	11	10	2
2. How much did you learn about learning activities?			5	14	6	2
3. How much did you learn about assessment decisions?		1	3	16	7	
4. How helpful was the support text for the video clips?		1	4	14	8	
5. How helpful was the option to print the support text?	1		2	10	11	3
6. How much did you learn about children's conceptual development in science concepts?	1	1	9	14	2	
7. How relevant was the website to your needs as a pre-service teacher?			4	12	10	1
8. How interesting did you find the website?			5	15	7	

N=27. 1 'unacceptable', 2 'can live with it', 3 'OK', 4 'good', 5 'very good'

Figure 17.1 *Student feedback on science education website (Hickey and Anderson, 2003)*

Van Horn (2004) reports that the convenience and time-saving features of web-based video is an important feature. He demonstrates that many pages of explanation in a book can be covered with a short video and this leads to a greater understanding. In addition, the use of slide bar controls enables quick locating of critical sections and still frames compared with traditional video. He acknowledges the limitations of video over dial-up modems, although in this is steadily changing as students have access to broadband at home and at their places of study. In the study by Hickey and Anderson (2003), the majority of students indicated that they were very satisfied with the download speeds of the video and this could be accounted for by the strategy of including different size video files, so that students could choose according to their bandwidth. Some students, however, reported that accessing even simple pages via an LMS can take longer than viewing standard web pages. One Singapore-based student commented:

> The high capability of Blackboard implies that it needs supporting structures in order to achieve good system performance. These supporting structures include network infra-

structure, bandwith/speed of access, availability of access points, PC capabilities etc. I am experiencing this limitation right now as I notice that it takes me long time to navigate in the Blackboard, compared to that for other web sites.

(Student posting, 2004)

When students can comfortably access digital video via reasonable bandwidth, it has been found to be particularly useful to demonstrate how to solve 'real-life' problems, particularly when the clips are limited to between five and ten minutes (Shore, Shore and Boggs, 2004).

Another group of undergraduate students at James Cook University was offered web-based case studies via the LMS as part of its early childhood education studies. In this instance, students were presented with scenarios known to have occurred in school situations. These scenarios were aimed at extending the students' practical knowledge of situations and they provided links to a range of human and web-based resources to help the students to develop possible solutions to these problems. Audio presentations in the form of radio plays were used to present the scenarios in preference to video. This had the advantage in terms of ease of production and enabled a better download rate for students using slower modem connections. In a similar style to the video example discussed earlier in the chapter, lecturers and students undertook the acting roles, thereby reducing costs. A web-based survey revealed that 88% of the students questioned either agreed or strongly agreed that it was valuable to participate in a community of learners such as this (Sorin, 2004). Students were encouraged to add comments and the following is typical of the positive response:

Discussing the various situations online with my colleagues was on the whole, a great learning experience. It accentuated the benefits of discussing problems to find the best possible range of solutions. A key element of teaching practice, I believe – discussion, collegiality and looking at a situation or problem from different perspectives.

(Sorin, 2004, 109)

Conclusion

Although encouraging examples of LMS use have been presented in this chapter an even greater number of examples of problematic use could have been highlighted. Changes need to occur in the technical make-up of an LMS, in the adoption of technologies such as wireless networking and mobile phone/PDA access and in the pedagogy embedded in LMS structure and educators' online mindsets. The JISC (2003, 19) claims that successful implementation will require 'organisational culture change, standards that are interoperable so data from different systems can be exchanged, support and information from central bodies, management administration and vendors should be encouraged to make the systems talk to each other'. As far as pedagogy is concerned this chapter has argued that LMS delivery requires a greater level of 'social presence' through increased use of synchronous communication, thoughtful use of video and audio and greater use of problem-based, collaborative learning. Gee (2002, 212), when outlining what he considers to be important principles for learning and literacy, argues that to be effective, learners should 'constitute an "affinity group" that, is, a group that is bonded primarily through shared endeavors, goals and practices'. It is the responsibility of educators designing and working within online spaces to provide a mixture of elements and tasks that take account of 'social presence' to enhance literacy development and learning.

References

Anderson, N. and Baskin, C. (2002) Can We Leave It to Chance? New learning technologies and the problem of professional competence, *International Education Journal*, **3** (3).

Baskin, C. and Anderson, N. (2003) *The Butterflies of Managed Learning Environments (MLE) and How to Get Them Flying in Formation – the promise of e-publishing*, Brisbane, Pearson Publishing Services.

Baskin, C., Barker, M. and Woods, P. (2003) Towards a Smart Community: rethinking the use of ICTs in teaching and learning, *Higher Education Research and Development*, **19** (2).

Brandl, K. (2005) Are You Ready to Moodle?, *Language, Learning and Technology*, **8**.

Brosnan, K., and Burgess, R. (2003) Web Bases Continuing Professional Development: a learning architecture approach, *Journal of Workplace Learning*, **15** (1), 24–33.

Burford, S. and Cooper, L. (2000) Online Development Using WebCT: a faculty managed process for quality, *Australian Journal of Educational Technology*, **16** (3).

Coghlan, M. (2004) The Role of Synchronous Interactions in eLearning Environments, *Proceedings of the Australian Computers in Education Conference*, Adelaide.

Everett, R. (2002) *Briefing Paper No. 1: What are VLEs and MLEs?*, Brighton, Social Informatics Research Unit, University of Brighton.

Gee, J. P. (2002) *What Video Games Have to Teach Us about Learning and Literacy*, New York NY, Palgrave Macmillan.

Hall, B. (2005) Low-cost LMSs, *Training*, (April), www.trainingmag.com (accessed February 2006).

Hickey, R. and Anderson, N. (2003) The Science Website: making judgements about science understandings. In Constantinos, P. Constantinou, Z. and Zacharia, C. (eds), *Proceedings of the Sixth Conference on Computer Based Learning in Science (CBLIS)*, Nicosia, University of Cyprus.

Hicks, O. and Ingram, D. (2001) *A Pluralist Approach to Managed Learning Environments*, University of Western Australia, www.itpo.uwa.edu.au/Pluralist-Approach-to-MLEs.html.

Hinton, B. (2005) Is Open Source the Answer?, *Learning and Leading with Technology*, (November).

Hong, K., Lai, K. and Holton, D. (2001) Web Based Learning Environments: observations from a web based course in a Malaysian context, *Australian Journal of Educational Technology*, **17** (3).

Huang, W., Yen, D., Lin, Z. and Huang, J. (2004) How to Compete in a Global Education Market Effectively: a conceptual framework for designing a next generation eEducation system, *Journal of Global Information Management*, **12** (2).

JISC (2003) *Managed Learning Environment Activity in Further and Higher Education in the UK*, Brighton, Social Informatics Research Unit, University of Brighton.

Johnston, M. and Cooley, N. (2001) Toward More Effective Instructional Uses of Technology: the shift to virtual learning, *Technology Source*, (November/December).

Lankshear, C. (1997) *Changing Literacies*, Buckingham, Open University Press.

Lankshear, C. (2003) *New Literacies*, Buckingham, Open University Press.

Lavooy, M. and Newlin, M. (2003) Computer Mediated Communication: online instruction and interactivity, *Journal of Interactive Learning Research*, **14** (2).

Moore, J. and Barab, S. (2002) The Inquiry Learning Form: a community of practice approach to online professional development, *TechTrends*, **46** (3), 44.

Morgan, G. (2003) Faculty Use of Course Management Systems, Educause Center for Applied Research, www.educause, edu/ecar/.

Pfaffman, J. (2005) Open Source Solutions – Moodle, *Learning and Leading with Technology*, (October).

Shore, M., Shore, J. and Boggs, S. (2004) Using Spreadsheets and Streaming Video for Developmental, Teacher Education Mathematics Courses, *Mathematics and Computer Education*, **38** (2).

Smith, G., Ferguson, D. and Caris, M. (2001) Teaching College Courses Online vs Face-to-face, *THE Journal*, **28** (9).

Sorin, R. (2004) Webfolio: an online learning community to help link university studies and classroom practice in preservice teacher education, *Australian Journal of Educational Technology*, **20** (1).

Stacey, E. (2002) *Social Presence Online: networking learners at a distance*, Dordrecht, Netherlands, Education and Information Technologies Publications.

Taylor, S. (2002) Education Online: off course or on track?, *Community College Week*, **14** (20).

Van Horn, R. (2004) Empowering Technology for Teacher Education, *Phi Delta Kappan*, **85** (9).

Walstad, J., Reed, M., Doescher, P. and Kauffman, J. (2003) Distance Education: a new course in wildland fire ecology, *Journal of Forestry*, **101** (7).

Wang, A. and Newlin, H. (2001) Online Lectures: benefits for the virtual classroom, *THE Journal*, **29** (1).

Wiesenberg, F. P. and Willment, J. A. H. (2001) Creating Continuing Professional Online Learning Communities, *Adult Learning*, **12** (1).

18

Approaches to enabling digital literacies: successes and failures

Alex Reid

Abstract

This chapter outlines a range of approaches that have been adopted in various universities in order to address the issue of achieving acceptable levels of information and communications technology (ICT) literacy among the staff and student body. Some of these have been successful, while others have failed. In each case an effort is made to identify the reasons for success or failure, including local factors; it then seeks to draw out general principles evidenced by these cases, which should lead to improved success in future.

Introduction

Information and communications technology (ICT) literacy is now universally considered an essential skill needed by university staff to undertake their research and teaching, and by students to undertake their studies. Graduates in almost all walks of life are expected to possess ICT skills, in varying depth. Many different approaches have been adopted by universities to improving the levels of ICT literacy among their staff and students. Some have been more successful than others but, since ICT literacy is rarely an end in itself, it is hard to assess the degree of 'success' or 'failure' of any particular approach. Much depends on the prevailing culture of the institution, what current levels of literacy exist, and what goals one has. What does seem clear is that the establishment of clear, achievable goals and an institutional commitment are vital, along with an understanding that 'ICT literacy' is not something that can be achieved once and for all, since the desired level of literacy is a moving target, which will continue to move (perhaps even accelerate) indefinitely (Winship, 2001; CEPIS, 2005). The following variety of approaches is presented to illustrate these claims, and to offer ideas that may be more or less appropriate in different cultural and technical environments.

Free and rich repertoire of classroom-based courses

Some universities have taken the approach of providing free-of-charge a wide range of (ever-changing) face-to-face courses. They are usually open to all staff (academic and general) as well as to postgraduate students and sometimes undergraduates. These courses are typically organized and managed by a small full-time staff contingent, supplemented by contributions made by technical specialists for more esoteric courses. The courses aim to cover a full spectrum of ICT skills, being constantly upgraded as technology and demand vary. A typical repertoire of courses that fits this model is offered by Oxford University (Oxford University Computing Services, n.d), where this has been done for many years, peaking at about 50,000 person-hours of training delivered per year between 1998 and 2002.

The emphasis at Oxford has always been on quality, and feedback from attendees is consistently very positive. The degree of usage of this service, together with the positive feedback, has ensured that the University has continued to support the necessary budget to meet the costs. Some institutions which do not charge for courses find that a significant portion of enrolments do not attend. Various approaches are adopted to deal with this, including overbooking and charging only for non-attendance. Experience at Oxford University has been that neither of these approaches is necessary as long as the quality and value are kept high.

As well as the cost of the staff involved, providing these courses also involves establishing and maintaining a suite of classrooms, equipped with reasonably current computers. Some universities, especially those which have succumbed to economic rationalism, assert that a charge should be levied for such services as these courses. This is necessary, they argue, on the grounds that people do not value what they do not pay for, that this is a natural test of real demand, that it serves to regulate demand, and that it ensures the provider is highly responsive to real need. There is some value in the notion that the service can automatically expand or contract in response to fluctuating demand (the classic 'market-driven' model), rather than wait for the lengthy budget cycles required of central funding allocations. However, this model fails to recognize that a university environment is certainly not a 'free economy', which requires a 'level playing field', disposable funds and perfect knowledge of alternatives on the part of the consumer, the ability of the provider to expand or contract in line with market demands (most employment contracts will not allow this), and the real possibility that a provider may 'become bankrupt'.

Other drawbacks of the market model include the cost of collection of course charges and, more significantly, staff and especially students often find it very difficult to gain access to the necessary funds. Most institutions are moving towards making the acquisition of ICT skills a strategic goal, so to make this a matter of 'personal preference', and to insert impediments to this action, are counterproductive. There are even those who argue that the market model saves the university money – not just because it reduces demand (a questionable objective anyway), but also because anything that reduces central budgets must be a saving – forgetting that it is a zero-sum game.

The discussion of the market economy has been something of a diversion from the main thrust of this approach to providing ICT skills training. However, the aim has been to present the various issues involved in whether or not to charge for training so that, if a discussion and decision are required, at least the pros and cons can be considered. The success of a free and comprehensive approach to skills training revolves around the quality and quantity of courses offered, the strategic support of the institution to ICT skill acquisition that it represents, and the generally greater penetration and skills acquisition that is achieved. Its principal drawback is its cost.

Extensive use of ECDL/ICDL

The European Computer Driving Licence (and its companion International Computer Driving Licence) has become a benchmark for ICT skills (www.ecdl.com), and is finding increased exposure within the university sector. It has widespread acceptance internationally and has become the world's leading ICT skills certification programme (ECDL/ICDL, n.d.).

The European Computer Driving Licence (ECDL) comprises seven modules covering:

- concepts of ICT
- using the computer and managing files
- word processing
- spreadsheets
- databases
- presentation and drawing
- information and communication.

The ECDL prescribes a curriculum and provides training material and tests, as well as certification. For a relative newcomer to ICT, it would require between 50 and 70 hours of study to achieve full certification. It is comprehensive and widely accepted as an independent measure of ICT competence in industry. Within the university sector, however, it represents a level of competence which is probably higher than necessary for many purposes required by staff and students. It is possible, of course, to pick and choose elements, and lower levels of competence are recognized.

Many universities now offer ECDL training, and some are accredited testers for certification. The key elements of the ECDL are the tests and certification; however, an ECDL textbook is available and it is also possible to acquire ECDL-specific online and face-to-face training courses from a range of providers, which are often then offered by universities alongside their other ICT training opportunities. They are sometimes closely integrated – for instance, so that typical short-course offerings can eventually build up to cover the full ECDL curriculum. Since the costs of proving some of these resources, and in administering the tests, involve significant outgoings, some or all of these costs are typically passed on to learners. This approach also reflects the fact that the certificate is a personal asset, typically representing a higher standard than required for ICT literacy within universities.

In summary, because of its costs and the higher standards than those required by most universities, it seems unlikely that the ECDL will become a primary element of institutional ICT literacy programmes, but it will remain at best a valuable supplement to them.

Reliance on peer support for just-in-time learning

At the opposite extreme from the approaches detailed above is total reliance on self-help and peer-help. This has been widely used in the past, especially among the scientific community within universities, and has its roots in the time when computers (usually mainframes) were the province of a handful of scientists and engineers. Like other pieces of scientific apparatus, it fell to the users themselves to learn how to use them, and to pass on this knowledge informally to colleagues and their own students.

This approach is still firmly entrenched in some parts of many universities. Often the prevailing sentiment tends to be 'We learnt to use this equipment ourselves, so why can't others?' However, it has rapidly declined, owing to the ubiquity of computer use, the increasing complexity of even 'simple' applications like word processing, and the retirement of the 'old brigade'. Nevertheless, some still hold this view, and they are often in positions of power and influence. In developing any strategy or agreement on an approach or blend of approaches to ICT skills training, it is important to recognize and understand this view. Actually, this approach does have a number of important merits. The just-in-time element is especially powerful because learning is best done at the point and time of need. The value of much course-based learning is lost because so little is actually applied immediately. Furthermore, there is a substantial convenience factor in being able to turn for help to a colleague next door, who is already known to you, speaks a language you understand, and can probably demonstrate on your own computer, with your real-life problem.

On the debit side of the ledger, reliance on a neighbouring colleague (often the most able ICT user) can be a great drain on that person's time and learning is often accomplished in a piecemeal fashion, with no coherent framework within which to assimilate knowledge. Furthermore, knowledge is often restricted to what the expert knows, and any misunderstandings they possess may be perpetuated indefinitely. And, the opportunity is rarely presented to open up new horizons or better ways of doing things offered by technological improvements.

When combined with self-help based on reading instruction manuals, guides or help files, some or all of these drawbacks can be overcome, but the approach does not suit everyone's learning style, and learning may still be constrained by a limited horizon. The costs of this approach are hard to quantify, since they are almost all hidden. In terms of pure efficiency, it is probably quite good, but it draws on a resource (one's academic peers) that is nowadays very limited, detracts from their primary function, and may undermine their research output (a totally hidden cost). Some instances of this approach in nearly all universities are almost inevitable, and indeed do have some merit, but this model is almost certainly best implemented in conjunction with other approaches.

Use of online self-paced courses

Online, self-paced learning is becoming a very important means of learning, either supplementing or replacing face-to-face learning. Universities know all about this, with very substantial initiatives and investments worldwide being made in exploring the capability and relevance of this approach to learning. The same is true of industry, where online learning (or e-learning) is gaining rapid acceptance. It is no surprise then that much effort has been put into developing online courses for learning ICT skills. There are many companies developing and providing these course materials. See the selection of online resources in the list of references at the end of this chapter for examples.

The effectiveness of such courses, especially when offered as the sole mode of learning, is questionable. The University of Western Australia acquired a licence to a large collection of online courses between 2000 and 2003. It provided few other (and no central) opportunities for the acquisition of ICT skills, but ended up not finding the approach very effective. The courses it bought were made available to all staff. A charge was levied for use, but it was heavily discounted. The courses were available also to students, but at the full cost.

The rationale behind this approach was that staff would be able to pick and choose the most relevant courses, and would be able to take them at their own desks, at times that suited them best, avoiding the deterrent of having to dedicate significant blocks of time to attend classroom sessions. Take-up grew for a while, though never reaching significant proportions, and then declined rapidly after about 18 months, to the point where it made no economic sense to continue with the licence, which was cancelled after the third year.

The reasons behind the failure of this approach to gain widespread usage include the impediment that any charging system imposes (see 'Free and rich repertoire of classroom-based courses' above); there may also have been inadequate promotion of the scheme. There are questions around the quality and relevance of the courses: for instance, the great advantage of online courses is that they run on your computer, and ideally interface and interact with the actual applications installed – in this case, they did not. Although some support was offered (by phone, e-mail or face-to-face), this may also have been inadequate or not widely advertised. The most telling obstacle to greater take-up, however, was almost certainly the fact that, despite the best of intentions, staff just did not make the commitment to spend time on the courses, in the absence of a specific time and place requirement (as exists for face-to-face courses). There was just not enough motivation to overcome the pressing other business that their lives entailed.

Many of these impediments to effective use of online course material may be overcome if much more compact, targeted, just-in-time online training material is used, for example Atomic Learning (n.d.).

Once again, there is clearly enormous value in making learning available by such means, but it almost always is used to best advantage when employed as a supplement to face-to-face courses, rather than as the sole means of learning. This blended approach to teaching and learning has gained wide acceptance among the e-learning community (Clark, 2003; Cardwell and Madigan, 2004; Heinze and Procter, 2004), and allows adaptation to the diverse learning styles of individuals and the diverse circumstances which may prevail.

Integrating tailored ICT literacy training into each discipline's curriculum

One proposition that is frequently voiced is that ICT literacy training (especially for students) must be undertaken within the context of the particular discipline within which a scholar works or which is being studied. The argument is that ICT skills should flow naturally from needs as they arise in the course of the unfolding of the curriculum; that highly relevant examples can be given; and that only the skills that are actually needed are developed. The University of Western Australia is one university which, among other things, adopted this approach, albeit by default rather than by conscious decision. However, it did not experience great success. The main problem has probably been lack of central leadership or follow-up to this strategy, so implementation has been enormously variable. In those (few) disciplines/faculties where there has been concerted support from the academic leadership, the approach has proved effective. For the most part, however, take-up has been haphazard and generally ineffectual.

This disappointing outcome is not strictly speaking due to an intrinsic failing of the approach – rather, it has been the lack of commitment and follow-through with the approach. To some extent, of course, any approach that depends on devolved action is prone to erratic implementation, unless there is strong central leadership. Typically, also, local areas have asserted that the cost of mounting appropriate ICT skills learning programmes, embedded in the discipline, has been too great; but this is simply a matter of varying local priorities.

This approach seems most suited to student ICT skills training. Where it is truly embedded into the curriculum, so that required skills are taught at the student's point of need, accompanied by suitable relevant examples, then learning is usually rapid and effective. However (as with all good teaching) this does require significant understanding, competence and effort on the part of the teacher. Accordingly, this approach generally is expensive, since substantial duplication of effort is involved. Indeed, with interdisciplinary courses increasingly being offered, considerable effort is necessary to avoid undue repetition of training. Furthermore, it can be argued that most ICT skills required by students are generic, with only limited scope for discipline-specific ones. Of course, the value of discipline-specific applications and examples is not to be denied.

There is clearly a place for such an approach, but once again it seems best applied in conjunction with other approaches – for instance, a generic basic ICT skills training course provided for all students, supplemented during academic sessions with discipline-specific examples. Knowing that all students can be expected to possess a standard knowledge base enables discipline teachers to concentrate just on discipline-specific ICT skill needs.

Self-assessment schemes

Self-assessment is frequently used as an adjunct to a training programme, and to help recipients to accelerate through the programme where they have existing skills (for example Glasgow Caledonian (n.d.), Monash (n.d.), Glasgow (n.d.), and Oxford (n.d.) universities). While not a distinct approach to IT skills training *per se*, there is one sense in which it represents an important component in an overall approach to IT skills training, and that is to raise awareness of need, to promote use of the IT skills training opportunities being provided, and thus to engender a measure of intrinsic motivation.

Self-assessment is best exemplified at the University of Bristol, where it has been used for several years successfully to raise awareness of training needs in the use of learning technologies (The eLearning Anorak, n.d.). All staff are invited to complete a short quiz, which provides an assessment of their readiness to make good use of learning technologies. Scores of all others completing the tests are retained, so that it is possible to compare your score with the average. The scores achieved by certain key figures within the university community, for example vice-chancellor and academic deans, are made available (with their permission) for comparison purposes. The scheme has a slightly light-hearted flavour, which entices participation. This university has found it to be a successful way of raising awareness of the need for training, and of promoting the whole notion of skills development. And it is simple and cheap to administer.

One can envisage a number of refinements to this scheme including, for instance, the ability to compare one's score with peer cohorts, and even the ability for managers to see the skill levels of their staff – either aggregated or anonymously, or (with permission) as individuals. One university has indicated that it plans to do just this, and is extending it to cover broader staff ICT skills, encompassing both generic ICT skills and application-specific skills. It is too early to say whether this approach will be successful in effectively raising an awareness of ICT skill needs, leading to an actual improvement in skill levels, but it is inexpensive and, when combined with other approaches, seems likely to be beneficial.

Conclusions

A number of principles have emerged from an examination of the several different approaches to ICT skills training discussed above:

- *Strategic alignment*. It is paramount for the success of any scheme or programme that the need to raise skill levels be firmly embodied in the university's overall strategic directions, so that it receives consistent top-level and cross-sectional support.
- *Blended approaches*. It is also clear that no one approach is likely to be fully successful on its own, but a blending of different approaches (e.g. online combined with face-to-face) is likely to have a greater chance of success.
- *Value of face-to-face*. The value of such training should not be underestimated. Apart from the obvious factors such as human interaction, responsiveness, engagement (as for other university teaching!), there are also the less obvious benefits such as the motivating effect of having to keep an appointment to attend a course, as well as the competitive element of learning with others.

- *Cultural context*. What may work effectively in one environment may not in another. The prevailing culture of each institution is different, and can have a profound impact on the success of any programme that seeks to develop the community in any direction, not just in ICT skills. Discover, understand and take into account this culture in designing a workable programme.
- *Avoid financial impediments*. Stand up to the economic rationalists where it is clear that cost-recovery will result in impeding demand, if there is an institutional commitment to improved ICT skill levels.
- *Harness peer support*. This can be a very powerful means of developing ICT skill levels, if it can be accomplished without imposing too great a burden on those who are already competent. One way may be to develop a mechanism to recognize and reward the contribution of such people.

References

[Websites accessed 14 February 2006]
A selection of online or CD-based ICT skills-training course providers:

- www.active-online-courses.com/computer-skills.html
- www.ed2go.com/
- www.freeskills.com/
- www.learningfast.com.au/
- www.netg.com/
- www.seeklearning.com.au/.

Atomic Learning Inc. (n.d.), www.atomiclearning.com.
Cardwell, C. and Madigan, D. (2004) Promoting eLiteracy: an open, blended approach in higher education, *JeLit*, 1 (1).
CEPIS (2005) *ICT-skills Certification in Europe*, March, www.cepis.org/download/ ICT-Skills_Certification_final_report_cedefop_v14_rev_bs_fgr_30_03_05.pdf.
Clark, D. (2003) *Blended Learning*, www.epic.co.uk/content/resources/white_papers/blended.htm.
ECDL/ICDL (n.d.), www.ecdl.com/main/index.php.
The eLearning Anorak (n.d.), www.ltss.bris.ac.uk/anorak/.
Glasgow Caledonian University (n.d.), www.learningservices.gcal.ac.uk/ictskills/index.html.
Glasgow University (n.d.), http://apps.iteu.gla.ac.uk/ITEU/html/needsanalysis/index.jsp.

Heinze, A. and Procter, C. (2004) Reflections on the Use of Blended Learning, *Conference Proceedings, Education in a Changing Environment*, 13–14 September 2004, www.edu.salford.ac.uk/her/proceedings/papers/ah_04.rtf.

Monash University's LearningFast (n.d.), www.learningfast.com.au/ICT/default.aspx?menu=ict.

Oxford University (n.d.), http://learnit.ox.ac.uk/.

Oxford University Computing Service (n.d.), www.oucs.ox.ac.uk/courses/.

Winship, J. (2001) *The First Step Forward: IT literacy policy project*, August, www.cau-dit.edu.au/information/projects/itlit_2001.html.

19

Professional development and graduate students: approaches to technical and information competence

Catherine Cardwell

Abstract

In recent years, institutions of higher education have increasingly recognized and emphasized the importance of improving, through a variety of initiatives, students' technical and information competence. The focus of these initiatives has generally been on undergraduate students and teaching faculty, not on graduate students. In their formal course work, graduate students concentrate on acquiring disciplinary knowledge and participating in disciplinary research. Relatively few opportunities exist for professional development activities designed to develop graduate students' technical and information competence. To remedy the situation, institutions of higher education need to rely on approaches typically used by faculty development centres in order to reach graduate students. An interdisciplinary learning community model used at Bowling Green State University in Ohio is presented in this chapter.

Introduction

Most initiatives regarding technical and information competence focus on undergraduate students or faculty, not graduate students. This is unfortunate since most graduate students will become faculty members or will follow equally challenging career paths requiring a high level of competence in these areas. As such, graduate students need more access to professional development opportunities. Their future employers and students will only benefit from their improved skills.

In the USA, graduate student preparation has recently gained more attention since several important studies found a mismatch between graduate student education and the kind of work expected of students once they complete their degrees (Pruitt-Logan and Gaff, 2004, 177). One area commonly identified as needing greater attention is teaching, specifically teaching with technology. Increasingly, faculty are expected to apply innovative technological approaches to their teaching (Adams, 2002, 3–4). Relying on the expertise of staff at faculty development centres is one possible solution to this problem for colleges and universities. Faculty development centres are able to employ strategies they typically use with faculty to reach graduate students because graduate students are more like faculty members in training, not undergraduates. These strategies may include but are not limited to offering workshops, fostering campus partnerships, providing incentives for participation, and creating cohort-based or topic-based learning communities.

A professional development project incorporating a variety of approaches used by faculty development centres is the focus of this chapter. In an attempt to improve graduate student information and technical competence, the Center for Teaching Learning and Technology (CTLT) along with University Libraries (UL) at Bowling Green State University (BGSU) launched an experimental interdisciplinary learning community. Now in place for two years, the programme has been successful in many ways. The programme history and possible future changes are presented in this chapter.

Background

The BGSU graduate student learning community began as a grant-funded project. The Ohio Learning Network offered competitive $25,000 grants for Ohio colleges and universities to integrate technology into teaching and learning and to promote the concept of learning communities. The staff at the CTLT brought together an interdisciplinary team of faculty and staff to explore the kinds technical and information competence important for graduate students. While more than ten potential areas were identified, only four were selected in order for a few areas to be developed in more depth. The final areas selected were computer literacy, rich media, document design and information literacy. The CTLT's grant proposal was successful; implementation of the grant was started in fall 2004.

Program logistics
Philosophy

The instructors in the learning community agreed up front on an instructional design philosophy: the content needed to be conceptual. The instruction and instructional material created by the team had to go beyond mechanical button pushing, the ins and outs of a software program or technical 'how-to' directions. In other words, the instructors wanted to develop in students the kind of thinking it takes to switch operating systems, survive a software upgrade or contend with an interface change. The instructors used another strategy to make students more technologically fluent. The students were lent laptops for the duration of the programme. However, for one semester, they had access to PCs; they had to switch to Macintoshes the next semester. While BGSU is a PC-oriented campus, students may need to work in a Mac environment after they graduate. Additionally, students were pushed to use a variety of software tools to complete a task instead of relying on only the most commonly used software. For instance, students were encouraged to experiment with Keynote, Apple's presentation software, instead of Microsoft PowerPoint. They were also pointed to freely available open-source software such as GIMP. Designed for image manipulation, GIMP works on many operating systems and is an alternative to more costly software such as Adobe Photoshop. The instructors believed students should be comfortable in any computing environment and should learn about alternative software tools as a means of decreasing their dependence on expensive software monopolizing the market.

The instructors had another goal. The programme had to have an immediate impact on graduate students' current research and teaching and at the same time had to prepare students for their future work and decision making. While the four content developers who were also the instructors agreed on these principles, they also decided that the instructors had freedom in the way they structured and delivered their modules. One instructor conducted his module in a completely online environment with little interaction among participants or the instructor. Another instructor delivered minimal content online, relying on discussion board activities to facilitate student learning. This variety of approaches created an environment in which participants experienced different methods of online teaching and learning and were able to enhance their own teaching repertoires.

Learning community

The project was structured around the concept of an interdisciplinary faculty learning community. The concept of interdisciplinary learning communities is one promoted by Milt Cox at Miami University of Ohio. Cox (2003) asserts that two long-term goals of learning communities are to 'investigate and incorporate ways that difference can enhance teaching and learning' and 'increase faculty collaboration across disciplines'. The four members of the teaching team as well the students who participated came from a variety of disciplines. The learning community instructors came from English, music, library science and visual communications technology. To attract graduate students, a call for participation was disseminated in a variety of ways, from a campus listserv directly targeting graduate students to the daily online announcement of university events. As a result, the learning community was able to draw 12 students from many disciplines, such as psychology, history, educational leadership, communication, computer science and sociology.

Structure

The learning community blended in-person and online approaches. Throughout the academic year, the community met once a month in-person while the content and assignments were delivered online.

The online content was divided into four modules with each module lasting about eight weeks, approximately half of the 15-week semester. The content was delivered in software created specifically for the project. Once content for a module was added to the software, a module was uploaded to Blackboard, BGSU's content management system. Typically, content wasn't made public until the appropriate time in the programme. That way, all students were theoretically in the same place. Instructors then made use of Blackboard's built-in features, specifically the discussion board, where students shared their questions and posted their projects for others to view. Students were also invited to contact the instructors individually if they had questions they didn't want to share with the group. Although content was delivered online, the learning community followed the academic calendar so that students were not expected to participate during vacations. Following this calendar was essential for instructors and students.

The in-person meetings were designed to promote community building, to provide time for students to present their projects, and to explore questions or issues the students raised. The in-person sessions also had an instructional element built into them to cover material not presented in the online modules. That content was sometimes determined by the instructors or driven by student requests. For instance, one in-person session reviewed the importance of netiquette. Additionally, the instructors used the in-person sessions to prepare students for a new module or to wrap up a module that the students had just completed.

Incentives for participation

Because of the way that graduate study is structured and accredited at BGSU, it is not possible to offer academic credit for this experience. However, the director of the CTLT was able to collaborate with BGSU's Department of Information Technology Systems and supply laptops to the participating students for the academic year in addition to providing a small stipend of $200 for additional professional development opportunities. Students, for instance, could use the stipend to buy books or attend a conference or workshop.

Content

The programme consisted of four modules: computer literacy, rich media, document design and information literacy. The content developed by the instructors focused on general principles or concepts. Typically, all of the instructors pointed students to already existing 'how-to' tutorials on the web rather than recreating them. For instance, in the database section of the information literacy module, students learned about database structure, controlled vocabulary and keyword searching. They did not learn a specific interface or database.

Computer literacy

The computer literacy module concentrated on hardware, software, operating systems, file management and networking. The goal of this unit was to increase students' knowledge of computers in order to make them better consumers and problem solvers. It is likely that graduate students will at some time in the future be in a position to buy computer equipment either for themselves or their departments. Understanding fundamental computing concepts will help them make appropriate selections and not waste resources. Another goal was to make students more self-reliant with computer equipment so that they are better able to solve or prevent problems when they teach with technology either in person or online.

Rich media

Perhaps the topic with most appeal for students, the rich media module concentrated on digital imaging (photography), digital media and digital video. The goals of this module were to encourage participants to think about how they might use rich media to enhance their teaching and learning and more generally to encourage students to think about the role media plays in their lives. See Figure 19.1.

In this unit, it was especially important to help students develop skills to incorporate media into their classes. For instance, one history graduate student participant wanted to include photographs in her classes but discovered that she and her students had trouble knowing how to talk about them. The leader for this module provided instruction on ways to talk about images both during the in-person learning community and on the Blackboard discussion board.

Document design

The overarching goal of this module was web documentation, that is creating web-based documents. Lessons included web-page design, usability, use of colours and graphics and file-management principles. Students had a series of mini-assignments requiring them to develop a web page, and then the learning

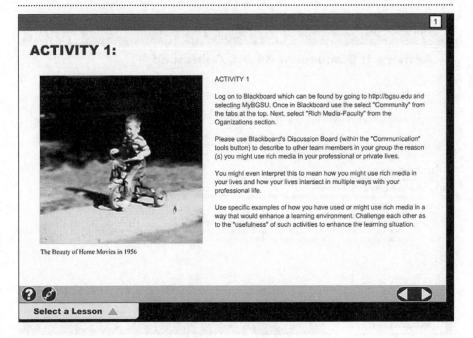

ACTIVITY 1:

ACTIVITY 1

Log on to Blackboard which can be found by going to http://bgsu.edu and selecting MyBGSU. Once in Blackboard use the select "Community" from the tabs at the top. Next, select "Rich Media-Faculty" from the Oganizations section.

Please use Blackboard's Discussion Board (within the "Communication" tools button) to describe to other team members in your group the reason (s) you might use rich media in your professional or private lives.

You might even interpret this to mean how you might use rich media in your lives and how your lives intersect in multiple ways with your professional life.

Use specific examples of how you have used or might use rich media in a way that would enhance a learning environment. Challenge each other as to the "usefulness" of such activities to enhance the learning situation.

The Beauty of Home Movies in 1956

Select a Lesson ▲

Figure 19.1 *Rich media activity*

community spent time online and in person critiquing student projects. At one in-person session, students debated the significance of faculty members creating personal websites or requiring students to create a website as a class assignment. They explored when is it appropriate for students to create a web page instead of writing a paper. Such dialogues encourage students to think more critically about the purpose of the web and reasons to develop web pages or to include development of a web page as a class assignment.

Information literacy

The goal of this module was to raise students' awareness of information literacy and to make students more efficient researchers. Many graduate students are unfamiliar with the meaning of 'information literacy', so the beginning of the module was dedicated to raising their awareness of the issue and its significance. See Figure 19.2.

Other lessons in this module included overviews of research database structure, search engines and the deep web. Because students learned to manipulate and create rich media, a lesson on ethical and legal issues relating to the use of information, particularly fair use of media, was included.

A common complaint of teaching assistants, just as with teaching faculty, is that their students rely too much on non-authoritative websites, so the instructor

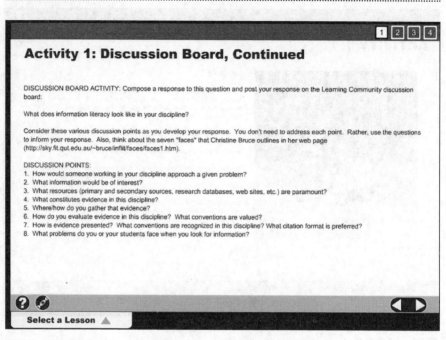

Figure 19.2 *Information literacy activity*

used discussion board conversations to address ways to help undergraduate students find relevant, high-quality information. The instructor as well as the students offered solutions to this problem.

In keeping with the project philosophy, the lessons focused on general principles about information literacy, research databases, search engines and the deep web. By learning general principles, students are better equipped to move from one database to another. For practice using a variety of databases, students were pointed to *Research Database Fundamentals*, a series of 'how-to' tutorials created by Carol Singer (2004), one of the UL reference librarians. The students were able to pick from among ten lessons to practise their skills.

Lessons learned for the future

Over the course of the two years that the programme was conducted, the instructors refined and improved the programme. For instance, during the first year, the learning community activities did not line up with the academic calendar, which caused some problems for the instructors and students. For the second year, the learning community followed the academic calendar and ran more efficiently and with less confusion as a result.

Another problem occurred in the first year when students were given access to their stipends at the beginning of the programme. Some students ended up being weak participants. For the second year, the stipend was available only at the end of the programme and only to those students who completed all four modules. This was a better way to motivate students.

Additionally, after discussing programme strengths and weaknesses with students, the instructors learned that a few graduate students had trouble maintaining participation because of other obligations that they had not anticipated at the beginning of the academic year when they made a commitment to the learning community. Offering mini learning communities lasting only half a semester and covering only two of the modules was a possible solution. Alternatively, they suggested that modules could be made available individually. That way, students would have greater ability to pick and choose modules that lined up better with the timing of their degrees and their interests. For instance, the information literacy module was the last in the series. Some students at the end of their degree programmes indicated that they would have benefited more from this module at the beginning of their degree programmes rather than at the end. This last suggestion of offering the modules individually would eliminate the benefits of belonging to a year-long learning community.

Conclusion

Because of future job expectations, graduate students need more opportunities to develop their technical and information competence. Their degree programmes rarely incorporate such prospects, so alternative approaches are necessary. Faculty development centres are one potential solution to this problem. They should rely on best practices and creative approaches and at the same time pursue collaborative relationships with other campus entities such as libraries to enrich their programmes.

References

Adams, K. A. (2002) *What Colleges and Universities Want in New Faculty*, Washington DC, American Association of Colleges and Universities.

Cox, M. (2003) *Faculty Learning Communities*, www.units.muohio.edu/celt/communities.shtml (accessed 13 June 2005).

Pruitt-Logan, A. S. and Gaff, J. G. (2004) Preparing Future Faculty: changing the culture of doctoral education. In Wulff, D. H. and Austin, A. E. (eds), *Paths to the Professoriate: strategies for enriching the preparation of future faculty*, San Francisco CA, Jossey-Bass.

Singer, C. (2004) *Research Database Fundamentals*,
www.bgsu.edu/colleges/library/infosrv/lue/rdfwelcome.htm
(accessed 13 June 2005).

20

Windward in an asynchronous world: the Antiguan initiative, unanticipated pleasures of the distance learning revolution

Cornel J. Reinhart

Abstract

This chapter explores the e-literacy impact of Skidmore College's University Without Walls (UWW) online asynchronous bachelor degree programme on the Caribbean island of Antigua. Primarily enrolling the island's teachers, mostly women, UWW's online courses, the author argues, have played a fundamental role in bringing a new pedagogical philosophy and digital literacy to this small and somewhat isolated island nation. For island teachers, participation in asynchronous courses offered wonderfully exciting opportunities to share ideas, teaching experiences, and community histories with other students located around the world. *Rum, Slaves and Molasses*, an online history course concerning the African slave trade, brought these teacher-students, via the power of the internet, new insights into their own Afro-Caribbean history. These valuable perspectives were quickly introduced into the teacher-students' own classrooms, offering new generations of Antiguan young people a more positive interpretation of their own African past and the important nation-building role played by their enslaved ancestors. In this learning process, these students were also taught how to create their own websites, to research archives around the world, and to access secondary sources totally unavailable on an island with almost no library facilities. The introduction of these web design skills and related valuable e-literacy tools to these teachers, and then to their students, ultimately brought their unique Antiguan story alive. The internet, coupled with constructivist e-learning strategies, allowed these island educators, previously isolated, to share their distinctive history with people around the globe.

In UWW's Antiguan initiative we see not only the power of e-literacy to transform learning architecture, but also a glimpse of the pedagogical future: the revolutionary impact of ICT and e-literacy on human societies. As educators, this experience allows us to marvel again at the enormous learning capacity inherent in allowing students to speak directly to each other across the world's vast distances; to share diverse cultural experiences and confront deep historical divides; to explore new ideas and information; and to 'construct knowledge' from common collective information. In that process, we also see in Antigua the earliest transformation of an entire culture's educational pedagogical foundation (albeit that of a small island nation).

Introduction

In the age of sail, windward and leeward described crucial attributes for ships, often slavers, bound for Caribbean sugar islands. In the distant learning age of the 21st century, the internet, and asynchronous learning, has again placed otherwise remote Caribbean islands to windward, to their advantage, as to ours.

Wind sails also powered Antigua's ponderous sugar mills, where cane and slaves alike were crushed, where stone ruins stand today, abandoned sentinels to Antigua's brutal legacy of slavery. From an historian's perspective, Antigua is both a typical English-speaking island in the eastern Caribbean and yet quite distinctive from others. Antigua is not as large in population or acreage as other islands, especially Barbados (not considered a Leeward Island) yet the entire panoply of the sugar plantation complex evolved there. Richard Dunn's excellent history of Caribbean sugar and slavery was made possible by the existence of the papers of the Codrington family, one of the most important Caribbean plantation families (Dunn, 1972). Dunn's careful scholarship provides a useful historical introduction to Antigua during the sugar plantation era. Sadly, but predictably, we have few or no written documents providing similar insight into the lives of the Africans enslaved on Antigua or of their proud descendants.

Yet, one of the most significant legacies of slavery is often overlooked in any discussion of the slaves' Antiguan descendants. The indigenous population born and raised on Antigua learns English only as a second language. The first tongue of native Antiguans is an entirely adequate language that Antiguans call, 'the dialect', but is not precisely an English 'dialect'.[1] I mention this historical anomaly only to help my reader appreciate how difficult and important education and literacy are on this small Caribbean island. For someone on Antigua to survive, much less prosper, in the contemporary world, he or she must master English and perhaps several other languages as well. Likewise, the information communication technology (ICT) age requires students everywhere, no longer isolated nor protected by oceans or deserts, to learn the emerging language, the digital grammar and vocabulary, necessary for efficient writing and computation; to learn the architecture of web design and web building, the internet tools necessary to share one's ideas with the world. In short, to be fully literate, to compete globally, today's citizens, similar to citizens of the age of sail, must master the language of their era, the digital language of the postmodern age.

In late 1987, Austin Josiah, then President of the Antigua and Barbuda Union of Teachers, had his first real experience of snow, and the fragility of Amtrak train engines, when he approached University Without Walls (UWW), Skidmore College, for his admission interview. Arriving on a cold and slushy Saratoga morning, Austin fondly recalls his taxi driver taking him directly from the train to a Saratoga Springs shoe emporium where the driver personally helped Austin select a proper pair of warm North Country boots.

Antigua and the University Without Walls

In June 1990, after much hard work, taking all his courses on Antigua by mail, telephone and e-mail, Austin Josiah became Antigua's first graduate of Skidmore College, through the UWW programme. Austin's final project, Public Education in Antigua and Barbuda: A Model for Developing an Effective Education System, reflected his deep commitment to transforming teaching, and thereby education, in Antigua from its older vocational, rote-learning colonial (and post-colonial) tradition, to a broader liberal arts, critical inquiry model. He credits his distance learning experience (via mail and telephone) as the catalyst for his lifelong quest for education and performance excellence. Mr Josiah's broad vision and evident capacity for leadership, coupled with his dynamic personality, quickly brought him into senior government leadership as the island nation's Labour Commissioner, and later as the nation's Chief Education Officer, the senior civil servant in the Ministry of Education.

Austin's example encouraged another student, Mr Colin Greene, to join UWW in the 1990s. When Colin Greene first walked into the UWW offices for his degree plan meeting he was essentially unknown to all but his two academic advisers. Mentored by Austin Josiah, Colin Greene was then serving as President of both the Antigua and Barbuda Union of Teachers as well as the Caribbean Union of Teachers. Like Austin, Colin was deeply committed to transforming Antiguan public education. Colin's extraordinary speaking talents and his passionate determination to bring liberal arts education to the training of Antiguan and Caribbean teachers seemed to suggest that closer ties between Mr Greene, the Union of Teachers and the University Without Walls, Skidmore College, might be beneficial to all.

It was a natural consequence of the friendship and mutual esteem that developed between members of the UWW staff and these strong island personalities that led to discussions concerning the extension of UWW's programmes to additional Antiguan teachers. In spring 2000 Deborah Meyers, UWW Academic Advisor, and I, UWW Director, were invited to speak to the annual Teacher's

Professional Development Day in Antigua. Deborah and I were overwhelmed with the warmth and professionalism exhibited by the some 700 Afro-Caribbean teachers we addressed that day. Emphasizing the value of a small liberal arts college, we had the pleasure of highlighting the UWW programme to the many teachers in attendance. A rousing address advocating the merits of a liberal arts education was given by a small, wiry speaker, Charlesworth Ephrain, soon to become UWW Skidmore's first permanent island faculty member. Dr Ephrain's views, similar to my own, reflected the guiding educational spirit of Skidmore College (Reinhart, 2005). After a few, thankfully successful, efforts at humour directly confronting the stark reality of these two white academics in a sea of black teachers, Deborah and I suggested that UWW could serve Antiguan students not only with traditional distance learning tools, but also by utilizing our rapidly developing online learning courses.

In the Summer of 2001, three members of the UWW staff returned to the island with hopes of admitting and enrolling new students to UWW. After a busy three days of interviewing, we admitted 26 new teacher-students to UWW Skidmore College. We also met senior members of the Ministry of Labour and other key individuals in Antigua. With their support, our students opened discussions with local banks concerning loans necessary to complete their education with UWW. After securing this vital financial support, 21 students enrolled.

What was new, if anything, about UWW Skidmore's presence on the island? In fact, nearly everything: UWW represented an American liberal arts college in an island nation whose entire institutional legacy was a product of the British colonial empire. When the British granted independence to Antigua and Barbuda in 1981, and subsequently departed, they left behind a two-year-degree-granting institution, Antigua State College, whose teacher training programme was sufficient to certify its students as teachers but not adequate to allow these professionals to be promoted. The University of the West Indies (UWI) was established to serve the English-speaking islands of the Caribbean with three institutions offering baccalaureate and graduate degrees: Jamaica, Barbados and Trinidad. Smaller islands, like Antigua, were served by two-year institutions. For teachers and other professionals on these smaller islands, opportunities for professional advancement necessitated leaving family and employment to attend residential programmes, either in one of the larger islands served by UWI, or to travel further a field, typically to Canadian or UK universities. And, though teachers were overwhelmingly women, this career advancement path provided scant opportunities for anyone, but those it did favour were primarily men.

Similarly, the pedagogical approach left by the departing colonizer was in most essentials a skills training model. When UWW's staff began enrolling students, we encountered a system very good at teaching skills emphasizing memorization, short answers and quizzes; in short, didactic, faculty-led classroom encounters providing few occasions for student-directed discussions or lengthy assessment efforts, essays, or papers encouraging critical analysis. This explains, of course, the impassioned speech delivered by Dr Ephraim to the island's teachers extolling the virtues of a broad liberal arts education. Born on Antigua, Dr Ephraim took his PhD in philosophy at Yale University and pursued a distinguished teaching career at the State University of New York, Purchase, among other American institutions. Returning to his island home to care for his ailing mother, Dr Ephraim was an ardent advocate of the powerful connections between a broad liberal arts education and genuine social transformation. For Dr Ephraim, the colonizers had unshackled the slave's limbs but left their minds bound by stifling convention and educational orthodoxy.

Now, in the summer of 2001, as UWW set out to enroll students, one of our first tasks was to determine what island resources were available to these new students. Phylise Banner, UWW's Instructional Technologist, conducted a person-by-person assessment of individual student computer skills, hardware capabilities and internet connections. Antigua's reality as an island in the third world became apparent quickly. Only a handful of students had individual access to the web; most shared a single portal with multiple (indeed often the same) e-mail addresses. Similarly, our choice for a headquarters, the Teachers' Place, a small wooden-frame structure serving the Teachers' Union as its administrative and social hub, was woefully equipped for online access despite serving as a small technology centre for island teachers and young students. These teachers, students and administrators were struggling with obsolete machines, many patched together from even older or partially damaged computers. Through the generous assistance of the New World Foundation we replaced these ageing machines with four networked computers at the Teachers' Place, immediately allowing 12 teachers to enroll in UWW's 2001 online summer courses.[2]

Asynchronicity and online learning

It is impossible to imagine UWW creating a genuine educational option for a significant number of Antiguan students without its own online, asynchronous courses. In the spring of 1997, University Without Walls, Skidmore College, experimented with its first online course hoping to better support its worldwide student population with high-quality liberal arts courses. With generous support from an Alfred P. Sloan Foundation grant, that goal began to be realized by early 2000. UWW was guided in the creation of its online courses by two critical principles: first, that each course be discussion, not lecture-centred, and, second, that courses be organized asynchronously. Recognizing that lectures were only another reading online, it seemed clear that to pursue true liberal arts excellence, faculty would have to be persuaded, indeed guided, to create genuine discussion forums that would serve as the intellectual and learning heart of their course (Payne, 2004). To facilitate that objective, classes would also have to be limited to a seminar-like size of 15–18 students. Asynchronicity was essential since UWW students were located everywhere in the world, removing any lingering notion of creating synchronous 'chat rooms' instead of asynchronous 'bulletin boards'.

Educators at all levels, including post-secondary, are only gradually coming to discover the enormous potentiality for learning inherent in web-based pedagogy. This is partially true, owing to the newness of the technology itself, but more so because of the need to redefine both the 'classroom' and the pedagogical paradigm that has for so long been the basis of the traditional face-to-face institutional environment. The web alters completely, literally transforms, the architecture of the traditional learning space, the classroom; it dissolves the institutional imperatives of time and space (synchronous physical space, rigid schedules), the necessity for lecturing in large halls and, perhaps more threateningly, makes the comfortable reliance on the didactic, lecture format itself obsolete. The internet offers instructors the opportunity to open their classroom to the world; to create enormously rich encounters between people of diverse cultural traditions who never before had affordable opportunities to talk directly with each other; to explore, discuss and compare the nuances of their cultures; and to discover the widely diverse institutional arrangements of their common human experience (Naudé and Reinhart, n.d.; Le Grange, 2004).

These two principles were also crucial in UWW's approach to education and literacy in Antigua. For Antiguan students to succeed with Skidmore faculty members teaching online, it was essential that these students quickly adjust their ideas of educational excellence from a behaviourist didactic top-down methodology to learner-centred constructivist pedagogy (Cooper, 1993). Similarly, online courses also naturally lent themselves to longer written assessments favouring critical thinking skills and analysis over memorization and regurgitation. Charles Ephraim's dream of transforming the island's post-colonial pedagogy and educational philosophy from its restraining orthodoxy to a more interactive and critical stance was realized in the variety of courses UWW provided online to its island students.

Naturally, all of UWW's online courses were available to our Antiguan students. But, because these students enrolled more nearly as a cohort (unlike UWW's typical individual admission) with common backgrounds in education courses, UWW was able to create several courses specific to serve these island students' curricular needs. Yet, wonderfully, these same learning experiences were open to UWW students located elsewhere in the world. Asynchronous technology created a remarkable opportunity to bring together students from enormously varied and diverse cultural backgrounds that could never have been reasonably expected to share the same classroom nor conduct extended conversations about topics as diverse as America's Caribbean foreign policy, new approaches to pedagogy, and the African slave trade.[3]

Globalization: the slave trade and the world wide web

It was exhilarating for me to offer the course 'Rum, Slaves and Molasses: Slavery and the Slave Trade in the Americas' to such a wonderfully diverse group of students scattered around the world. Imagine: six Afro-Caribbean students living on the former sugar-producing island of Antigua, all descendants of slaves; African–American students living in Washington DC, Euro-American students living in the former slave-trading ports of Boston, Providence and New York City; a single student living on an island off the coast of Maine; and a true 'outlier', one young woman living in Switzerland! Asking each student to introduce themselves was equally amazing but no moment more electrifying than the introduction in the 'seminar space' (asynchronous bulletin board) of one Antiguan man, a high school principal:

> I am the product of a 15 year old girl and a 17 year old boy who went to pleasure themselves in one of the many canefields their parents were working in 57 years ago. . . . I live in Parham which is a maritime old town situated on the North Eastern part of Antigua. I grew up on three sugar estates (plantations) of the many that are situated around the town of Parham.
>
> I have a farm on which I raise goats. I still give them molasses today as the sugar planters gave their animals during slavery. The molasses called 'Fuzie' by the slaves was given to the cows, horses, mules and donkeys to improve their rations and control diarrhoea. The slaves also used to drink molasses in water to enhance libido.
>
> I believe that I will enjoy this course very much. I have been listening to, and been taught His-story for many years. I have come to the conclusion that His-story is also Mis-story. Since I met with Corky and the Skidmore Experience, I have been given a chance to tell My-story.

Suddenly, before the course had fairly begun, we glimpsed a few of the products of slavery and oppression; we envisioned plantations of masters and slaves; we sensed the pervasive role of sugar and molasses in the lives of these black slaves and their descendants; we felt the pride and joyfulness of these proud people.

History, identity and e-literacy

I proposed that students create groups of two or three to produce collaborative web-based projects, exploring the issues slavery and the slave trade presented in the places they lived (Gilbert and Moore, 1998; Palloff and Pratt, 1999; Janicki and Liegle, 2001). This interactive, student-led assignment yielded truly exciting results. For the Antiguan students – themselves teachers – this assignment posed real challenges to their technological literacy but also offered an enormous opportunity to explore their island's history and their identity as descendants of African slaves. Essentially abandoned after emancipation and the end of colonization, to build their own society on this impoverished island in the middle of the Caribbean basin, these strong Afro-Caribbean people nourished a somewhat fragile economy into a healthy and stable one while developing the island's infrastructure of roads, water desalinization facilities, hospitals and schools. It was no small achievement when the island's citizens successfully elected a new government after over 40 years of one party – indeed – one family rule.

Overcoming their fears about building group websites and the related technical obstacles proved to be easier than exploring their history. Slaves left no written records; the only extant manuscripts were the papers of colonial Antigua's largest land and slave owners, the Codrington family, papers preserved in microfilm in the island's historical museum. One group of Antigua students explored these records for evidence of the condition of slaves on the island prior to emancipation. A second, equally rich source of historical information, however, came from the island's fascinating oral tradition. Two other teams of students utilized oral interviews with older members of the Antiguan community to uncover a treasure of stories describing the plantation system and slaves' daily lives, religious beliefs and many wonderful stories passed orally from generation to generation. Little or none of this rich tradition had been formally preserved. Now, utilizing the power of the internet, these students created websites that brought this history alive allowing them to share it with the world. As teachers themselves, suddenly they had the power to use this fascinating historical tradition to offer their own students a positive historical image – not just a history of oppression and domination by the white master – but an alternative and parallel story of a people who created and shaped their own lives, their own destinies, who lived forceful and creative individual existences inside the stifling, brutal systems of slavery and colonization.

The comments of one such teacher in the 'seminar space' suggests the impact of our assigned historical readings and the powerful role that 'conversation' itself plays in the learning process:

First, I was very impressed to see that my country Antigua was mentioned in *The Diligent*. I knew that my island was involved in the slave trade, as were many other islands, but I have never come across any historical data directly linking Antigua to the trade, well not in high school anyway. Antigua's name was first mentioned on page 186, as part of a strange, peculiar and somewhat ironic tale involving an Englishman, Bulfinch Lambe, a young African, Captain Tom and a great African ruler, King Agaja. ... When the demand for slaves could not be met by 'panyarring', plots of attacks on neighbouring kingdoms were deliberately conceived to meet the demand for slaves as POW's were normally sold into slavery. Well at least that's the way I see it. In my previous history lessons (or 'his' 'story') to use the term coined by Foster to mean history from the 'white man's' point of view, I was taught that the Africans then were wild brutes, or pagans and idolaters who frequently made war with themselves and sold their brothers into slavery. The question of why this was so never came to mind and I never thought of or was encouraged to find reasons for this. I believe I now have the answer. . . . The Slave Trade did a lot to create certain stereotypes of Black people, which are still very evident today.

For this student, the course Rum, Slaves and Molasses, brought to her small island nation via the power of the internet, gave her new and valuable perspectives into her Afro-Caribbean history. These insights and this new ICT literacy were quickly used in her own classroom to offer a new generation of Antiguan young people a positive alternative interpretation of their African past and the role their ancestors played in building Antigua and the New World.

Nearly as important, these Antiguan stories could now be shared with their fellow classmates, mostly, but not entirely white, situated along the American eastern seaboard and in Europe. Responding to her Antigua colleague, a student born in Massachusetts commented:

I was surprised to find mention in Mannix of my home town, Marblehead, Massachusetts, (p. 61). 'The first definitely authenticated American-built vessel to carry slaves was the Desire, built in Marblehead and sailing out of Salem.' My home town advertises itself as the 'Birthplace of the American Navy' because most of the first American ships were built there. But they do not say publicly that they outfitted the Slave trade.

The internet allowed these island educators, otherwise somewhat isolated, to share their distinctive histories with people around the globe. For a historian with a long-standing interest in the power of local history to excite students often bored by national stories, to observe students sharing unique historical experiences across deep multicultural divides was exciting and profoundly moving.[4]

Skidmore College's University Without Walls Antiguan initiative offers an especially interesting glimpse into the pedagogical future. Educators at all levels, including post-secondary,

are only gradually coming to discover the enormous potentiality for learning inherent in web-based pedagogy. This is partially true due to the newness of the technology itself, but more so because of the need to redefine both the 'classroom' and the pedagogical paradigm that has for so long underlay the traditional face-to-face institutional environment.

(Naudé and Reinhart, n.d.; Payne, 2004).

Conclusion

In Antigua, we see not only the power of the internet to transform learning architecture but the revolutionary impact of this technology on human societies. As educators, we experience the enormous learning capacity inherent in allowing our students to speak directly to each other, to share ideas and information, to 'construct knowledge' from information (Winn, 1997; Payne, 2004). In that process, we also see the beginning of the transformation of an entire island culture's educational pedagogical system. All of us quickly grasp, indeed marvel, at the internet's power to communicate globally, to create opportunities for human artistic expression, and to make the world's archived information widely available. Less acknowledged is the internet's capacity to nourish older communities while building new ones, giving Third World peoples, once forgotten or isolated, a technological edge, and finding themselves once more windward in an asynchronous age.

Notes

1   Rather remarkably, the Antiguan 'dialect' is unintelligible on Barbados (and Barbadians cannot understand Antigua speakers) but it is understood in Jamaica and Antiguans can also understand Jamaicans.

2   Currently, UWW-enrolled students, mostly Antiguan teachers, are paying UWW fees without recourse to financial aid. Senior teachers in Antigua earn on average US$12,000 a year. The UWW yearly enrolment fee and course fees (assuming six courses a year) cost students about $8000 per year, or two-thirds of their yearly salary. This startling statistic demonstrates as little else the Antiguan students' extraordinary level of commitment to further their education, often only in order to make a difference in the lives of their own students on this small island nation.

3   Space does not allow for an extended discussion of the remarkable online course, New Approaches to Pedagogy, initially offered by Professors Joyce Rubin and Donna Brent who introduced our Antiguan students, all of whom were experienced teachers, to the most recent ideas for effective teaching in the contemporary classroom. I also want to thank my friend and colleague David Glaser, who offered America's Caribbean Foreign Policy online, for sharing his ideas and pioneering experiences with internet learning with me.

4   Owing to copyright concerns, if you wish to access these student projects it will be necessary to e-mail me at creinhar@skidmore.edu or UWW's Instructional Technologist, Phylise Banner, at pbanner@skidmore.edu).

References

Cooper, P. A. (1993) Paradigm Shifts in Designing Instruction: from behaviorism to cognitivism to constructivism, *Educational Technology*, **33** (5).

Dunn, R. S. (1972) *Sugar and Slaves: the rise of the planter class in the English West Indies 1624–1713*, Chapel Hill NC, University of North Carolina Press.

Gilbert, L. and Moore, D. L. (1998) Building Interactivity into Web Courses: tools for social and instructional interaction, *Education Technology*, **38** (3), 29–35.

Janicki, T. and Liegle, J. O. (2001) Development and Evaluation of a Framework for Creating Web Based Learning Modules: a pedagogical and systems approach, *Journal of Asynchronous Learning Networks*, **5** (1), www.sloan-c.org/publications/jaln/v5n1_janicki.pdf (accessed 14 July 2005).

Le Grange, L. (2004) E-learning: some critical thoughts, *South African Journal of Higher Education*, **18** (1).

Naudé, L. and Reinhart, C. J. (n.d.) The Power of Engagement: a new pedagogical model in online service learning, unpublished manuscript.

Palloff, R. M. and Pratt, K. (1999) *Building Learning Communities in Cyberspace*, San Francisco CA, Jossey-Bass.

Payne, C. R. (2004) Design for Success: applying progressive educational principles online. In Vrasidas, C. and Glass, G. (eds), *Online Professional Development for Teachers*, Greenwich CT, Information Age Publishing.

Reinhart, C. J. (2005) The Liberal Arts Ideal in an Asynchronous Age. In *Elements of Quality Online Education: into the mainstream: wisdom from the Sloan Consortium*, Sloan-C Series, Books on Online Education, www.aln.org/publications/books/wisdom.asp (accessed 14 July 2005).

Winn, W. (1997) *Learning in Hyperspace*, www.umuc.edu/ide/potentialweb97/winn.html (accessed 14 July 2005).

21

A tale of two courses

Gill Needham and David Murphy

Abstract

This chapter describes a case study of two courses on information literacy presented by distance-teaching institutions from opposite sides of the world. The courses are 'Mining Information in the Internet Age', from the Open University of Hong Kong, and 'Mosaic: Making Sense of Information in the Connected Age', from the UK Open University, both of which are taught online. Designed and developed entirely independently, the courses have distinct similarities and differences, which will be explored in the chapter.

Introduction

In July 2002 the authors of this chapter, two course developers, one from the Open University Hong Kong (OUHK) and one from the UK Open University (UKOU), met for the first time in Hong Kong and began to discuss a mutual interest in information literacy. Information literacy is an important topic, particularly in the context of an online environment, but not one that at that time featured in stand-alone course offerings, particularly outside the USA and Australia. In the conversation, it transpired that both authors had been proactive in developing and delivering short courses in information literacy in their respective countries.

Both courses were developed in response to similar circumstances. Both institutions are distance-teaching universities. The UKOU was founded more than 30 years ago and was the first university of its kind; the OUHK followed 20 years later using the same model of 'supported open learning'. Before near-universal internet access enabled the use of digital library resources, students of these institutions were not required to use libraries as part of their studies. The philosophy of equitable access meant that students had to be able to complete their studies without visiting a library. Instead they were provided with a rich array of multimedia course materials – now referred to as 'the course in the box'.

Both institutions have invested heavily in developing their digital library collections over the last eight to ten years, but had to wait until the majority of students had internet access before their use could be integrated into courses. As students were introduced to the use of digital library resources, it became evident that many lacked the most basic information literacy skills. Many students who had studied for several years with the UKOU had never learned to use libraries, databases or other tools. They had no experience equivalent to the library induction mandatory in most traditional universities. This was confounded by the fact that many of the tutors (part-time academic staff) who supported the students were not used to using libraries in an online environment.

These extreme circumstances provided an ideal environment for developing a new and creative approach to information literacy.

The courses

The two courses discussed in this chapter are 'Mosaic: Making Sense of Information in the Connected Age', from the UKOU, and 'Mining Information in the Internet Age', from the OUHK. Both courses are taught online, and were developed to meet similar needs identified within the respective institutions. This is reflected in the stated aims and objectives of the courses, reproduced in Table 21.1 overleaf. Although there are differing levels of detail, it is plain that the courses have essentially identical aims.

Background and course development

Both courses are unusual in their respective institutions because they are generic skills development courses, relevant to students in all disciplines. For this reason both are unconventional in the way they were developed.

Making Sense of Information in the Connected Age

In the UKOU courses are developed by multidisciplinary course teams. Although membership may be inter-faculty, the course team will be led and owned within one particular faculty. The short course Mosaic: Making Sense of Information in the Connected Age had a very different origin.

The importance of information literacy was first articulated by the UKOU in its 2001 Learning and Teaching Strategy, which included as one of its strategic objectives 'Preparing students for the knowledge society'. This was in part influ-

Table 21.1 *The aims and objectives of the two courses*

Mosaic: Making Sense of Information in the Connected Age	Mining Information in the Internet Age
Introduction This course has been developed as a response to the growing importance of information in all our lives. People increasingly need skills in finding, using and handling information, particularly in an electronic environment. We hope that through Mosaic you will develop skills that will both equip you to be a more effective student and help you to function more confidently in 'the information society'.	*Introduction* This course has been designed to help you to improve your skills in searching for information that you require in your work. That is, once you've completed the course, you will be able to find the information you want quickly and efficiently, secure in the knowledge that what you've found is the best available to you.
Aims and objectives The course aims: To help you to develop skills and confidence in finding, using and handling information. By the end of the course we hope you will: • Be familiar with a range of information sources • Be familiar with tools and techniques for searching for and organising information • Be able to plan and carry out a systematic search for information • Be able to use a systematic approach to judge the quality of information and • Be able to organise information and present it in an appropriate way.	*Course aims* Information Literacy and the Internet aims to provide you with the skills required to support lifelong learning. In particular, the course will teach you how to access, search, select and evaluate electronic and online information resources from the internet, with a focus on the OUHK's Electronic Library. *Course objectives* The course is divided into three study units, with the following objectives. By the end of *Unit 1*, you will be able to: • describe a strategy you would follow to obtain relevant and useful information for a problem or question you face; • determine the key concepts of your question; • understand the terms involved; • decide what search terms to use; and • determine where to look for the information. By the end of Unit 2, you will be able to: • choose an appropriate tool for the search you are undertaking; • use the chosen tool appropriately; and • store the information for later use. By the end of Unit 3, you will be able to: • critically evaluate the information you have located; • acknowledge your information sources; and • list your information sources.

enced by national higher education policy, particularly a series of subject bench-marking statements produced by the Quality Assurance Agency.

As staff on the Library's helpdesk identified the students' lack of skills and confidence in accessing, finding and evaluating information, the University funded the Library to work with colleagues in the University's production unit to develop an online, flexible, interactive tutorial called SAFARI (Skills in Accessing, Finding and Reviewing Information) – freely available to all UKOU students. The content was written by Library staff with academic colleagues acting as critical readers. At the same time, a UK national task force on information literacy, set up by SCONUL (the umbrella group for all UK higher education directors of library services) identified a need for a credit-bearing introductory course to be available nationally.

The UKOU had at that time embarked on a short courses initiative: this provided some funding to explore the possibility of reversioning the material to form a ten-point short course at level 1. The Dean of the Faculty of Education and Language Studies (FELS) subsequently agreed to host the course in his faculty.

The course was developed by reversioning and supplementing the SAFARI materials in less than three months, going live in April 2002 for a 1 May start date. This was made possible by flexible and effective teamwork and expert course management. The timescale required presented particular challenges to production, as did the technological solutions necessary to repurpose material for an accredited-learning environment. The co-ordination of design and web development was particularly important and overall the initiative required the close collaboration of all partners.

Mining Information in the Internet Age

This course was developed by a course team of OUHK staff, with members from the Library, academic units and the Educational Technology and Publishing Unit (ETPU). Instructional design and the drafting of the study units was the responsibility of one of the authors of this paper, who is a senior course designer in the ETPU. Unlike Mosaic, the course was developed 'from scratch', and consequently took twice as long (approximately six months) to complete.

Overall, the aim of the course is to improve participants' skills in searching for, evaluating and using information from the internet. At the same time, access is provided to the OUHK's extensive Electronic Library, and a significant part of the course is devoted to elaborating how best use can be made of this resource. Background resources were gathered and ideas gleaned and refined from a large array of materials from university libraries around the world. Particular attention was paid to existing online library guides, some of which are included as links in the course.

Course delivery
Mosaic: Making Sense of Information in the Connected Age

This course, delivered entirely online, incorporates a range of design features to break up the text and interactive activities to help to engage the learner. The level of interactivity within Mosaic is kept high throughout with a mixture of activities located within the course and opportunities to seek out and explore electronic resources elsewhere. The course's accessibility features include text alternatives for all graphic images and tables, flexible fonts and colours, and the ability to navigate by keyboard. The entire course was tested by a visually impaired colleague using screen-reading software. Supported discovery of online resources gives students with a range of disabilities access to a wealth of information not otherwise easily available.

The technology used to deliver the course is particularly innovative. It is underpinned by its own personalization system, identifying individual students, and allowing them to record their work. The site itself draws on ColdFusion technology, allowing the course team to manage and update the content of many pages of the website themselves.

Online conferencing is used for specific activities in the course and for informal discussion and support. The course is delivered twice a year (May and November). A study support team provides advice by telephone, conferencing and e-mail. In addition, this course uses an online portfolio submitted electronically as an end-of-course assessment and also marked online. Students receive feedback in the form of a skills profile as well as an overall pass/fail result.

Mining Information in the Internet Age

This course is built on the WebCT platform. However, due to dissatisfaction with the standard interface of the software, a purpose-designed interface was developed by the team with the assistance of graphic and programming staff of the ETPU. The online discussion group facility of WebCT was left unchanged. Multimedia elements in the course include audio introductions to each unit and demonstrations of the use of software, developed using Camtasia.

The course presents a five-step strategy for searching for information, which forms the basis for the course content. Participants are presented with a number of scenarios of persons seeking information from a variety of perspectives, and stages of the scenarios are integrated with the study units, culminating in final outcomes at the end. In addition, participants are led through a series of activities (with generic feedback included) that allow them to apply the steps to their own information-searching needs. Assessment is carried out through a series of online quizzes, one for each of the three units. Each consists of multiple-choice items, and participants are given up to three attempts to pass.

Implementation
Mosaic: Making Sense of Information in the Connected Age

After two pilot presentations, the course was formally approved to be offered for five years. As of May 2005, more than 1400 students have taken the course. The collaboration between Library, Faculty and Learning and Teaching Solutions has proved effective. More recently, the course has been used as part of the University's strategy to help to develop the information and ICT skills of the 8000 part-time tutors. An initial cohort of 25 tutors took the course and evaluated it in terms of its potential value for their colleagues. Responses were generally very positive with the majority recommending that the course be included as part of induction for new tutors. A typical comment follows:

> I am tutoring both a Project and a Postgraduate course and I now feel much more comfortable discussing electronic searching techniques, databases, evaluating websites, etc. with them.

> (A tutor)

Mining Information in the Internet Age

As it turned out, initial enrolments for the course were disappointing, with only 11 students opting to take the course. However, it was believed that the course would be of benefit to staff of the University, and when soon after a slightly modified version was offered to full-time staff, 40 persons enrolled. Encouragingly, these enrolments included both academic and administrative staff. Given this positive outcome, Mining Information in the Internet Age has also been made available to the large pool of part-time tutors of the OUHK. Two cohorts of tutors, at 60 participants per cohort, have completed the course.

Further consideration of the potential of the course led to the decision to develop a version for student use. Using a new title, Information Literacy and the Internet, the course is provided free to all newly enrolling students, who are encouraged to study it during the period after enrolment during which they are waiting for the semester to commence. Initial indications are that nearly 20% of the new students attempt at least part of the course, and that their reactions to it (from completed evaluation questionnaires) are positive.

Assessment

Both courses have relied heavily on feedback from participants in order to stimulate ongoing refinement of content, delivery and support. Survey instruments were prepared to gather evaluative data, which turned out to be strongly supportive of each course.

Mosaic: Making sense of Information in the Connected Age

After the first year of the course, students were surveyed. Questionnaires were sent out to 186 students who completed the course in 2002 and 75 returns were received, a response rate of 40%. Of these returns, 68% (51) were from new students and 32% (24) were from continuing students.

In terms of general satisfaction, 85% of students considered the course *fairly* or *very* good value for money. Further, while 88% of students were *fairly* or *very* satisfied with the academic quality of the course, only 23% were *very* satisfied.

Concerning skills development, Table 21.2 shows the percentage (and number) of students who felt studying the course had *fairly* or *very much* enabled them to achieve some generic/key skills.

Table 21.2 Student skills development

Generic/key skills	Percentage responding	
	Fairly successful	Very successful
The use of information technology for study	86	61
Study skills	84	55

Participants were also asked 'Will you be able to use any of those generic/key skills you have developed through study of this course?' In all, the following percentages (and number) of students indicated ability to use generic/key skills they have developed through study of their course in further study, other activities and in paid employment:

- further study – 97% (61)
- in other activities – 87% (53)
- in paid employment – 76% (44)

Additional overall comments included:

> I really enjoyed the course and felt that it has taught me considerable information skills. I would really like to see another course, which builds on what the course taught.

> This was my first experience of an on-line course and I was quite worried about that. I found the course was reassuring and allowed me to gain confidence. I thought the self-assessment parts were stimulating and useful. I now feel much more confident in information searching as well as now feeling able to assess the quality of the information I find.

Mining Information in the Internet Age

From the first two iterations of Mining Information in the Internet Age with staff of the OUHK, 66 returns were received from 98 participants. A selection of particular items that concentrate on skills development and the usefulness of the course is shown in Table 21.3.

One particular item that has consistently had the most 'spread' of responses concerns the incidence of printing pages for later reference and study. It seems that participants are evenly divided on the issue; that is, about half of them print the pages for study purposes.

Overall comments from participants include the following:

> The course gives us a systematic approach of doing a search in the WWW and lots of useful tips for evaluating the information obtained. This course alerts me of important issues when doing search on the WWW, things that I have not paid much attention before the course.

> This is the first online course I studied in OUHK. It is good that I can study at office, home or during business trip when I can arrange my time in flexible way. The content of the course is relevant and appropriate.

Table 21.3 *Selected evaluation questionnaire responses*

Item	Number (%) who agreed/strongly agreed
3. I found it easy to navigate the online course materials.	59 (89.4)
7. The course content was clear and easy to follow.	62 (93.9)
9. I now have a useful strategy for locating and evaluating information.	59 (89.4)
10. I am confident that I can evaluate the quality of a web site.	52 (78.8)
11. The course satisfied my learning needs.	57 (86.4)
23. I found the activities useful to my learning.	59 (89.4)
30. I would recommend this course to my friends.	59 (89.4)

The wider context

Since the development of the two courses, information literacy has moved into the spotlight both nationally and internationally. In the UK, the Higher Education Funding Council's strategic plan (HEFCE, 2003) states:

> The student body is changing, with more part-time and mature students and people from diverse backgrounds. In the modern world, people increasingly need skills of evaluating and managing information, in both their personal and working lives. Curriculum design and pedagogy within HE must support and develop these skills and encourage students to take responsibility for their own learning.

In September 2003, 40 representatives from 23 countries met in Prague to discuss information literacy. The Prague Declaration (2003) articulates the representative's mission and goals:

> To date, advancements in information and communication technologies have only increased the divide between the information rich and the information poor.
>
> Prague participants acknowledged the need for three elements to improve this situation: 1) ready access to information and communication technologies; 2) unrestricted availability of needed information; and 3) an information literate citizenry. They agreed that an information literacy citizenry is required to mobilize an effective civil society and create a competitive workforce.

At the same time, the World Summit on the Information Society is considering the importance of information literacy and ICT skills for the developing world, focusing particularly on the needs of teachers in this respect. As part of the United Nations Literacy Decade 2003–2012, UNESCO's Information Literacy Programme is being launched during the 2004/5 biennium. One of the objectives is to 'promote innovative curricula about Information Literacy' (Abid, 2004). These international developments suggest that courses like the two discussed in this chapter are likely to be in considerable demand in many parts of the world.

Conclusion

The similarities between these two courses reflect similar thinking about the skills and knowledge required by students in the two institutions with respect to information literacy in the early years of the 21st century. Certainly it would seem that each development team can be justly proud of the outcome of its efforts. Mosaic: Making Sense of Information in the Connected Age has won a UKOU teaching award and, as mentioned, Mining Information in the Internet Age has become a standard 'taster' course for all new OUHK students. Neither institution can afford to be complacent, however. While the policy initiatives described above suggest that information literacy education will assume a still higher profile as the century unfolds, we cannot assume that students' needs will stay the same. The challenge will be the ability to adapt and build on these courses to reflect the needs and expectations of tomorrow's distance learners in the context of a changing social and technological environment.

References

Abid, A .(2004) *Information Literacy for Lifelong Education*, paper presented at the World Library and Information Congress, Buenos Aires, Argentina, August.

Higher Education Funding Council (2003) *HEFCE Strategic Plan 2003-8*, www.hefce.ac.uk.

Prague Declaration (2003) Towards an Information Literate Society, press release (15 October).

Index